The "Unknown" Reality:
A Seth Book

Volume 1

The "Unknown" Reality: A Seth Book Volume 1

by Jane Roberts

notes and introduction by Robert F. Butts

Prentice-Hall, Inc., Englewood Cliffs, New Jersey

The "Unknown" Reality: A Seth Book
Volume 1
by Jane Roberts
Copyright © 1977 by Jane Roberts

Printed in the United States of America

Prentice-Hall International, Inc., London
Prentice-Hall of Australia, Pty. Ltd., Sydney
Prentice-Hall of Canada, Ltd., Toronto
Prentice-Hall of India Private Ltd., New Delhi
Prentice-Hall of Japan, Inc., Tokyo
Prentice-Hall of Southeast Asia Pte. Ltd., Singapore
Whitehall Books Limited, Wellington, New Zealand

10 9 8 7 6 5 4 3 2 1

Library of Congress Cataloging in Publication Data
Roberts, Jane,
    The "unknown" reality.

    Includes index.
    1. Psychical research.   I. Seth.   II. Title
BF1031.R634 1977   133.9   77-1092
ISBN 0-13-938704-8

TO ROB

Contents

The "Unknown" Reality:
A Seth Book

Volume 1

Summer Is Winter

Today is tomorrow, and present, past,
Nothing exists and everything will last.
There is no beginning, there was no end,
No depth to fall, no height to ascend.
There is only this moment, this flicker of light,
That illuminates nothing, but oh! so bright!.
For we are the spark that flutters in space,
Consuming an eternity of a moment's grace,
For today is tomorrow, and present, past.
Nothing exists, and everything will last.

(A note by R.F.B.: This is the second and last verse of a poem Jane wrote in April, 1952, when she was 23 years old. Even in this immature work, which she produced 11 years before she was to initiate the Seth material, her mystical nature was asserting its innate knowledge.)

Introductory Notes
by Robert F. Butts

I started the first rough draft for these notes on April 16, 1975. Although they bear my name, before I was finished with them I'd had plenty of help from my wife, Jane Roberts, and from Seth, the nonphysical entity who speaks through her while she's in trance. In fact, Jane and Seth are the ones who so beautifully bring these notes to their conclusion; and in that order—Jane with some excellent material about her relationship with Seth, and Seth himself with his new letter to correspondents. Yet Jane isn't particularly turned on by dates, session numbers, information about footnotes, and some of the other material I'll be discussing here.

Seth began dictating *The "Unknown" Reality: A Seth Book*, in the 679th session for February 4, 1974, and finished it with the 744th session for April 23, 1975. In the beginning we anticipated another intriguing Seth book, the successor to *Seth*

Speaks and *The Nature of Personal Reality.* We thought the new work would probably be a long one, but we hardly expected that it would require publication in two volumes.

The firm decision to do this was made when we were visited by Jane's editor at Prentice-Hall, Tam Mossman, and a business colleague who accompanied him. By then it was obvious that in a couple of weeks Seth would be through with *"Unknown" Reality,* as we'd taken to calling it. For some time all of us present had been aware that as a single volume this new work would be more massive than we wanted it to be. Jane and I were really pleased, then, to get the official word. Not only would the expanded format be something out of the ordinary in itself, but it meant that with two volumes I'd have the room I needed for notes and references; excerpts from Jane's ESP class sessions, as well as from "regular" sessions dated before and after the production time of *"Unknown" Reality;* a little of Jane's poetry; and appendixes—all of which I thought would add extra dimensions of consciousness to the books. (And, of course, I couldn't begin these notes until such a decision had been made.)

Seth presented his sessions for *"Unknown" Reality* as usual, but dispensed with any chapter framework. He did group his material into six sections, though, with headings. As he told us in the 743rd session, a few days after the visit of Tam and his associate: "This book had no chapters [in order] to further disrupt your accepted notions of what a book should be. There are different kinds of organizations present, however, and in any given section of the book, several levels of consciousness are appealed to at once." Seth gave no headings for individual sessions, so after each one as it's listed in the Table of Contents (in each volume), Jane plans to insert a few words indicating at least some of the subjects discussed in that session.

Seth himself said nothing about publishing *"Unknown" Reality* in one volume, two volumes, or even more while he was producing it. He referred to it as one unit until the very last session, the 744th, when he said in answer to a question I asked: "The Seth material is endless. I organize it for your benefit. If you want to divide it into two volumes, that is fine. You will find several points where this can be done . . ." In our final view, however, the obvious point of division is also the best one: three sections in each volume. I'll note a little more about this natural point of separation in the Epilogue of this book.

Since the sections themselves are of unequal length, for a while I contemplated trying a four-and-two division; but as Jane commented, "Three sections in one book are enough of a bite for the reader." We do think most people will find it more convenient to have *"Unknown" Reality* presented, with indexes, in two shorter works, whether or not they're of equal length. Volume 2 will be published a year or so after the first printing of Volume 1. After that initial waiting period, the two can always be read together.

I'm sure that that "energy personality essence," as Seth calls himself, regarded with some amusement our gropings about how best to publish his work as the sessions began to pile up. I think that basically he was unconcerned with ideas of length or time; that Jane's and my own willingness to continue delivering and recording the body of the material were the true arbiters of its length. In that sense, then, the creative processes involved with these two volumes *were* endless—at least until Jane and I called a halt to them for sheer physical reasons. (Those processes are still without end, of course, as is all creativity.)

We think now that *"Unknown" Reality* could continue for the rest of our lives, really. In other, larger respects, it could go on for centuries. For all we know in ordinary conscious-mind terms at this "time," there *could* be a third volume to the set (as Jane herself speculated in the 730th session, in Section 6), and a fourth and fifth. . . .

Now I'd like to briefly comment on the handling of the notes, excerpts, and other such matter. After Jane began delivering this work it soon became apparent that my notes for it were going to be longer than they are in *Seth Speaks* and *Personal Reality.* The very way Seth was presenting his material required this. Jane and I liked the idea because it meant something different from the two previous Seth books, but at the same time I was concerned that the notes would become too prominent. (I felt this way even though Seth told me in a private session in June, 1974: "The notes will take care of themselves. Do not worry.")

Once we'd decided to publish in two volumes, Jane, Tam, and I agreed that we didn't want to move all of the supplementary data to the back of each book, as is often done in such cases. Not only would the reader be constantly involved in looking up specific items, but we felt that the shorter notes especially

would be too far removed from their intimate positions within
the sessions; we wanted these to enhance individual sessions
directly without getting in the way, so I worked out a compro-
mise which offers some sort of orderly presentation without
being too rigid.

　　As in *Seth Speaks* and *Personal Reality*, the usual notes
are presented at break times, but I've indicated the points of
origin of what would ordinarily be footnotes by using consecutive (superscription) numbers within the text of each session;
then I've grouped the actual notes at the end of the session for
quick reference. For consistency's sake, these notes are printed in
the same smaller type throughout both volumes. Footnotes will
be found "in place" only when they refer to a specific appendix
in the same book. So for the most part, these approaches keep
the body of each session free of interruptions between breaks.

　　The appendix idea worked well in both *The Seth
Material* and *Seth Speaks*. Here in *"Unknown" Reality* the individual excerpt or session in an appendix, with whatever notes *it*
may have, is usually pretty complete in itself. These pieces can be
read at any time, but I prefer that the reader go over each one
when it's first mentioned in a footnote, just as he or she ought to
check out all other reference material in order throughout both
volumes.

　　Without carrying the idea too far, I designed the notes
and appendixes so that to some extent they reinforce each other,
as the sessions themselves do. In Volume 1, I refer to certain
sessions—the 681st, for instance—every so often because in them
Seth comes through with key concepts that should be stressed.

　　As *"Unknown" Reality* progresses into Volume 2, it's
natural that I use notes more and more often to call attention to
earlier sessions. When those sessions are in Volume 1, think of
that book as a separate entity used for reference in the same way
that *Seth Speaks, Adventures in Consciousness,* or any of Jane's
other books are. At the same time, in an effort to build some
mental bridges between the two parts of *"Unknown" Reality,*
I've made it a point occasionally to lift something out of one
volume for inclusion in the other, or at least to include that kind
of reference.

　　In the notes I've tried to say exactly what I mean, no
more and no less, and to watch out for unwitting implications.
Things can get complicated, though, and at times while preparing

these volumes I found myself wondering just how to make clear
certain points of reference without leaving the reader confused
by dates, session numbers, or other matter. Although I think my
system of presentation has a kind of order, still it'll take study at
times, and I can only ask the reader to patiently go along. I don't
believe such instances are too many.

I've noted the time every so often during each session
to show how long it takes Jane to deliver a particular passage
(and shortly I'll explore further the time elements involved with
the production of *"Unknown" Reality*). For obvious reasons I've
deleted most of Seth's instructions for punctuating his material,
beyond leaving a few examples in place at the start of his Preface,
or in an occasional session. But Seth is far short of overdoing
such directions. Once in a while Jane or I recast his sentence
structure for clarity's sake, or we eliminate a repetitive phrase—
for all of this is *verbal* work as opposed to prose work, which can
be easily revised on the spot. Except for such changes the
material is presented as received throughout both of these volumes. Whenever anything is deleted from a session—personal
information, say—it's always indicated; occasionally such material is summarized.

During our book sessions, which are almost always
private—held without witnesses, that is—Seth speaks at a mod-
erate enough pace so that I can take down his dictation verbatim
in my own kind of shorthand. Although it's often hard work, I
find this approach more intimate and meaningful than passively
using a tape recorder; I also have time to insert my own comments as we go along. Then, later, I type the sessions. I can do
this much more quickly and comfortably from my notebook
than I can from a tape. As I wrote in *Personal Reality,* I believe
that Jane's ability to deliver Seth's material with so few changes
being made in it "says important things about these sessions."
(See my notes at the end of the 610th session, in Chapter 1 of
that book.) And concerning my objective observations of Seth
himself, I'll let my notes in the sessions build up whatever com-
posite picture I'm able to construct.

Like the other Seth books, then, each volume of
"Unknown" Reality contains not only the Seth sessions, but
Jane's and my own ideas about them, as well as our notes on the
circumstances surrounding their production.

The next four paragraphs contain some information on

our publishing schedule that I'll present as simply as I can. Originally I hadn't planned on dealing with such material in these
notes, but after talking it over, Jane and I agreed that it should
be given here after all. There are various titles, section numbers,
and dates to keep in mind, so these passages may take some
rereading.

     As I note in the Epilogue for this volume, Section 6 in
Volume 2 contains the story of how we moved into our "hill
house," just outside Elmira, N. Y., a month before Seth completed that section—and his part in *"Unknown" Reality* as a
whole—in April, 1975. But in October, 1974, long before our
move from the two apartments we occupied in downtown
Elmira, Jane started her *Psychic Politics: An Aspect Psychology
Book*; that book is the sequel to *Adventures in Consciousness*,
and is to be published this Fall (in 1976) by Prentice-Hall, Inc.
Politics is also mentioned in the Epilogue to Volume 1 of *"Unknown" Reality*, and my first session notes on it show up in
Section 4, in the second volume.

     We'd intended to publish Volume 1 before *Politics*, but
since Jane finished her book before I could complete the notes
for the two Seth books (I found it necessary to do many of the
notes for both volumes together), we decided to publish *Politics*
first instead. Our move to the hill house also cost me considerable working time on the manuscripts. So it's obvious, then,
that *Politics* jumps ahead of *"Unknown" Reality* as far as a
strictly correct publishing chronology is concerned.

     In *Politics* Jane also refers to certain blocks of material
that first appeared in *"Unknown" Reality*, so I've adjusted the
appropriate notes in the latter to account for their earlier discussion. Intrinsically there's no conflict between Jane's latest and
Seth's latest, however. Each one enhances the other. I simply
want to stress that our overall goal is the publication of Jane's
books (including those produced with Seth), and that each work
is a complete entity while containing within itself the necessary
references to others in the series.

     We want those references to help the reader place each
one in a time sequence, regardless of when any particular book
might have been first published. For the more time passes, the
less important the date of publication becomes. When I note, for
example, that *Psychic Politics* "is to be published this Fall (in
1976)," I know, of course, that by the time the first volume of

Seth's work is in print in the spring of 1977, *Politics* will actually have been on sale for several months. Yet, as I see it, that's the most accurate way to present that bit of information in this Volume 1.

One can have a lot of fun with numbers. They can, for instance, be used to explore different perspectives of the same subject—in this case, time, the quality that's just been under discussion. The two volumes of *"Unknown" Reality* contain 65 sessions. Jane delivered these for Seth over a period of a little more than 14½ months. This elapsed time includes more than a few weeks during which she gave no book dictation at all, of course, but I was curious to get an approximate idea of the number of hours she actually spent in producing the entire work.

I averaged 40 of the sessions, just the parts devoted to dictation, for two things: the time Jane spent in trance only, and her trance time plus relevant break times. I obtained figures of 1:39 and 2:02 hours respectively. Then I multiplied each of these by 65. I found the low results difficult to believe; they speak volumes (the pun is deliberate) about the great speed that creativity—at least Jane's—can show under certain conditions. For she completed the two volumes of *"Unknown" Reality* in a total trance time of 90:35 hours, or a total trance-plus-break time of 131:30 hours (sums which translate roughly into times of 45 hours and 65 hours per book). Keep in mind that these figures result from averages, and that the remaining 25 sessions would yield very similar results, since they include no extremes of brevity or length. So either hourly total is most remarkable for the involved creative accomplishment of *"Unknown" Reality,* regardless of the larger context in which those hours were really expended. For comparison, think of *one week* as consisting of 168 hours.

Every so often I've thought of averaging Jane's dictation time for *Seth Speaks* and *Personal Reality* in the same way, but haven't done so. I'm somewhat puzzled to note, however, that her very short working times for the Seth books seem to be either ignored or taken for granted by practically everyone—or, perhaps, those factors just aren't understood in terms of ordinary linear time. Maybe I'm alone in my interest here, for even Jane doesn't express any great curiosity about the time she has invested in the Seth material; she just delivers it. But given her abilities, I think her speed of production is a close physical approach to, or translation of, Seth's idea that basically all exists at once—that really there is no time, and that the Seth books, for example, are "there" to be had in final form for just the tuning in. (In Section 3 of this volume, Note 2 for Session 692 contains information on another way by which we can move closer to Seth's idea of simultaneity from our physical reality, but that method grows out of material not discussed here.)

Since Jane began publishing the Seth material in 1970, she's received many hundreds of calls and letters about her work. We're very grateful for all of those communications (including the letters we haven't answered yet), but I don't recall this fantastic time element being mentioned in even one of them.

Do I think that Jane, in trance, could actually deliver a complete, book-length manuscript in just 45 hours? The question must be hypothetical, but I'm sure she could as far as having Seth's material available is concerned; she'd need only the necessary physical strength. Even now, while speaking for Seth she can easily outtalk my writing capacity by many hours. The information from Seth would be there. The work produced would be different from the "same" work delivered over a longer time. Seth wouldn't have our current daily activities to draw upon for some of his analogies, for instance, but in such cases I think he'd either call upon similar episodes from our pasts, or cast his material in different ways—which would yield the same results.

I think it important to periodically remind the reader of certain of Seth's basic ideas throughout both volumes of *"Unknown" Reality*. As an example, I'll continue with the subject of time—but Seth's time now—and couple it with his notions of a durability that is at the same time spontaneous and simultaneous, as he's explained to us more than once. The durability is achieved through constant expansion in terms of value fulfillment. Part of my paragraph of commentary following the 724th session, in Volume 2, fits in here: "As he [Seth] quite humorously commented in the 14th session for January 8, 1964, '... for you have no idea of the difficulties involved in explaining time to someone who must take time to understand the explanation.' Yet Seth's simultaneous time isn't an absolute, for, as he also told us in that session: 'While I am not affected by time on your plane, I am affected by something resembling time on my plane ... To me time can be manipulated, used at leisure and examined. To me your time is a vehicle, one of several by which I can enter your awareness. It is therefore still a reality of some kind to me [my emphasis]. Otherwise I could not utilize it in any way whatsoever.' "

I think Seth's concept of simultaneous time will always elude us to some extent as long as we're physical creatures, yet it gives clues to invisible mechanisms—we can better understand that Jane speaks *her version* of what Seth is. The very casting of the idea into words (as best Jane can do it) helps one grasp what Seth means: We can make intuitive nonverbal nudges, or jumps, toward understanding that to some degree transcend our trite ideas of that quality or essence we call time, and take so much for granted in our Western societies that to even question its seeming one-way flow appears to be quite futile.

I'll continue these notes by quoting Seth in two short passages, then follow those with a longer contribution from Jane.

The first Seth excerpt is in keeping with the idea of creating bridges between the two volumes of *"Unknown" Reality* by lifting something out of one for inclusion in the other. Once more from the 743rd session in Volume 2: "No book entitled *The "Unknown" Reality* can hope to make that reality entirely known. It remains nebulous because it is consciously unrealized. The best I can do is to point out areas that have been relatively invisible, to help you explore, actually, different facets of your own consciousness . . . I am well aware that the book raises many more questions than it presents answers for, and this has been my intent. . . ."

And Jane's intent and mine, too. Jane's books are records of her use of certain abilities that we think are very creative; the questions she raises present us with larger fields to investigate. Ordinarily we don't think of those questions—and challenges—as being mystical in origin, not from our Western-social viewpoint. Seth discusses Jane's early religious background, her "deeply mystical nature," in the first session of this volume (the 679th), and I add some material on mysticism in an appendix to that session. That information is related to these introductory notes, yet it should be separate.

However, the work we do deals with concepts that consciously we'd paid little attention to in earlier life. (I was 44 years old and Jane was 34 when she initiated the Seth material late in 1963). Jane's early poetry, as I show in certain notes, clearly reflected her intuitive understanding of some of the

concepts Seth came to elaborate upon much later. (This was true
even when she was consciously unaware of what she was up to.
See the verse from her early poem, *Summer Is Winter,* which
precedes these notes.) As I see it, her task with the Seth material
is to place these basic artistic ideas at our conscious service, so
that their use in our daily lives can change our individual and
collective realities for the better; and by "artistic ideas" here I
mean the deepest, most aesthetic and practical—and, yes, *mystical*—truths and questions that human beings are capable of
expressing, then contending with. Much of the response to her
work that Jane receives by mail and telephone indicates this is
happening. (That response, incidentally, will be discussed briefly
at the end of these notes, when Seth's letter to correspondents is
presented.)

In the Seth books we've deliberately refrained from
commenting upon the similarities that exist between Seth's ideas
and those of various religious, philosophical, and mystical doc-
trines from the Near, Middle, or Far East. This approach fits our
natures, of course. Jane and I know that such correlations exist—
indeed, we'd only be surprised if they didn't. Others have often
mentioned them to us, and we've done a little reading on Buddhism, Hinduism, Zen, and Taoism, for example, not to mention
subjects like shamanism, voodooism, and obeah. It's obvious, we
think, that a book could be written comparing the Seth material
with other systems of thought, whether religious or not, but Jane
and I, being individualists, have chosen not to concentrate upon
those areas. Nor is what I'm writing here meant to be taken as an
attempt to put down other approaches to "basic" reality.

Although there are similarities, then, in our view there
are vital differences, too, between Seth's philosophy and that of
many other organized systems. Jane and I prefer to think about
the unities we find in our world as *including* religions, not being
defined by them, and we think Seth stresses this. We go along in
our own stubborn ways, knowing that our outlooks are rooted in
the Western traditions of the world, but also knowing that there
exist all about us these numerous other philosophies or systems,
some of them many centuries old, that the human race has
created to help it explain reality. Yet we feel no compulsion to
intimately know the *details* of, say, Sufism or Brahmanism. (A
simile I often think of here compares Eastern and Western life
and thought with the right and left hemispheres of the brain;

they're separate, yet united; each half performs functions that complement and to some extent overlap those of the other, and together they operate as a whole.) But we dislike the idea of nirvana in Buddhism and Hinduism, which calls for the extinction or blowing out of individual consciousness, and its absorption into a supreme spirit, usually after a series of lives. And we object to the notion that "nature," in those terms of linear time, has so arranged things that the individual has to pay a karmic debt in one life as the result of actions in a previous one. Why should nature punish any*one* if it doesn't punish any*thing*? The realities of nirvana and karma are not ones that Jane and I want to create.

We prefer instead Seth's—as well as our own—concepts of the inviolate nature of the individual consciousness, before, during, and after physical existence, in ordinary terms, and whether or not any theory of reincarnation is involved. It may be natural enough for us in the West not to enjoy the idea of surrendering our individual natures upon physical death, even if intellectually we can understand, for instance, the Buddhist teaching that "perfect" joy can be found in the eventual, blissful surrender of the self to a supreme spirit—although I note with some humor that personally I've yet to determine how the self who surrenders knows it's done so if it's been so thoroughly absorbed.

I'm more inclined to agree with what Seth told us in the 590th session in Chapter 22 of *Seth Speaks*: "You are not fated to dissolve into All That Is. The aspects of your personality as you presently understand them will be retained. All That Is is the creater of individuality, not the means of its destruction." And whenever I read about conventional Eastern conceptions of a supreme spirit, I remember what Seth had to say in the 596th session in the Appendix of *Seth Speaks*: "I have used the term 'expansion of consciousness' here rather than the more frequently used 'cosmic consciousness' because the latter implies an experience of proportions not available to mankind at this time. Intense expansions of consciousness by contrast to your normal state may <u>appear</u> to be cosmic in nature, but they barely hint at those possibilities of consciousness that are available to you now, much less begin to approach a true cosmic awareness."

It's plain that many arguments can be brought against all I've written in the last four paragraphs, I suppose, yet the material in them briefly approximates the ways Jane and I look at the Seth material these days in relation to other philosophies. Especially do I like the fact that Jane's work, her contribution to our thought, comes out of her psyche unaided by laboratories, statistics, or tests. That is, our idea of real testing consists in watching to see how the Seth material can assist in practical, everyday living. Other kinds of tests, more "formal" ones that we carried out in 1965-66, are detailed in Chapter 8 of *The Seth Material*; it's easy for us to forget now that those early tests were quite successful, and could be resumed at any time. When they were held I wondered (as I still do) why the human animal, of all the creatures on earth, felt it necessary to construct laboratories in which to "prove" what it really *is*, what its abilities— telepathic, metabolic, or whatever—really *are*. This subject alone is so vast that Jane and I could write about it indefinitely, so I can barely mention it here.

In his laboratories, man thus has great opportunities to obtain preprogrammed answers, based on what he thinks he already knows; his exteriorized equipment can hardly produce anything else. (A scientist doesn't call an atom of oxygen, or one of any other element, alive, let alone conscious. Yet a collection of certain atoms assembled into a human form *calls itself* alive— and vehemently denies the same status to identical atoms that have the misfortune to exist outside of that human framework.) But some of the reasons for our exceedingly poor understanding of the general human state are discussed by Seth in the material he's given over the last decade, and I'm sure there is much more to come.

I feel extremely cheered by the idea that Jane, simply by using her chosen physical apparatus and nonphysical mind, is consistently demonstrating abilities human beings are not supposed to possess. We aren't satisfied with the answers to our questions that our social orders, whether Eastern or Western, give us. So, we say, each reader can make his or her own sense out of what the Seth material has to offer on such questions as the meaning of life, its depths and mysteries, its infinite possibilities.

Here's Seth from the 750th session, held on June 25, 1975, two months after he finished Volume 2. In it he not only sums up his motives in producing *"Unknown" Reality*, but comments on another one of his basic ideas that I think it important to stress every so often; this time, perception is involved. *"The*

'Unknown' Reality was written to give . . . individuals glimpses
into alternate patterns of reality. It was meant to serve as a map
that would lead, not into another objectified universe *per se*, but
into inner roads of consciousness. These inner roads or strands of
consciousness bring elements into play so that it becomes possible to realize that the content of a given objectified universe
may actually be perceived quite differently. You are part of what
you perceive. When you alter the focus of your perception you
automatically change the objectified world. It is not simply that
you perceive it differently while it remains the same, regardless
of your experience. The act of perception itself helps form the
perceived event and is a part of it."

And what of Jane's feelings about her relationship with
Seth? The mechanics of her mediumship? Our idea at first was
that she'd write her own introduction to accompany these notes,
but finally she decided that wasn't necessary; nor did she want to
repeat much of the material she's already covered in her own
books. Instead, in March, 1976, she produced the following
essay, which I consider to be an excellent summation of the
combined inner and outer realities she experiences while speaking
for Seth:

"The *'Unknown' Reality* itself is a product of the
unknown reality of the mind, of course, since I produced it entirely in a trance state, as Seth. In a way the
two volumes are the products of an inner psychic
'combustion'—the spark that is lit in our world, as
Seth's reality strikes mine—or vice versa. For me, this is
an accelerated state. I would compare it to a higher
state of wakefulness rather than to the sleep usually
associated with trance—but a different kind of wakefulness, in which the usual world seems to be the one
that is sleeping. My attention is not blunted. It is
elsewhere.

"As Jane, I'm not discarded when I'm in such a
trance. Yet I step out of my Jane-self in some inde-
scribable way, and step right back into it when the
session is over. So there must be another 'I' who leaves
Jane patiently waiting at the shore while 'I' dive headlong into those other dimensions of experience and
identity. Once the almost instant transformation is
over, 'I' become Seth or Seth becomes what I am. And

in that state, the conditions of perception are those native to other lands of consciousness than ours.

"Such sessions never wear me out. Instead, I'm often more refreshed than I was earlier. Usually I have little idea of time. As Seth I may speak for an hour, but when I 'snap back' I'll look at the clock in surprise, thinking that perhaps 15 minutes have passed at most. The trance is not static, though. It has gradations and characteristics. These are almost impossible to explain, but the state isn't always the same—it has peaks and valleys, psychological colorations and intensities that mark its nature.

"The trance state is characterized by a feeling of inexhaustible energy, emotional wholeness, and subjective freedom. At times Seth's voice is very loud and powerful. Even in trance I'm aware of this, and I'm swept along in its energy. In the first years of my mediumship Seth's voice and accent seemed very odd to me, whether I heard myself speaking for him during sessions or listened to tapes. But in the trance, what is known is known. Returning to my usual condition, the words that I've just spoken as Seth vanish in dreamlike fashion. Although I've read 'Unknown' Reality since it was finished, and had looked portions of it over during the time of its production, it seems alien to me in the strangest fashion.

"I appear to be more than ordinarily opaque, as if a part of me refuses any conscious consideration with my trance manuscripts; perhaps so as not to confuse myself. For one thing, I like to keep the boundaries of my subjective states separate; it seems like an economical and practical way to handle exotic conditions as naturally and easily as possible. The Seth state remains inviolate in its fashion. So does the Jane state.

"When I'm Seth, I'm just a small part of his reality, maybe only the portion I can grasp, but I bask in that personified energy. When Seth turns his attention to people, addressing them or answering questions, then I sense an almost multidimensional appreciation of their worth and individuality. He understands the validity of each person, or salutes it, approaching people in an

entirely different light than we do. That experience of
his reaction to others leads me to suspect the existence
of an emotional experience far more vivid than the one
we know.

"Yet I'm sure that Seth stands for something else, a
different kind of personhood, and that Seth 'happens'
when that kind of being intersects with my subjective
world.

"In many ways, we're a lonely species. We seem to
be forever prowling around the confines of our own
nature. Maybe our idea of identity is like a magic circle
we've drawn around our minds, so that everything outside seems dark and alien, unselflike. There may be
other psychic fires lighting up that inner landscape
with a far greater light than ours; other aspects of consciousness to which we're connected as surely as we're
connected also to the animals in a chain of being we
barely comprehend.

"We love to look 'backward' at our animal origins.
We take it for granted that evolution in those terms is
over, and here we are—aha, kings of the mountain. But
maybe we're just in the middle, sensing imperfectly the
existence of other remote versions of ourselves that
will appear in a 'future' too far ahead of us to know.
Maybe I'm some distant ancestor of Seth's in those
terms, alive in my life but only a memory in his. But
he insists there's fresh action in the past; so if that's
the case, I'm still searching out my own paths.

"When I get this far in my own thinking, a peculiar acceleration seizes me. My body grows very
relaxed, but my mind has a strange feeling of motion
as if something I'm trying to comprehend is going
past me too fast to follow; yet I keep trying to twirl
faster myself to catch up. If one of my cells tried to
comprehend my own subjective reality, it might feel
the same way. I think that I'm alive in Seth's subjective 'body' in the same way that one of my cells is
alive in my physical body. Only I keep groping . . .
and sensing events that my own reality can't really
understand.

"This may just be the conscious mind's reaction as

it tries to glimpse its own source. Perhaps when we try
such feats we pause, figuratively speaking, on our conscious platforms, looking upward and downward at the
same time. Like weightless spacemen we know who we
are, but we aren't sure of our position, which shifts
psychologically in inner space. We grow momentarily
dizzy, dazzled by an inner cosmos of selves and self-
versions, and feel that we are traveling through some
gigantic psyche that spawns selves the way space
spawns stars."

And, finally, what of our efforts to handle the steadily
increasing volume of mail that's resulted from the publication of
Jane's books? (Incidentally, we have on file most of the letters
and cards we've received over the years.) Our latest attempt to
cope here consists of three pieces we've prepared for correspondents: a short form letter from Jane and me; a longer one
dictated by Seth in April, 1975, soon after he finished Volume 2
of *"Unknown" Reality*; and a list of all editions of Jane's books.
(We prepared such a list in answer to many requests, and it's
being continually updated, of course.) Yet the form letters aren't
really a satisfactory answer for the correspondent who'd like a
personal response from Jane and/or Seth; given our characteristics, they merely represent the best we can do within the
time we have available. Jane handles most of the mail herself
these days, and tries to add a few individual lines to each reply.
With this system she acknowledges more letters than ever before,
yet it's ironic that there are still more to answer simply because
of the greater number received.

Once before (in January, 1973), Seth dictated a letter
for us to send to those who wrote, and it can be found in the
633rd session in Chapter 8 of *Personal Reality*. Many people
liked that letter (they still do)—and some wrote back in response
to *it*! Because of this, Jane and I suggest that Seth's earlier letter
be read in conjunction with the one below, for as Jane says, the
two complement and reinforce each other. We feel that both
messages from Seth reflect much of the essense of his material,
and our own circumstances and attitudes surrounding its production. Certainly we think that presenting Seth's new letter here
makes an ideal way to conclude these notes. (Seth refers to Jane
by her male entity name, Ruburt; and to me as Joseph, for the
same reason.)

Dear Correspondent:

Ruburt has read your letter. So has Joseph. I am aware of its contents. We have no organization yet of an exterior kind, so there are no secretaries to take dictation, no middlemen—or women—to write flowery, prepackaged replies.

Ruburt and Joseph, or Jane and Rob if you prefer, are private people. They also have a kind of one-to-one relationship with the universe. This particular quality means that they resist forming any kind of organization, even though such an organization might help in answering the mail. I am, therefore, dictating this letter. While it will be sent to many of you, it is written to each of you, and I only regret that I cannot go into your aspirations, challenges, and problems on a more individual basis.

Some of you have written in joy, some in sorrow. Some of you have written to tell of answers you have found, and some of you have written requesting answers. In any case, energy is being sent out to you with this letter.

That energy will arouse in you your own abilities. It will lead you to insights and solutions that can be yours alone. It will put you in touch with the ground of your being—from which, eventually, all exultation and answers spring. My purpose is not to solve your problems for you, but to put you in touch with your own power. My purpose is not to come between you and your own freedom by giving you "answers," even to the most tragic of problems. My purpose is to reinforce your own strength, for ultimately the magic of your being is well equipped to help you find fulfillment, understanding, exuberance, and peace.

Your problems are caused by your own doubts. These doubts arise because you have been out of touch with the validity of your own existence. Let me here reinforce that validity. Let me reinforce my faith in your innate ability to find joyful acquiescence, and to rise above any problems that you have. If I presume to solve problems for you, then I deny you your own power, and further reinforce any feelings of

powerlessness that you have. I know that you can grow
tired, however, and that sometimes a gift of energy can
be quite a boost; so, again, with this letter I send my
joyful recognition of your existence—and energy that
you can use to reinforce your own vitality and
strength.

All mail does not come from the postman, so each
of you should have your own kind of inner response
from me whatever letter you have sent by mail. I serve
in many ways as a speaker for your own psyche, however, so the inner message will be from your own
greater being to yourself; and at that multidimensional
level of reality, I salute you.

                                              Seth

Preface by Seth

(The circumstances surrounding Jane's delivery of Seth's Preface, while she was in trance, are given in the 685th session for February 25, 1974, in Section 1. After a break midway through the session, Seth began the material below at 10:57 P.M. He always indicates each word, phrase, or sentence to be underlined. This time he also called out each paragraph as he went along, and some of the other punctuation; to show Seth's own sense of organization on such occasions, I've left a few of his instructions in place in the first three paragraphs.)

Now: Preface: There is an "unknown" reality, in quotes as given. I am part of it, and so are you.

New paragraph. *(Long pause.)* Some time ago[1] I suddenly appeared within your space and time. Since then I have spoken to many people. Period. This is my third book.[2] There would be nothing strange to anyone in any of this if I had been born into your world in a body of my own, in usual terms. Instead I began to express myself by speaking through Jane Roberts. Period. In all of this there has been a purpose, and part of that purpose lies in this present book.

New paragraph. Each individual is a part of the unknown reality. Because of my position, however, I am obviously more a part of it than most. My psychological awareness bridges worlds of which you are consciously aware, and others that seem, at least, to escape your notice. The woman through whom I speak found herself in an unusual situation, comma, for no theories—metaphysical, psychological, or otherwise—could adequately explain her experience. She was led to develop her own, therefore, and this book is an extension of certain ideas already mentioned in *Adventures in Consciousness*.[3] To write that book, Jane Roberts drew on deep resources of energy.

(*11:11*.) The unknown reality, however, is unknown enough to usual reaches of the most flexible consciousness, in your terms, that it can only be approached by a personality as couched in it as I am. Once expressed, however, it can be comprehended. One of my purposes then has been to make this unknown reality consciously known.

Man thought once, historically speaking, that there was but one world. Now he knows differently, but he still clings to the idea of one god, one self, and one body through which to express it.

There is one God, but within that God are many. There is one self, but within that self are many. There is one body, in one time, but the self has other bodies in other times. All "times" exist at once. (*Long pause.*) Historically speaking, mankind chose a certain line of development. In it his consciousness specialized, focusing upon sharp particulars of experience. But inherent always, psychologically and biologically, there has been the possibility of a change in that pattern, an alteration that would effectively lift the race into another kind of weather.

(*11:22*.) Such a development would, however, necessitate first of all a broadening of concepts about the self, and a greater understanding of human potential. Human consciousness is now at a stage where such a development is not only feasible, but necessary if the race is to achieve its greatest fulfillment.

Jane Roberts's experience to some extent hints at the multidimensional nature of the human psyche and gives clues as

to the abilities that lie within each individual. These are part of
your racial heritage. They give notice of psychic bridges connecting the known and "unknown" realities in which you dwell.

While you have highly limited concepts about the
nature of the self, you cannot begin to conceive of a multidimensional godhood, or a universal reality in which all consciousness is
unique, inviolate—and yet given to the formation of infinite
gestalts of organization and meaning.

In my other books I used many accepted ideas as a
springboard to lead readers into other levels of understanding.
Here, I wish to make it clear that this book[4] will initiate a
journey in which it may *seem* that the familiar is left far behind.
Yet when I am finished, I hope you will discover that the known
reality is even more precious, more "real," because you will find
it illuminated both within and without by the rich fabric of an
"unknown" reality now seen emerging from the most intimate
portions of daily life. Give us a moment. *(Pause at 11:35.)* Your
concepts of personhood are now limiting you personally and *en
masse*, and yet your religions, metaphysics, histories, and even
your sciences are hinged upon your ideas of who and what you
are. Your psychologies do not explain your own reality to you.
They cannot contain your experience. Your religions do not
explain your greater reality, and your sciences leave you [just] as
ignorant about the nature of the universe in which you dwell.

These institutions and disciplines are composed of
individuals, each restrained by limiting ideas about their own
private reality; and so it is with private reality that we will begin
and always return, period. These ideas in this book are meant to
expand the private reality of each reader. They may appear esoteric or complicated, yet they are not beyond the reach of any
person who is determined to understand the nature of the unknown elements of the self, and its greater world.

So the book had a private beginning. Jane Roberts's
husband, Robert Butts, wondered about the death of his mother
(on November 19, 1973). In a session *(the 679th for February 4,
1974)* he brought out some old photographs. Now: Life after
death has usually been described quite in keeping with the old
accepted ideas about one self, and limited concepts of personhood. I took that opportunity, however, to begin this book.

(Long pause.) The self is multidimensional when it is
physically alive. It is a triumph of spiritual and psychological

identity, ever choosing from a myriad of probable realities its own clear unassailable focus *(very intently)*. When you don't realize this, then you project upon life after death all of the old misconceptions. You expect the dead to be little different from the living—if you believe in afterlife at all—but perhaps more at peace, more understanding, and, hopefully, wiser.

(Pause at 11:51—then with much emphasis:) The fact is that in life you poise delicately and yet perfectly between realities, and after death you do the same. I used the opportunity, then, to explain the great freedom available to Robert Butts's mother after death—but also to explain those elements of her reality present during life that had been closed to him consciously because of mankind's concepts about the nature of the psyche. I comment now and then about photographs that belong to the Butts family [including Jane Roberts], yet any reader can look at old photographs and ask the same questions, applying what is said here to private experience. The "unknown" reality—you are its known equivalent *(again, louder)*. Then know yourself. Your consciousness will expand as you become acquainted with these ideas.

I speak, myself, for those portions of your being that already understand. My voice rises from stratas of the psyche in which you also have your experience. Listen, therefore, to your own knowing. Period.

(Jovially:) End of Preface.

(12:01 A.M.)

NOTES: Preface by Seth

1. Seth first announced his presence by name to Jane and me in the 4th session, held on December 8, 1963. See Chapter 1 of *The Seth Material*.

2. Seth's two previous books are *Seth Speaks* and *Personal Reality*—but they're also Jane's too, of course. See the frontmatter for a list of her books as published by Prentice-Hall, Inc. (To make the record complete, it should be noted that Jane's first book on psychic phenomena was *How to Develop Your ESP Power*. It was published in hardcover and paperback editions in 1966 and 1974, respectively, by Frederick Fell Publishers, Inc., New York, N. Y. 10016. Then in 1976 it was issued in paperback by Pocket Books, New York, N. Y., 10020, under a new title: *The Coming of Seth*.)

3. Actually, Jane began the final draft of her manuscript for *Adventures in Consciousness: An Introduction to Aspect Psychology,* earlier this month (February, 1974). She's worked out all of her themes for it in detail, however.

4. The decision to publish *"Unknown" Reality* in two volumes followed receipt of this preface by some 13 months. See my Introductory Notes.

Section 1

**YOU AND THE
"UNKNOWN" REALITY.**

Session 679
February 4, 1974
9:41 P.M. Monday

*(Before the session I showed Jane a childhood photo-
graph of herself, and one of me. The two pictures are roughly the
same size, about 3¼" by 5". They also look remarkably alike in
their brittle and discolored condition—almost as though they'd
been snapped at the same time—yet mine is older than Jane's by
20 years.*

*(The photograph of me, taken and dated by my father
[Robert Sr.], has been kept in one of the Butts family albums
for 53 years. In it the time is June 1, 1921. I'm almost 2 years
old. I have curly light-colored hair. I wear a one-piece suit, long
white stockings, and black shoes. I stand in the side yard of the
house my parents rented in Mansfield, a small college town in
northeastern Pennsylvania. Perhaps a dozen chicks cluster in the
grass at my feet while I stare down at them, quite entranced. In
blurred focus behind me an unknown teen-age girl sits on a swing*

that's suspended from a tree limb, and an empty wicker stroller-type carriage [mine?] stands beside her. Parked in a driveway in back of her is a four-door touring car with a fabric top. I might add that Mansfield is only 35 miles below Elmira, N. Y., where Jane and I live now.

(The photograph of Jane is 33 years old. It was taken by an older lady friend who was treating her to an outing at a spa just outside of the New York State resort of Saratoga Springs, where Jane lived with her bedridden mother, Marie, and a house-keeper. In a childish hand Jane had scrawled her friend's name on the back of the picture, along with the date. Many years later she was to tell me, "My mother hated that woman." In the snapshot it's a sunlit day in August, 1941. Jane is 12 years old. She sits on the grass before some evergreen shrubs; she leans slightly back on her right hand, her bare legs rather primly folded. She wears a print dress that had been given to her in the Roman Catholic orphanage in Troy, some 35 miles from Saratoga Springs; she'd spent the previous 18 months there in the institution while her mother had been hospitalized in another city for treatment of rheumatoid arthritis. Jane also wears a short-sleeved pullover sweater. Her mother had knitted it during her stay in the hospital.

(Jane's blond hair—which was to turn quite black—is neatly parted and combed, and she wears a barrette in it. Her face is youthfully round, but quite unsmiling. She's not scowling. Rather, from her position on the grass she just stares directly out of the photograph at the viewer, displaying a sober, almost controlled regard that seems out of place for one of that age. . . .

(To me, both photographs had a certain mysterious quality that I'd often found intriguing—an aura due partly to their being old, personal, and so irreplaceable, I suppose. But for a long time I'd been aware of other feelings connected with them. Jane had begun delivering the Seth material late in 1963, and soon afterwards Seth started developing his ideas on probabilities.[1] Many times while looking at the snapshots since then I'd found myself speculating about the probable realities surrounding their two young subjects. I told Jane now that I understood the course of action each of us had chosen to make physical, or "real" in our terms. But what of all the other paths our probable selves had embarked upon since those pictures had been taken? By now, did those photographs actually depict the

immature images of us, *the Jane and Rob we knew and had
always been, or from our standpoint did they show a probable
Jane, a probable Rob—two individuals who long ago had set out
upon* their *own journeys through other realities? I wasn't clear
on what I wanted to know, and had trouble expressing myself to
Jane. Maybe I just wanted Seth to comment on probabilities in a
more personal way. [And added later: At the time, I had no idea
that my questioning would trigger a new Seth book.*[2]*]*

*(The outward signs of Jane's trance performances as
Seth are very interesting in themselves, and I don't intend to mini-
mize them: indeed, I describe them every so often. My real fasci-
nation, however, lies with what I call the greatly enhanced consciousness, or energy, that she displays in the sessions—and always I
sense an even more powerful flow of that quality just beneath the
surface of her delivery. I thought of this as Jane sat quietly in her
Kennedy rocker, waiting for Seth to come through. After a few
minutes, her right hand lifted to her glasses. As she took them off
her eyes were much darker and more luminous than they usually
are: She was dissociated—in trance. Seth was there, staring at me.)*

Now: Good evening.

("Good evening, Seth."

*(As Seth, Jane briefly handled the two photographs I'd
placed on the coffee table between us.)*

I am doing two things here—but you can also have the
material on any picture separately if you choose to.

("Yes.")

Each of you, again, chose your parents and environment. You spoke in your notes *(two days ago)* of precognition in
connection with art—an excellent point. Precognition in those
terms also applies at your birth, when ahead of time you are
quite aware on unconscious levels of those conditions that you
will meet. You have chosen them and projected them ahead of
you, out into the medium of time.

The conditions, however, while "set" in one fashion,
are highly plastic in another, so that a multitudinous variety of
probable events can flow from them. Precognitively you are unconsciously quite aware—again in your terms—of the results of
any given action or cause. When this *(photograph)* of Ruburt[3]
was taken, he had already become aware of the overall interests
and concerns that would dominate his future life, although the
particular course of it had not been chosen.

Some of this throws light on current experience. The religious background was there. At his preference and demand, he changed from a public to a Catholic school after the third grade.[4] This was against his mother's judgment. She felt that public schools were better and more socially beneficial. Ruburt, at that age—when he changed at the third grade—had quite a will then, in that he forced his mother to acquiesce to the change of schools. He put up such a fuss, Ruburt, and held such temper tantrums, that permission was given. He was stubborn even then.

Now: He was always highly imaginative, as was his mother. His mother was socially defiant, flaunting her beauty with the "disreputable" elements of society. Much later, Ruburt would date the "disreputable" men in his environment, yet neither mother or daughter saw that parallel. Ruburt's mother by then wanted a respectable, hopefully rich husband for Ruburt, and could not understand why he chose men who did not conform.

Ruburt chose a background in which he was poor, as did the mother. The mother was also bright, but chose to bank upon beauty for escape *(from her environment)*. Ruburt tried his brains instead. That material has been given *(over the years in a series of personal sessions)*.

("Yes.")

Ruburt's nonconformance took the larger framework of unconventional ideas. In the background, as a child under the organization of the Welfare Department, self-indulgence, small luxuries or too-unconventional behavior, were all dangerous in the framework chosen—the neighbors could report any transgressions to Welfare. At about this time *(tapping the photo)* Ruburt sat on the lap of an adult man on the front porch, and neighbors duly reported this—the idea being that sexual depravity could be involved.

Ruburt's mother knew that the child could be taken away were it proven that she was an unfit mother in any way, or unable to give the child proper care. Well over a year before this picture was taken, in fact, Ruburt was sent to a Catholic home.[5] There, unconventional thought was not tolerated. The inflexibility of dogma conscientiously applied to daily action was experienced, and within it Ruburt tried to apply himself and to focus his deeply mystical nature.*

*See Appendix 1.

He remembered his mother's constant criticism of him, but barely recalls his scandalized disapproval of her swearing, for example, on his return home. He threw himself headlong into the Catholic reality, pursued it with great stubborn diligence, used it as a framework of conventionality in which he could allow his mystic nature to grow.

When that nature grew out of the framework, he left it. All the beliefs that had once seemed so legitimate were then seen as hampering, and all their defects became plain. While he followed the framework, nothing could swerve him from it, and here (touching the photo) in this child's picture, you already have the unswerving nature, the great spontaneity, looking for a structure that will allow it growth, and yet give the illusion of safety.

The placid-looking child (in the photo) was as dogmatic and unyielding in some respects as Ruburt has ever been. Yet leaving the church framework, Ruburt fastened upon the mind as opposed to the intuitions. The child here was convinced that statues of Christ moved. Without a framework to contain that kind of experience, the growing girl began to squash it. Mystical experience became acceptable only through poetry or art, where it was accepted as creative, but not real enough to get him into trouble, or to upset the "new" framework. The new framework threw aside such superstitious nonsense. The mind would be harnessed, and art became the acceptable translator of mystical experience, and a cushion between that experience and the self. He threw some of the baby out with the bathwater.

The mystical went underground, reappearing as science fiction.[6] Again, in the social and religious background of the child, unconventional mental or physical actions could bring penalties. For a while the child could interpret mystical experience within the church—but even then, there was always conflict with church authorities.

(10:19.) Without this experience of following such a belief in the church so fervently, however, he would not understand the need of people for such beliefs, or be able to reach them as well as he does. His questioning mind was exercised originally as he began to examine religious beliefs. He was afraid that psychic experience, when he encountered it much later, might lead to a new dogma, and was determined not to use it in such a way.

His "conservatism," meaning his strong recognition of conservative ideas, is used as a springboard. He leaps from where he knows other people are into new areas. He combats the dogma of spiritualism as much as he did the dogma of the church.

He leaped, however, from the framework of the church into another framework, one in which mysticism was experienced secondhand, under the guise of artistic production. *Idea Construction*[7] literally shattered that framework.

(Pause.) For various reasons already given, concerning your joint relationship, and your own purposes *(to me)*, it has taken some time for a newer, suitable framework to form itself—one in which Ruburt is free to pursue mystic experience in a practical structure; one in which unconventionality of thought is allowed to continue freely. He felt that this could outgrow the framework of his art, as it did that of the church. The physical symptoms[8] served quite literally as a framework in which spontaneity was to some extent at least allowed a mental and psychic freedom, until he felt secure.

Take your break.

(10:31. Jane came out of trance very easily and quickly, as she usually does. The speed of her delivery for Seth had been average, which to me means that I'd been able to just comfortably keep up with my verbatim "shorthand" notes. Jane remembered little of what she'd said, yet now she felt the emotional impact of the material in her stomach—the reaction she often gets, she told me, when the information is of a personal or "charged" nature.

(I reminded her that I hoped Seth would comment on the old photograph of her in connection with probable realities, although now I could see that it would take him longer to develop answers than I'd thought it would. I didn't think we'd get any material on my own picture tonight.

(Resume in the same manner at 10:42.)

Now: You were correct. Probabilities are of course involved. Remember the first few sentences of this session. The general overall conditions were chosen, but many probable courses were concerned.

(As Seth, Jane pointed to the photograph of herself, taken when she was 12 years old.)

That child took a different course than this woman did *(Jane indicated herself as she sat in her rocker).* The dogmatism prevailed. The child's mystical nature, while strong, was not strong enough to defy the church framework, to leave it or to rise above its provided symbolism. It [the mysticism] was to be expressed, if curtailed, relatively speaking. The mind would be harnessed so that it would not ask too many questions. That child (*in the photo*) joined a nunnery, where she learned to regulate mystical experience according to acceptable precepts—but to express it nevertheless with some regularity, continuously, in a way of life that at least recognized its existence.

In your terms, the intersection with probabilities occurred one day in an interview the child had with a priest. The event, in Ruburt's terms, with its results in your probability, is mentioned in his *Rich Bed* (*see Note 4*). The child in seventh or eighth grade wrote a poem, expressing the desire to be a nun, and brought it to a parish priest. In your probability, the priest told the child that she was needed by her mother; but intuitively he saw that Ruburt's mysticism would not fit into the church organization.

In the other probability, Ruburt's desire at that time won. He managed to water down the extent and dimensions of his mysticism enough so that it was acceptable. In that other probability, there will be no long period of time in which the mystical experience would lie latent, and no necessity at all to put it into new terms.

The writing ability would follow as its handmaiden. In this world the artistic abilities were put first, but the mystical nature was given greater chances to expand and develop. And both were given the opportunity and the challenge of shattering old, historic frameworks, and of rising beyond them.

(*Intently:*) Ruburt here chose the writing structure, and has stuck to it as unswervingly as he once stuck to the church, yet always seeking a new framework. For a while he idealized you. Your guidance and strength were his framework. When it became apparent that you were also human, and not a framework, he became frightened. When you encouraged the emergence and expression of his mysticism, then you could no longer act, he felt, as a framework to contain it. By then it seemed to threaten the joint structure of your lives. He knew intuitively that you also used artistic creation as a buffer between yourself and mystical expression.

For all of the reasons given—and they are clearly given

(in personal sessions)—he was afraid that spontaneity, mental or physical, would threaten the long-accepted framework of your joint lives. If he went spontaneously forward in mystical experience, then, given his ideas, it threatened the conventional acceptance of his art. Conventional ideas of art and writing, upon which the old framework, now, was dependent, no longer fit.

Once again his natural experience, he felt, was leading him beyond structures he had considered safe.

(11:05.) He had you to consider. This experience of his was taking time from your art as well as his own, to his way of thinking. At the same time, the mystical nature rejoiced at its opportunity, and sensed its potential. Ruburt was determined to go ahead *(louder)*—he was also determined to keep the old structures and to ignore the cracks in them. In part his loyalty to you was connected, and his responsibility as he saw it to keep you focused as an artist, and to let nothing distract you. Yet here he was distracting you.

For a while your joint communication system was shaky. He was afraid to go ahead. The symptoms kept him at his job, at home, and allowed him to concentrate without outside distractions; kept him writing, with mystical experience dutifully translated into art.

The symptoms also served to focus that fantastic energy while he figured out how it should be used. He could not accept a new psychic framework while within it there were questions concerning your joint ideas of business, and divided loyalties about writing and painting; your personal fears, jointly, about spontaneity in general, and the need to protect your talents both from your own sexual natures and the distractions of others.

He could not accept a new framework, and he dared not let the old one go, so the symptoms became the physical materialization of these conflicts, and served many purposes. This child *(in the photo)*, grown up in its own probability, has no such problems. The challenges are not there, either—only in latent form.

Give us a moment . . . Ruburt greatly needs to realize that you love him, and accept him, as he is now in your terms. He gets from you what feeling of creaturehood acceptance he has, that you received in your way from your family in early years.

Your questioning, Joseph *(see Note 3)*, and your deep
distrust of the world's current theories, are shared as intensely by
Ruburt, and your joint insistence upon discovering new answers
is responsible for these sessions, and what will come from them.

You see his joyful potential, and he knows that you
do. Sometimes he feels lost, however, as an emotional human
being, groping toward that potential, and he needs to be com-
forted. As you know now, comforting him can be frightening to
you, because it returns you both to deep emotional realizations
and feelings that you sublimate in your paintings, and even to
mystical experiences that you also channel through your work.

Take a break.

*(11:25. "I've got that feeling again," Jane said, after
she'd come out of a deep trance. "Empty inside, you know, as
though it's all hitting home . . ."*

*(From Seth's delivery following last break, I've deleted
less than two short sentences of very personal material. Obviously, Jane and I did choose to meet the challenges presented by
the emergence of her psychic abilities 11 years ago. Those "new"
abilities offered creative possibilities so apparent that, given our
natures, we had little desire to do otherwise; beneath our doubts
and questions we intuitively felt the rightness of our decisions. I
found that I was able to contribute psychically in certain ways,
other than just recording the sessions. And to have at least some
of our deepest desires and motivations brought so clearly to conscious awareness, through psychic means or any other way, was
more than we'd thought possible in previous years. We found
such information especially valuable within the larger social context. With all of this, I was also eager to acquire whatever knowledge was available about both the philosophy and the act of
painting.*

*(I hope the [very slightly edited] information Seth
gives about my own family will trigger insights for others.
Resume at 11:37.)*

Now: Let us briefly, for now, attend to this.

*(Seth-Jane held up the photograph of me, taken when
I was almost 2 years old.⁹)*

That child enjoys great feelings of vigor <u>and</u> safety. In
your family relationship so far, so good. You were mainly surrounded by love and affirmation. Your parents were young. Your
mother had produced two beautiful boys; and she was also a

perfectionist in her way, and in her framework—one never understood by your father.

It was on the surface a very conventional structure, yet underneath, highly unwieldy. There were dogmas. The mother was expected to bear perfect children and to be subservient to the male, at least in outward fashion.

Your mother felt, then, that each played a fitting part in the marriage, in that your father had in her eyes great prospects, and she had given him two sons. It was only later that she felt he had not fulfilled his part of the bargain, and that you began to feel insecure. She had forced herself to focus all of her great emotional power into the marriage structure as they both understood it; but your father would not concentrate his own abilities into the cultural and financial structure as he had agreed to do in the tacit contract.

She had forced herself to contain her own reality in conventional terms—but to her way of thinking, he refused to use his energy in the accepted social and financial structure that each of them had accepted.

You began to feel, years later, as Ruburt did: that creativity was in its way dangerous, that it would lead you outside of accepted social structures, and definitely must be protected against normal family life.

(Picking up the photo of me:) Not in this picture, but quite alive, was your brother Linden. You insisted upon using your abilities, and tried for years to fit them into the commercial pattern, where they were accepted financially and socially, and in terms of your self-image. Finally you grew outside of the structure. [10] When you did, you made the artificial division in which good art would not sell—but you would do it anyway.

You would make your creativity real, in sense terms. Linden would not. He would keep it safely inside a "play" structure—not play necessarily in basic terms, but a structure in which he would work with models, cleverly, never applying his creative abilities in certain ways to a practical reality. They would be outside, safely, in that context.

The abilities that he possessed, that could be channeled into society as he understood it, were [so handled]. In such an eventuality, fragmentation occurred so that the abilities were dispersed, some directed into school, some into drawing, and others into his models. Those creative attributes were separated so that they could be safely handled, yet expressed to some degree, and not completely denied.

Your own character is in its way more direct, meaning that you maintained a more immediate focus. When that picture was taken, however, your parents were beginning to realize their difficulty. Your first year was one in which your father and mother were filled with expectation. Linden sensed that lack. He was secure, but not as secure as you had been, as the division between your parents was beginning to show.

Linden uses words now as a framework to contain creativity and communication, rather than to express them. You were more free-roaming here *(in the photo)* as a child because you felt safer physically. Linden was far less venturesome in that respect. . . .

(After a pause at 12:02, Seth delivered a page of material for Jane before ending the session at 12:16 A.M. As I interpret his information on the photographs, then, Jane's depicts an individual who was to become a probable Jane to the one I know, while mine is pretty much an early version of the self who's always lived in this reality . . .)

NOTES: Session 679

1. Seth tells us that all actions are initially mental in nature. Very simply, probable realities flow from the multitudinous actions—or events—we may envision, but choose not to actualize physically. But any motion of ours remains quite valid once it's conceived, and is carried out in all of its variations by probable selves in other realities. There can be communication between at least some of these worlds. Jane has had a modest success in touching upon a few of her probable selves, and plans to write about those experiments and others she hopes to conduct.

Seth, in his material on probable systems in Chapter 16 of *Seth Speaks*, says: "The soul can be described for that matter as a multi-dimensional, infinite act, each minute probability being brought somewhere into actuality and existence; an infinite creative act that creates for itself infinite dimensions in which fulfillment is possible."

Then see Chapter 15 of *The Seth Material:* Probable Selves and Probable Systems of Reality.

2. Indeed, Jane was to hold several sessions before we realized that Seth *had* begun a new book—see the 683rd session in this section. Seth had finished *Personal Reality* over six months ago. We suspended our regular sessions after that, yet were as busy as ever. My mother died in November,

1973. For some months we'd known her death was coming, and so had arranged our affairs around that irrevocable event; I spent weeks preparing the final manuscript of *Personal Reality* for the publisher; Jane conducted her ESP class whenever she could, and worked on her two books, *Adventures in Consciousness* and *Dialogues of the Soul and Mortal Self in Time.* She also gave a number of private Seth sessions for the two of us on a variety of subjects. We ended up calling a portion of one of those the 678th session and added it to our records, since the material, which Jane received at my request, concerned probabilities and Jerusalem. We hope to publish it some day.

3. Almost always Seth refers to Jane by her male entity name, "Ruburt"—and so "he," "his," and "him."

To sum up Seth's somewhat amused comments in the 12th session for January 2, 1964: "Sex, regardless of all your fleshy tales, is a psychic phenomenon, merely certain qualities which you call male and female. The qualities are real, however, and permeate other planes as well as your own. They are opposites which are nevertheless complementary, and which merge into one. When I say as I have that the overall entity [or whole self] is neither male or female, and yet refer to [some] entities by definitely male names such as 'Ruburt' and 'Joseph' [as Seth calls me], I merely mean that in the overall essence, the [given] entity identifies itself more with the so-called male characteristics than with the female."

4. Jane is treating the many, often chaotic details of her life in her autobiography, *From This Rich Bed.* She's been working on the project for some time along with her other books, and it may develop into more than one volume.

In a very simplified summary from *Rich Bed*: Jane was the only child of Marie Burdo and Delmer Roberts. She was 2 years old when her parents were divorced in 1931. With her daughter, the young Marie then returned to her own parents, and the home that the family had rented for a number of years: half of a double dwelling in a poor neighborhood in Saratoga Springs, N. Y. Marie began experiencing the early stages of rheumatoid arthritis, but worked as much as possible.

Eventually Jane's grandfather, Joseph Burdo, with whom she shared a deep mystical identification, was unable to support two extra people, and the family had to rely upon public assistance. Jane's grandmother was killed in an automobile accident in 1936. The next year, her grandfather moved out of the house. By then Marie was partially incapacitated, and the Welfare Department began to furnish mother and daughter with occasional (and often unreliable) domestic help. Thus, Jane was 9 years old in 1938, when she changed schools after finishing the third grade.

Always, when Jane and I present personal material in *"Unknown" Reality,* we have several things in mind. We not only want to give necessary background information relative to the sessions themselves, but to offer glimpses into the very complicated emotional and physical forces that lie beneath close long-term relationships. We think Seth's comments about our situations can help the reader better understand his or her own beliefs, motives, and desires.

5. See the notes about Jane and the photographs at the beginning of this session.

6. It took more than a little while for Jane's mystical nature to show itself in prose. Two years after we married, she published her first work of fiction, a short story about reincarnation called "The Red Wagon": It appeared in the December, 1956, issue of *The Magazine of Fantasy and Science Fiction* [© 1956 by Fantasy House, Inc., New York, N. Y.]. She was 27 years old, and most pleased with the beginning of her professional career. Within the next several years she sold a number of additional stories to the same magazine, as well as two short novels, and also published poetry and a little fiction in other markets.

Jane regarded all of these works as being science "fantasy" rather than "straight" science fiction. Her fictional themes especially were extensions of much of her earlier poetry, and contained the same kind of thinking that had led to her breaking with her church. She had no conscious intimations that within a decade she would develop the Seth material. "My mind just worked that way," Jane said of her stories. "I was concerned with those themes so I wrote about them."

I remember being a little surprised at her subject matter for "The Red Wagon"—for it's not contradictory to write here that even though she was so interested in reincarnation as a theory, we seldom talked about it. "The Red Wagon" is included in the collection *Ladies of Fantasy/Two Centuries of Sinister Stories by the Gentle Sex,* © 1975 by Manley and Lewis, and published by Lothrop, Lee & Shepard Co., New York, N. Y., 10016.

7. While writing poetry on the evening of September 9, 1963, Jane had her first consciously recognized psychic experience. It was a massive one, lasting at least two hours, astonishing her with the "barrage" of new ideas she discovered while immersed in it. During part of that time her consciousness left her body; and during it she produced through automatic writing a manuscript called *The Physical Universe As Idea Construction.* Later Seth told us that Jane's alteration of consciousness had represented his first attempt to make "formal" contact with her, although she wasn't aware of it then.

Idea Construction did serve as a psychic trigger, however; it led Jane to her outline for *How to Develop Your ESP Power* (see Note 2 for Seth's Preface in this book), then to the beginning of the Seth sessions two months later. "Enough energy was generated in that evening to change the direction of my life and my husband's," she wrote in Chapter 1 of *The Seth Material.* In that chapter she examines the experience in some detail, and

gives excerpts from *Idea Construction* itself. In *Seth Speaks*, see her Introduction and Session 596 in the Appendix for further references to that
original manuscript.

Idea Construction still charms Jane whenever she reads it over.
It's never been published, but she feels that all of her subsequent work is
directly related to it.

8. As Seth, Jane delivered several excellent pages of material on
her physical symptoms in the 645th session for March 5, 1973, in Chapter 11 of *Personal Reality*.

It's taken us some years to understand that behind Jane's
symptoms lay her efforts to understand and express the very strong creative
energy she's sensed within herself since childhood. Yet the conflict that
developed between her writing self and her mystical self, as explained by
Seth in *Personal Reality*, was only one facet of her intuitive drive toward
that expression: As Jane matured, she realized that there were other challenges for her to contend with too. Among them were the resolution of
some old family relationships—and nowhere in this note am I talking about
past lives or probable lives, but just the working out of hard questions
rooted in this present physical reality. From Seth and ourselves we've
accumulated much unpublished material about Jane's symptoms and atten-
dant matters. The bulk of it is often applicable to others, and eventually she
may write a book about the whole subject. Should she do so, it would
certainly be a history of one person's long efforts to grapple as fully as
possible—and not always successfully—with her own human qualities. But I
also think that in many ways it would be her most illuminating work. She
fully accepts the idea that she creates her own reality.

In the meantime, Jane's making good progress in handling her
personal challenges; now her work consists mainly of dissolving the set of
protective, symbolic body beliefs that she placed about the use of her great
energy.

9. I described that childhood photograph of myself at the beginning of the session. My parents had three sons. As the oldest, I was born
on June 20, 1919; next came Linden, 13 months later; the youngest,
Richard, followed me by 9 years. (Both names have been changed.)

The three of us got along well as children, although our natures
and interests varied considerably. All of us went through grade school and
high school in Sayre, a railroad town in northeastern Pennsylvania: Our
father settled his family there in 1923 when he opened an auto-repair and
battery shop. The separations in the family began to happen after Linden
and I graduated from high school, left Sayre, and started to work our
respective ways through college and an art school. Then came long periods
of military service for the three of us (World War II for Linden and me).
Years passed before I understood how much my parents had been affected
by the departure of their children.

Seth has discussed the members of the Butts family at times, including some of their reincarnational aspects. Six months before starting *"Unknown" Reality,* however, he made a few remarks that I've applied ever since to life in our physical reality: "Each person chooses his or her parents, accepting in terms of environment and heredity a bank of characteristics, attitudes, and abilities from which to draw in physical life. There is always a reason, and so each parent will represent to each child an unspeakable symbol, and often the two parents will represent glaring contrasts and different probabilities, so that the child can compare and contrast divergent realities . . . Your two brothers also chose the family situation. Each parent [both of whom are now deceased] represented opposites to them—but individual ones, and so they saw your parents differently [than you did]. Do not lose contact with them. . . ."

From this, it also follows that my mother and father saw *their* individual creations, or versions, of each of their children.

10. I gave up my commitment to commercial art in 1953, when I was 34 years old. My intuitive desire to do so had been growing slowly for several years. The act of separation finally became conscious and deliberate when I moved to a small community near Saratoga Springs, N. Y. (where Jane lived), to temporarily help an artist-writer friend produce a syndicated "comic" strip. This was the last commercial work I was to do for some time; I finally understood that I was simply more interested in painting pictures than in doing anything else. Since I believe that each of us creates our own reality in the most precise terms, it can hardly be a coincidence that at this time of decision my friend introduced Jane and me—for she was just as devoted to writing as I was to painting.

Session 680

February 6, 1974
9:21 P.M. Wednesday

(*In the last session, Seth began discussing separate photographs of Jane and me [taken at the ages of 12 and 2, respectively] in connection with his ideas about probable selves. Since we wanted Seth to continue with the same material tonight, we looked the pictures over again while waiting for him to come through. Then, without greetings:*)

Now: When I speak of probable selves, of course I am not speaking of some symbolic portion of the personality structure, or using the idea of probabilities as an analogy.

Consciousness <u>is</u> composed of energy, with everything that implies. The psyche, then, can be thought of as a conglomeration of highly charged "particles" of energy, following rules and properties, many simply unknown to you. On other levels, laws of dynamics apply to the energy sources of the self. Think of a given "self" as a nucleus of an energy gestalt of consciousness.

44

That nucleus, according to its intensity, will attract to it certain masses of the entire energy patterns available to a given identity.

In those terms the identity at birth is composed of a variety of such "selves," with their nuclei, and from that bank the physical personality has full freedom to draw. Ruburt's mystical nature was such a strong portion of the entire identity that in his present reality, and in the probable reality chosen—as mentioned when I discussed this picture *(of Jane)*—the mystic impulses and expressions were given play. Intersections with probable realities occur when one psychic grouping intensifies to a certain point, so that fulfillment as a self results.

Within the entire identity there may be, for example, several incipient selves, around whose nuclei the physical personality can form. In many instances one main personality is formed, and the incipient selves are drawn into it so that their abilities and interests become subsidiary, or remain largely latent. They are trace selves.

On many occasions, however, such latent selves will be as highly energized as the "main" personality. Since physically a certain personality structure must be maintained, traces are made. Therefore, when such situations arise, one or two of the other energized selves will literally spring apart from the time-space structure that you know.

From your viewpoint these offshoots of energy become unreal. They exist as surely as you do, however. In terms of energy, this multiplication of selves is a natural principle. *(To me:)* Your "sportsman self"* was never endowed with the same kind of force as that of your artistic or writing self. It became subsidiary, yet present to be drawn upon, taking joy through your motion and adding its vitality to your "main" personality.

Had it been given extra force through your environment, circumstances, or your own intent, then either your artistic self would have become subservient or complementary; or, if the energy selves were of nearly equal intensity, then one of them would have become an offshoot, propelled by its own need for fulfillment into a probable reality. Do you follow me?

(Yes."

(9:44.) Give us a moment . . . Your parents literally did not share the same reality at all. This is not as unusual as you

*See Appendix 2.

may think. They met and related in a place <u>between</u> each of their
realities. It was not that they disagreed with each other's interpretation of events. The events <u>were</u> different.

In terms of energy, intent is stabilizing. There is a
center to the self, again, that acts as a nucleus. The nucleus may
change, but it will always be the center from which physical
existence will radiate. Physically, intent or purpose forms that
center, regardless of its reality in terms of energy.

In your family life in <u>this</u> reality, your parents acted
opaquely to each other. There were strong energy shifts, so that
the personalities did not meet directly. Give us a moment . . .
Some of this is difficult to explain. In a way they were un-
focused, yet each with strong abilities, but dispersed. There was a
reason for this.

They contained within themselves intense and yet
blurred talents that were used as energy sources by the children.
Give us time . . . They came together precisely to give birth to
the family, and for no other main reason as far as their joint
reality was concerned. They seeded a generation, then.[1]

Your mother loved physical reality and took the
greatest pleasure in its most minute aspects, for all of her com-
plaints. Your father loved it but never trusted it. Each of your
parents had their strongest reality, this time, and in your terms,
in a probable system of reality—and <u>here</u> *(in this reality)* they
were offshoots. To them this system always seemed strange.[2]

In another system of reality your father was—in fact,
still is—a well-known inventor, who never married but used his
mechanically creative abilities to the fullest while avoiding emotional commitment. He met Stella *(my mother)*. They were going
to be married—and in terms of years, the same years are involved,
historically. At one time, then, in your father's past as you think
of it, having met Stella, he did <u>not</u> marry her after all. His love
was for machinery, the speed of motorcycles, mixing creativity
with metal. At that point of intersection, equal desires and
intents within him became like twin nuclei. Whole regroupings of
energy occurred, psychological and psychic implosions, so that
two equally valid personalities were aware in a world in which
only one could live at a time.

By far, the creative, mechanically inventive personality
began to outstrip the other. The father that you knew was the
probable self, therefore. That probable self, however, dealt with

emotional realities that the other avoided, and this was indeed his sole intent.

(*Pause at 10:07.*) This does not mean that such a personality is limited, basically, or that he does not collect about him new interests and challenges, for he is himself mobile. He even has many of the characteristics of the other self, though these of course are latent. But through having children your father brought about the birth of emotional existence, full-bodied and alive, in sons.[3]

This was a great fulfillment on his part, for the inventor did not trust himself to feel much emotion, much less give birth to emotional beings. In that other probability in which your parents originally met, your mother married a doctor, became a nurse, and helped her husband in his practice. She became an independent woman, and—again in your historical context—when it took some doing for a woman to distinguish herself.

She had one son, then a hysterectomy, on purpose. She schooled herself rigorously, moved in social circles, hid the unschooled, naïve aspects of herself. In that life, for example, she would certainly not wear red bows in her hair. All of the controlled energy made her somewhat bitter, though she was successful. She died in her 50's—do you follow me?

(*"Yes."*)

Her energy was such that it spilled over into this system with your father, however. Someday I will try to explain this more clearly, in terms of energy patterns. Historically, however, many probabilities exist at once. When your mother died in her 50's in one probable system, your mother in this system was the recipient of energy that then returned.

Your father's greatest vitality was in the inventor's reality, and so in your terms this one suffered. This does not mean that each personality, regardless of probabilities, is not endowed with free will, and so forth. Each is born, in whatever system, from a source gestalt energy, and develops.

When your picture was taken, therefore, your parents were already living in a probable reality, but you and [your brother] Linden were not. Now take your break.

(*10:25. Jane's trance had been an excellent one. She said that while immersed in it she'd thought the material "fantastically complicated ... like: 'Where are you in all of this— where's your soul?' "*)

(Some quick figuring showed us that the 50's for my mother had encompassed the years 1942-51. From my present viewpoint I had no idea if she'd consciously or unconsciously experienced any influx of energy resulting from the death of a probable self during that decade. In those days the Buttses didn't think in such terms, for one thing; for another, I was absent from the family home in Sayre for much of that time. In 1947, for example, when my mother was 55 years old, I was 28 and living in New York City. I wasn't to meet Jane for five years. And even if Stella Butts were still living, I think it would be difficult to question her about an event that would have taken place approximately a quarter of a century ago.

(I told Jane now that had my mother received any additional energy during her 50's, she might have expressed its benefits through the habitual mores of our society, in terms of changes rather than of probabilities, say: "My life changed for the better at that point, when I made that decision." I added that perhaps the important thing for us now was to observe our unfolding lives with Seth's ideas of the larger, or whole self, in mind, and so achieve insights we could interpret in terms of probabilities. So we decided not to ask Seth to backtrack and give us material about the son my mother's probable self had had in her reality, even though that son was a probable self of mine.

(As we talked, Jane decided to go back into trance; she was getting so many "bleed-throughs" on the material herself that she was beginning to feel consciously confused. But Seth had all the data there, she said, if she had the time to give it. Resume at 10:45.)

Now: There are basically no limitations to the self, and all portions of the self are connected—so the probable selves are aware, unconsciously, of their relationships.

Because no system is closed,[4] there are flows of energy between them, and interaction. Some of this is <u>exceedingly</u> difficult to verbalize, since the word "structure" itself is not only serialized, but <u>particle-ized</u>.

(Pause.) You think of entities as particles, for example, rather than as waves of energy, aware and alert, or as patterns. *(A one-minute pause.)* Think of Ruburt's living area in *Adventures*,[5] for example. Imagine that at age 13, three strong energy centers come to the surface of the personality—highly charged, so that one person cannot adequately fulfill the desires or abilities

presented. You may have a three-way split at age 13. At [age] 40, each of the three selves may recognize age 13 as a turning point, and wonder what might have happened had they chosen other courses.

None of this is predetermined. An offshoot probable self might leave your reality at age 13, say, but could intersect with you again at age 30 for a variety of reasons—where to you, you suddenly change a profession, or become aware of a talent you thought you had forgotten, and find yourself developing it with amazing ease.

(*To me again:*) Your birth (*in 1919*) coincided with the birth of your mother's child in that other reality, hence her stronger feelings toward you. Your birth, and that of your youngest brother (*Richard*), were highly charged for her—yours for the reasons just given, and your brother's because it represented the time of your mother's hysterectomy in that other reality. In this reality, Richard's birth represented your father's final attempt to deal with emotional reality. Both of your parents imbued the third son with the strongest emotional qualities of their natures. Your mother had him defiantly, after the usual childbirth age (*she was 36*), almost reacting against that [probable] hysterectomy. In this world, she could and would have another child.

Linden was the one "natural" child of this marriage. Watch how you interpret that, but he was the child least affected by other realities. For that reason, however, and because of your parents' personalities here, the same amount of attention was not paid him psychically, and he felt that lack.

(*11:02.*) Give us a moment . . . I told you (*in the last session*) that in one probability Ruburt was a nun, expressing mysticism in a highly disciplined context, where it must be watched so that it does not get out of hand. Because there is an unconscious flow of information and experience here, you have one of the reasons for Ruburt's caution in some psychic matters, and his fear of leading people astray. There were three offshoots: one, the nun, with mysticism conventionally expressed, but under guarded circumstances; one, the writer who veiled mystical experience through art; and one, the Ruburt you know, who experienced mystical experience directly, teaches others to do the same, and forms through writing a wedding of the two aspects. You have known two of those selves, then, and

you were present at Ruburt's birth with *Idea Construction.*
Give us a moment . . . The birth of Joseph took place
at York Beach with the dancing episode,[6] so you have in your
own experience examples in adult life. I cannot give you everything in one evening, of course. A few glimpses before a word for
Ruburt. Sportsmen make good money, so for this and other
reasons you early turned to commercial art—a field in which
artistic ability would be well paid for.

There were other connections, seemingly trivial yet
pertinent. You enjoyed doing comics with outdoor scenes: animals in motion, the body performing. As an audience watches a
sportsman perform, so those who read the comics watched your
characters perform in action across the page. All hidden patterns,
yet each one making sense. I will go into the birth of Joseph.
Now, however, a word to Ruburt.

(*11:15. After giving two pages of material for Jane,
here deleted, Seth closed out the session at 11:33 P.M.*)

NOTES: Session 680

1. See Note 9 for the last session.
2. I think that as a child I often sensed my parents' feelings of
strangeness about this reality, although I was quite unable to express myself
in those terms. Perhaps I'm reinterpreting old memories in the light of
Seth's material here. Consciously, however, I knew nothing then about
probable realities or the power of belief; I was just acutely aware of the
unending differences of opinion between my mother and father, and of my
unformed questions about the reasons for their behavior; at the same time I
saw them struggling to live like others I knew. I don't think I even discussed
my confused feelings with my brothers as we grew older. On several occasions Seth has given very blunt, very perceptive interpretations of the churn-
ing relationship involving my parents. That material is too long and complex
to excerpt here, but I'd like to treat it separately sometime.
    I do know a deeper compassion for my parents now than I did
when they were alive. To paraphrase a remark one of my brothers made
recently, I miss them in ways I couldn't have anticipated before their
deaths. Each of them died at the age of 81—my father in 1971, my mother
in 1973. For those who are interested, I drew a likeness of my father for
one of my pen-and-ink illustrations in Jane's *Dialogues,* and incorporated an
image of my mother in another one. See pages 89 and 137 of that book.
    3. While dealing with emotional realities in this life, my father
also exercised very considerable mechanical abilities. According to Seth's

ideas, these would have represented bleed-throughs from his "inventor" probable reality.

The Butts family albums contain numerous photographs of my father as a young man, many of them self-taken with the aid of a timer; he poses with a variety of automobiles and motorcycles through the years before his marriage to my mother in 1917, and afterward, too. Sometimes he'd assembled the vehicles himself, or modified them in his own ways. In 1922 he took his wife and children (I was 3 years old, Linden not yet 2) on a six-month motor trip from the East Coast to California. When our touring car broke a rear axle on a remote dirt road in Montana, he fashioned a substitute in a blacksmith shop.

Returning east to Sayre, Pa., he opened his auto-repair and battery shop. (Again, see Note 9 for the 679th session.) Through our early school years Linden and I had part-time "jobs" at our father's shop, and many chances to watch him work. I think that his exacting mechanical abilities are reflected in Linden's very realistic models, and are transmuted in the methods I use to solidly "construct" my paintings and to keep the records for the Seth material.

4. Seth has insisted from the very beginning of these sessions (late in 1963) that there are no closed systems—and in so doing has given us clues about his own ability to travel through at least some of them.

From the 12th session for January 2, 1964: "I have more senses, so to speak, in operating use . . . than you have, because not only am I aware of my own plane [or reality], but of yours and other parallel planes, even though I myself have not existed in some of those others . . ." And: "There are certain environments that I cannot glimpse from my viewpoint, although I have greater understanding of these things than you. I realize that the changes that must occur before I can view those other planes will occur in me, and not in the planes."

From the 13th session for January 6 of the same year: "If I speak in analogies and images, it is because I must relate with the world that is familiar to you."

From the 14th session for January 8: "Everything on your plane is a materialization of something that exists independently of your plane."

From the 15th session for January 13: "Imagination allows you to enter into these planes . . . Pretend that you not only understand your cat's concept of time to some degree, but could also experience his sense of time through the cat [Willy] himself. In doing this you would in no way bother, inhibit, or annoy the cat. He would not be aware of your presence. Nor could this be represented as any sort of invasion.

"Imagine further that you actually experienced the feeling of such a furry coat, and all the other feline equipment from the inside, purely as a spectator. This would loosely represent an analogy to my traveling to other planes. It follows that I could not travel to 'higher' environments than my own, where more acute senses would instantly perceive me. . .On many planes, we are fully visible to others on that plane. To some we are invisible; and to us, some are invisible.

"As I have mentioned earlier, the senses change according to the plane of materialization. If you are speaking about my present form, I can be many forms. That is, within limits I can change my form, but in doing so I do not actually change my form as much as I choose to become part of something else.

"My incipient form is a man's form, if this is what you want to know, but it is not materialized in the same fashion as yours—that is, as your form [is] —and I can dematerialize it whenever I choose. It is not at all physical in your terms, however, and so here I suppose we will run into a block [in your understanding] . . . ."

Jane quotes Seth's material from the 12th session much more extensively in Chapter 3 of *The Seth Material*; see Seth's analogy involving cubes (realities) within cubes.

5. Jane is now working on the final draft of her own theoretical work on psychic matters, *Adventures in Consciousness: An Introduction to Aspect Psychology*. She started *Adventures* in July, 1971, and has stayed with it through all of her other writing projects. It's first mentioned (as *Adventures in Consciousness*) in Chapter 21 of *Seth Speaks*; see the 587th session. In her glossary for *Adventures* Jane defines the living area as "The 'paths' our lives follow from birth to death."

A note added later: *Adventures* (or *Aspects*, as we also call it) was published in September, 1975, by Prentice-Hall, Inc. I did 16 schematic pen-and-ink drawings for it, many of which contain representations of Jane's "living area."

6. Jane covers our York Beach "dancing episode" in Chapter 2 of *The Seth Material,* and also quotes information Seth gave us on it in later sessions. The mystifying event took place during our vacation in York Beach, Maine, in August, 1963, a few months before Jane began to speak for Seth. At the time we understood little of what happened; yet the event represented a key episode at the very beginning of our psychic education; for in a crowded, smoky hotel barroom Jane and I unknowingly created physical "personality fragments" of ourselves—then came face to face with them. In the 9th session for December 18, 1963, Seth explained what we had been up to, and called our creations "fragments of sour selves, thrown-off materializations of your own negative and aggressive feelings." (Naturally, the more Seth told us about the human ability to generate such forms, the more questions we had!) In that 9th session Seth also used his term, "probable self," for the first time.

I might add that if the York Beach adventure was a strong sign for us of psychic development to come (even if we weren't able to interpret much of it at first), then Jane's reception a month later of her manuscript, *Idea Construction*, was another; and that experience contained obvious psychic elements. See Note 7 for the last session.

Session 681
February 11, 1974
9:28 P.M. Monday

("I'm just waiting," Jane said at 9:25, after we'd been sitting for the session since 9:10. "Seth's around, I can tell. I was getting stuff earlier, but I'm just waiting until it's ready. I can feel concepts in my head, but they aren't clear yet, not the way they should be. It's as though Seth's going to have a hard time explaining them.")

Now: Good evening—

("Good evening, Seth.")

—and Ruburt is correct, so give us a moment . . .

What I am about to explain is difficult. Purposely, it is not as yet in any of the books, simply because certain beliefs must be dispensed with before these ideas can be at all accepted.

It is not that I am holding back so much as that, in your terms, what follows is dependent upon an understanding of concepts presented earlier. People who are still worrying about one soul, gods, and devils, must be helped to relate to greater realities from their own framework, and gently led away from it if possible. Probabilities have been mentioned in such a way that alternate realities are presented, showing such people that choices are available.

The deeper explanations, however, demand a further expansion of ideas of consciousness, and a certain reorientation. It is extremely important that you bear in mind the importance of free will, and the presence of your own identity as you think of it. With that preamble, let me continue then.

It is not so much a matter of Ruburt's vocabulary, incidentally, since even a specialized scientific one would only present these ideas in its own distorted fashion. It is more a problem of basic language itself, as you are acquainted with it. Words do not exist, for example, for some of the ideas I hope to convey. We will, at any rate, begin.

All probable worlds exist now. All probable variations on the most minute aspect in any reality exist now. You weave in and out of probabilities constantly, picking and choosing as you go along. The cells within your body do the same thing.

(Slowly:) I told you once that there were pulses of activity in which you blinked off and on—this applying even to atomic and subatomic particles.[1] "You" assign as real—present here and now—only that activity that is your signal. "You" are not aware of the others. When people think in terms of one self, they of course identify with one body. You know that the cellular structure of it changes constantly. The body is at any given moment, however, a mass conglomeration of energy formed from that rich bank of probable activity. The body is not stable in the terms usually thought of. On deeper biological levels the cells straddle probabilities, and trigger responses. Consciousness rides upon and within the pulses mentioned earlier, and forms its own organizations of identity. Each probability—probable only in relation to and from the standpoint of another probability—is inviolate, however, in that it is not destroyed. Once formed, the pattern will follow its own nature.

(A one-minute pause at 9:50, head bowed, eyes closed.) The organizations of consciousness "grow" even as cells grow into organs. Groups of probable selves, then, can and do form their own identity structure, which is quite aware of the probable selves involved. In your reality, experience is dependent upon time, but all experience is not so structured. There are, for example, parallel events that are followed as easily as you follow consecutive events.

The structure of probabilities deals with parallel experience on all levels. Your consciousness picks and chooses to accept as real the results of, and ramifications of, only certain overall purposes, desires, or intents. You follow these through a time structure. Your focus allows other just-as-legitimate experience to become invisible or unfelt.

In the same way that you latch upon one personal biological history, you latch upon but one mass earth history. Others go on about you all the time, and other probable selves of your own experience their "histories" parallel to yours. In practical terms of sense data, those worlds do not meet. In deeper terms they coincide. Any of the infinite number of events that could have happened to you and Ruburt [do] happen. Your attention span simply does not include such activity.

(10:00.) Such endless creativity can seem so dazzling that the individual would appear lost within it,[2] yet consciousness forms its own organizations and psychic interactions at all levels. Any consciousness automatically tries to express itself in all probable directions, and does so. In so doing it will experience All That Is through its own being, though interpreted, of course, through that familiar reality of its own. You grow probable selves as a flower grows petals. Each probable self, however, will follow through in its own reality—that is, it will experience to the fullest those dimensions inherent to it. You pick and choose one birth and one death, in your terms.

(To me:) You died as a young boy in an operation, however, in this life as you think of it. You died again in the war, where you were a pilot—but those are not your official deaths, so you do not recognize them.[3]

Science likes to think that it deals with predictable action. It perceives such a small amount of data, however, and in such a limited area, that the great inner unpredictability of any molecule, atom, or wave is not apparent. Scientists perceive only what appears within your system, and that often appears predictable.

Give us a moment . . . True order and organization, even of biological structure, can be achieved only by granting a basic unpredictability. I am aware that this sounds startling.

Basically, however, the motion of any wave or particle or entity is unpredictable—freewheeling and undetermined. Your life structure is a result of that unpredictability. Your psychological structure is also. However, because you are presented with a fairly cohesive picture, in which certain laws seem to apply, you think that the laws come first and physical reality follows. Instead, the cohesive picture is the result of the unpredictable nature that is and must be basic to all energy.

Statistics provide an artificial, predetermined framework in which your reality is then examined. Mathematics is a theoretical organized structure that of itself imposes your ideas of order and predictability. Statistically, the position of an atom can be theorized, but no one knows where any given atom is at any given time.[4]

(10:22.) You are examining probable atoms. You are composed of probable atoms. (A one-minute pause.) Give us a moment . . . (A one-minute pause.) Consciousness, to be fully free, had to be endowed with unpredictability. All That Is had to surprise himself, itself, herself, constantly, through freely granting itself its own freedom, or forever repeat itself. This basic unpredictability then follows through on all levels of consciousness and being. A certain cellular structure may seem inevitable within its own frame of reference only because opposing or contradictory probabilities do not appear therein.

In your terms, consciousness is able to hold its own sense of identity by accepting one probability, one physical life, for example, and maintaining its identity through a lifetime. Even then, certain events will be remembered and others forgotten. The consciousness also learns to handle alternate moments as it "matures." As it does so mature it forms a new, larger framework of identity, as the cell forms into an organ on another level.

In your terms—the phrase is necessary—the moment point,[5] the present, is the point of interaction between all existences and reality. All probabilities flow through it, though one of your moment points may be experienced as centuries, or as a breath, in other probable realities of which you are a part.

(Pause at 10:36.) Ruburt is at this moment feeling massive.* He is experiencing several things. The inner cellular

*See Appendix 3.

body consciousness feels itself massive, while to you cells are minute. The sounds of the package, for example *(as Seth, Jane crumpled an empty cigarette package)*, or the fingernails across the table *(demonstrated)*, are magnified, for in the cellular world they are an important outside-the-self cosmic event—messages of great importance. The cellular consciousness experiences itself as eternal, though to you the cells have a brief life. But those cells are aware of the body's history, in your terms, and in a much more familiar fashion than you are aware of the earth's history.

The cells are also aware of probabilities in a more familiar fashion than you are, as they manipulate the past and future history of the body. Ruburt now, again, is experiencing massiveness, as in your idea of probabilities the cellular structure feels its vast endurance. Working with events not even real to you, it produces a physical structure that maintains identity and predictability out of a vastly creative network. That network is unpredictable, yet from it Ruburt can predictably put ashes into that shell. *(Jane held up her favorite ashtray, the abalone shell we'd found in Baja California in 1958, and tapped some ashes into it from her cigarette.)* The predictability of that gesture rests upon the basis of an unpredictability, in which multitudinous other actions could have occurred, and in other realities do occur.

(10:46.) You had better give us a moment, and rest your hand.

(Jane had been speaking steadily in trance, if with many pauses, for 78 minutes. Now she still sat upright in her chair, sipping beer, eyes closed. A minute passed.)

Now: Your beliefs and intents cause you to pick, from an unpredictable group of actions, those that you want to happen. You experience those events. *(To me:)* "Your" desire to live straddled the death of the child in an operation. The child's desire to die chose that event. People are as free as atoms are. Give us a moment . . . In no way could you predict what would happen to the child in that photograph of yourself.[6] In no way now can you "predict" what will happen to you now. You can choose to accept as your reality any number of given unpredictable events. In that respect, the choice is yours, but all the events you do not accept occur nevertheless.

In a very small measure you can see how this works when you think of your mother in, say, her last years, and compare your idea of her with those of [your brothers] Linden and Richard. She was a different person to each of you. She was herself; but in the interweavings of probabilities, while certain agreed-upon historic events were accepted, she admitted into her reality whatever portions of your probable reality she chose. Each of you had a different mother.

Probabilities intersect then in your experience, and their intersection you call reality. Biologically and psychically these are intersections, coming-togethers, consciousness adopting a focus.

Again, Ruburt is still experiencing massiveness. . . . All of the atoms and molecules that have composed your body since your birth, and will compose it until your death, in your terms, exist now; so even your knowledge of the body is experienced in a time form—that is, bit by bit.

(Long pause at 11:05.) Part of Ruburt's feeling of massiveness comes from the mass experience of the body, existing all at once. Therefore to him the body feels larger. Calculations impossible to describe occur, so that from this basic unpredictability you experience what seem to be predictable actions. This is only because you focus upon those actions that "make sense" in your reality, and ignore all others. I am not speaking symbolically, of course, when I say you died as a youngster. Nor was any harsh reality forced upon the mother by the dying child, for that portion of your mother was the part that regretted having had the child.

Now: Atoms can move in more directions than one at once.[7] You only perceive scientifically the probable motion you are interested in. The same applies to subjective experience.

Now, take your break.

(11:10. Jane slowly came out of one of her longest session trances; she'd been under for an hour and forty-two minutes. I've indicated but a few of the many long pauses she took.

(She still felt massive. Her eyes rolled up, then closed again. "Things are really weird, like the sky's cracking . . . Seth talking about it sort of controlled things, but now my head's getting really big . . ." I roused her with a call, and she said, "Yeah, it's wild . . . I don't know whether I should break it or go along with it. I feel like my head is real big now, and going around to the right and spinning—it's huge . . ."

(11:15. "And when there isn't any sound outside, everything's ringing—the way your ears do, only more so . . . Now my whole body's really big. Massive. I might end it. It's funny: It's not terribly pleasant. My teeth seem really huge—everything—my feet . . ."

(11:17. Jane smiled as I called her again. "I just got the image of being a giant in a giant room. Then something I don't understand: an image of myself as a gorilla, or something like that. I'm as tall as the ceiling, trying to knock the walls down . . . I'm not understanding what's going on very well. Now I'm getting bigger. I think I'm going to come out of it . . . My face isn't doing anything, is it? Changing in any way?"

("No.")

(11:21. "I had the feeling of my hair being long and parted in the middle, as though I've got some kind of humanoid features; you know, with the hair hanging down on each side of my face, which is something like an animal's—but with very intelligent eyes, very warm and soft."[8] Jane finally opened her eyes. Her ears still rang, so loudly that she asked me if I heard the same sound. I told her I didn't. We walked around the room. I made her half a sandwich. "It's sort of frustrating," she said. "It's as though I'm seeing or feeling what I'm capable of at the moment, but I know there's more there behind that. I can feel it, but I can't get it out."

(As she ate Jane said, "The noises in my mouth are real loud—you're not used to it." When she sipped beer, she felt the cold liquid descend inside her body, but displaced to the right of her esophagous. She recited a list of opposing feelings in her own body that she was simultaneously aware of in her "bigger body": Her right foot was very cold, her back very hot . . . I got her a sweater, for our living room had cooled off. The February night was very cold.

(Resume, finally, at 11:47.)

Now: Only out of unpredictability can an infinite number of <u>orders</u>, or <u>ordered systems</u>, arise.

Anything less than complete unpredictability will ultimately result in stagnation, or orders of existence that in the long run are self-defeating. Only from unpredictability can any system emerge that can be predictable within itself. Only within complete freedom of motion is any "ordered" motion truly possible.

From the "chaotic" bed of your dreams springs your ordered daily organized action. In your reality, the behavior of your consciousness and of your molecules are highly connected. Your type of consciousness presupposes a molecular consciousness, and your kind of consciousness is inherent in molecular consciousness—inherent within your system, but not basically predictable. Predictability is simply another word for significance. Unpredictability, looking at itself in a variety of different fashions, finds certain portions of itself significant, and forms certain orders, or ordered sequences, about itself. In one of our very early sessions, I told you that you perceive from a vast field only certain data that you find meaningful. That data could only arise from the bed of unpredictability. Only unpredictability can provide the greatest source of probable orders.

Your cells are quite able to handle different orders of events; therefore in the dream state they are able, in their individual ways, to perceive your experience, and from it to choose those actualities you want made real in your terms.

In dreams you are acquainted with probable events, from which you then choose; *(to me:)* so before you died as a child, you knew that you could pick or choose that death. In greater terms you chose both life and death, and the picture of you at the age of 16[9] was never taken in one reality.

(Pause.) We have quite all that Ruburt can handle this evening, and this is a beginning.

(Now Seth came through with half a page of material for Jane, then wound up the evening's work with this joking comment:)

His probable brain can translate only so much of this at one time.

("Yes. Good night." 12:06 A.M. Jane still felt somewhat massive. A few notes added the next day: She slept restlessly, and found herself "giving material on probabilities just about all night." She woke up often, and at such times was relieved to discover that she hadn't been holding a session that I wasn't recording. As it was, she laughed, the material was still "safe"—we'd get it at a regular session.

(Jane has often told me that usually on such nighttime occasions she doesn't feel Seth's presence or hear his voice. Instead she's just aware of the material "running through her.")

NOTES: Session 681

1. In several of the sessions he delivered in 1970-71 for *Seth Speaks*, Seth explained how atoms and molecules phase in and out of our physical system. See especially the 567th session in Chapter 16: "Now the same sort of behavior occurs on a deep, basic, secret and unexplored psychological level." Some of the probable systems arising out of such activity would be quite alien to us: "One such fluctuation might take several thousand of your years . . . [which] would be experienced, say, as a second of your time . . ." Jane elaborates upon related ideas from her own viewpoint in Chapter 10, among others, in her *Adventures in Consciousness*.

2. Long before this, Seth was concerned that Jane and I might feel insignificant once we attempted to grasp the endless ramifications of consciousness as he was explaining them to us. As he said in the 29th session for February 26, 1964: "Later I will attempt to show you where the boundaries are—though *(with a laugh)* there really are no boundaries—that form a variety of such planes [realities] into a sphere of relation in which, to some extent, cause-and-effect operates as you understand it. Beyond that for a long time there will be no need for me to go any more deeply. I will speak of the entity, the personalities, the reincarnations, the diverse personality fragment groupings, the planes with which you are familiar or can understand, and ultimately try to deal with your questions, implied if not spoken, as to where entities came from to begin with.

". . . Needless to say, I wanted you to know that there is much more than even this, complexities that are truly astounding, intelligences that operate in what I suppose you would call a gestalt fashion, building blocks of vitalities of truly unbelievable maturity, awareness, and comprehension. These are the near ultimate [as I understand such things].

"This material should not make you feel unimportant or insignificant. The framework is so woven that each particle [of consciousness] is dependent upon every other. The strength of one adds to the strength of all. The weakness of one weakens the whole. The energy of one recreates the whole. The striving of one increases the potentiality of everything that is, and this places great responsibility upon every consciousness.

"I would even advise a double reading of the above sentence, for it is a keystone, and a vital one. Rising to challenges is a basis for existence in every aspect of existence. It is the developer of all abilities, and at the risk of being trite, it is the responsibility of even the most minute particle of consciousness to use its own abilities, and all of its abilities, to the utmost. Upon the degree to which this is done rests the power and coherence of everything that is."

See also the 453rd session for December 4, 1968, in the Appendix of *The Seth Material*.

3. According to Seth, then, in one probability I failed to survive the operation I underwent for appendicitis in this reality when I was 11

years old. My second probable death took place sometime during the years of my military service (1943-46) in World War II. It's interesting to note that Seth says I was a pilot, and hence an officer, in that probability. In the reality *I* know, I served in the ATC—the Air Transport Command—as an aircraft instrument specialist and mechanic, with the rank of staff sergeant. While on duty in some of the remote islands of the Pacific, however, I managed to get in some flying time, though not as a pilot.

4. I thought that in his last sentence especially Seth was flirting with the principle of uncertainty, or indeterminacy, as postulated in 1927 by the German physicist Werner Heisenberg. In quantum mechanics this axiom maintains that it's not possible to simultaneously ascertain the momentum and position of a subatomic wave-particle like an electron, say— electrons being one of the qualities that make up atoms. The day after this session was held, I asked Jane if she'd heard of Heisenberg. She hadn't; nor did she understand his work, as best I could explain it to her.

Just before break at 11:10, Seth offers up another fillip about atoms . . .

5. Seth's concept of the moment point is implicit in his material as I quote it in Note 1 for this session. Also see the 514th session in Chapter 2 of *Seth Speaks,* and the 668th session in Chapter 19 of *Personal Reality.*

At the age of 25, however, (nine years before the beginning of the sessions), Jane expressed an intuitive grasp of the moment point in these lines of her poem, *More Than Men*:

> *Between each ticking of the clock*
> *Long centuries pass*
> *In universes hidden from our own.*

6. Seth referred to the photograph my father had taken of me when I was about 2 years old; see the appropriate note at the beginning of the 679th session.

Since Seth mentioned predictions in connection with the photograph, this is a good time to present a few of the things he said in an earlier session about his own ability to predict, and about the subject in general. Jane and I have found this very useful material to keep in mind. From the 234th session for February 16, 1966:

"Now: Often precognitive information will appear to be wrong. In some cases this is because a self has chosen a different probable event for physical materialization [than the one predicted]. I have access to the field of probabilities and you do not, egotistically. . . . To me, your past, present, and future merge into one.

"On the other hand, as I have told you, you change your past continually. It does not appear to change to you, for you change with it. . . You alter your future in the same manner. In such cases it is necessary that the correct channel of probable events be perceived—correct meaning the channel which shall be ultimately chosen [for actualization by the subject].

"These choices, however, are based upon your changing perception of past and present. Because I have a larger scope of perception than you, I can with greater facility predict what may happen. But this is dependent upon my prediction as to which choice [of probable events] you will make, and the choice is still your own ... Predictions, *per se*, do not contradict the theory of free will, though free will is dependent upon much more than any freedom of the ego alone. If the ego were allowed to make all the choices, with no veto power from other layers of the self, you would all be in a sad position indeed.

"I can, therefore, perceive far more than you can of your own future. I am hardly omnipotent, however. Nor, strictly speaking, is such omnipotence possible."

7. As an artist, my intuitive reaction to Seth's remark that an atom can move in more than one direction at once was to associate that ability with his notions of simultaneous time and probabilities. The artist, since he isn't any kind of a scientist (even though he might be interested in science in general), attempts to grapple with the statement as best he can, in light of the *feeling* he has for what Seth is trying to say. At the same time he realizes that from his artistic viewpoint he may not be able to understand the paradox of "contradictory" motions.

To simplify a great deal: In modern physics it's said that atoms are *processes*, not *things*; that atoms and/or their constituents can appear as either waves or particles, depending on how we observe them; and that these qualities exist outside of our coarse world of space and time. Atoms are patterns of probabilities. It's further said that our attempts to describe or visualize such nonphysical qualities inevitably cause us to misinterpret them; so the artist wonders whether the atom's movement in more than one direction at once may not be perfectly "natural" in its own environment—some sort of ability quite separate from any play we may indulge in with words while trying to consciously comprehend it.

8. Jane's assertion tonight that she felt a humanoid aspect of herself reminded me of the material she'd given almost a year ago in Chapter 12 of *Personal Reality*, on "the idea of natural therapy in animals," and animal medicine men. She came up with that information on her own, too, and during a session break. On that occasion she was more of an observer. There was quite a difference in "physical size" between the images she had seen then and her visions of herself this evening; yet there were similarities also, for of that earlier experience she said: "I saw creatures who walked upright—hairy, with brilliant compassionate eyes ..." See the 648th session at 11:30.

9. On facing pages in our album, Jane and I have a pair of large, rather formal photographs of ourselves that we've often joked about. As it happened we looked at them earlier this evening. Both of them were taken

in 1936. Jane, in her photograph, is 6½ years old. I'm 16 in mine, and one year short of finishing high school. More than once Jane has asked me what I'd have thought at that age had I been aware that my wife-to-be was a "round-faced little kid, still playing with paper dolls . . ."

Session 682
February 13, 1974
9:27 P.M. Wednesday

("I think Seth's heading toward something new," Jane said at 9:20, as we sat waiting for the session. "Funny—not that we're going to come up with new words, but some new ideas. I feel like I've had three or four drinks, or as though I'm in a different state of consciousness already—and here I haven't had anything except this apricot juice..."

(Indeed, we were out of beer, which Jane usually drinks during the sessions, and she didn't want any wine. "I feel him—Seth—around now," she said, "but it's like last time: I'm getting stuff, but I'm waiting until it's clear... I don't really feel looped, but the center of focus I always use in the sessions seems strange. There's an unfamiliarity about finding it. I'd say, although I don't know, that I'm already in a deeper state than usual..."

(A note: The night was very warm, and followed a series

65

of really cold ones through most of this month. Much snow had melted today. The change in the weather was quite exhilarating.)
Now: Good evening.
("Good evening, Seth."
(Pause.) The Nature of Personal Reality[1] is an excellent handbook, one that will enable people to manipulate in the world they know with greater effectiveness. It will not matter whether or not they understand deeper issues upon which the whole nature of <u>physical</u> reality itself depends. The material I am giving now will attempt some explanation of those deeper issues.

Ruburt's own development makes this possible, for it was necessary that he progress to the point that he has in *Adventures*,[2] and reach the level of certain theories so that these could be used as springboards. Give us a moment . . .

We must unfortunately often deal with analogies, because they can form bridgeworks between concepts. There are units of consciousness,[3] then, as there are units of matter. I do not want you to think of these units as particles. There is a basic unit of consciousness that, expressed, will not be broken down, as once it was thought that an atom was the smallest unit and could not be broken down. The basic unit of consciousness obviously is not physical. It contains within itself innately infinite properties of expansion, development, and organization; yet within itself always maintains the kernel of its own individuality. Despite whatever organizations it becomes part of, or how it mixes with other such basic units, its own identity is not annihilated.

It is aware energy, identified within itself as itself, not "personified" but <u>awareized</u>. It is therefore the source of all other kinds of consciousness, and the varieties of its activity are infinite. It combines with others of its kind, forming then units of consciousness—as, mentioned often, atoms and molecules combine.

This basic unit is endowed with unpredictability. That very unpredictability allows for infinite patterns and fulfillments. The word "soul" unfortunately has been so used in regard to your species that it becomes highly difficult to unravel the conceptual difficulties. Using usual definitions, you would call a soul the result of a certain organization of such units, which you would then recognize as a "soul."

(9:47.) That leads to the old inevitable questions: Do

animals have souls—or do trees, or rocks? In line with the usual definition then, in your terms, this smallest unit would be "soul stuff." That viewpoint however is highly limited, for "above you," using that scale, there are other more developed organizations of these units; and so from that "more exalted viewpoint," you would seem to be junior souls indeed.

So I prefer, here at least, to speak of these units of consciousness instead. *(Long pause.)* Their nature is the vitalizing force behind everything in your physical universe, and others as well. These units can indeed appear in several places at once, and without going through space, in your terms. Literally now, these basic units of consciousness can be in all places at once. They are in all places at once. They will not be recognized because they will always appear as something else.

Of course they move faster than light. There are millions of them in one atom—many millions. Each of these units is aware of the reality of all others, and influences all others. In your terms these units can move forward or backward in time, but they can also move into thresholds of time with which you are not familiar.[4]

All probabilities are probed and experienced, and all possible universes created from these units. Therefore, there are realities in which the endless probabilities of one given event are probed, and all experience grouped about that venture.

There are systems in which a moment,[5] from your standpoint, is made to endure for the life of a universe. I do not mean that a moment is simply stretched, or that time is slowed down alone, but that all the experiences possible within a moment become realities within that framework. Such systems have little to do with you in any practical manner, nor is such information given to dwarf your idea of what your own consciousness is. It is important, however, that you realize the fact that there is more creativity and variety in an inner reality than you ever physically perceive.

(10:06.) These units of consciousness do not have human characteristics, of course. They do, however, possess their own "inclinations," leanings, propensities—and perhaps "propensities" comes closest to the term I want. I do not want you to think of them as miniature people. Nevertheless, neither are they clumps of "idle" energy. They are vitalized, aware, charged, with all the qualifications of being.

All psychological structures then are composed of such organizations, however long- or short-lived in your terms. They are innately endowed with the desire or propensity for growth and creative organization. They are not found alone, then, in isolation. Since these units of consciousness exist at once, they are aware of all the organized self-structures of which they are a part. To this extent, all probable realities are connected in that basic manner. These units grow out of themselves. Since I have told you that in your terms your past, present, and future exist at once, these units are constantly emerging out of your now-point from both the future and the past.

(*Long pause, one of many.*) I do not want to ruin your idea of stability, and I do not want to confuse you. The fact remains that in speaking of probabilities thus far, I have simplified the issues considerably. (*To me:*) I said, for example, that you died as a child in one probability, and again in the (*military*) service, and I gave you a small sample of your parents' probable history. (*See the last two sessions.*) In doing so I used ideas and terms quite easily grasped. The larger picture is somewhat more difficult—by far—to express.

(*10:21. "Are you saying that you* have *to keep things that simple for us?" I asked.*)

I am saying that I am now ready to lead you beyond those necessary preliminaries.

All matter is based upon the units mentioned, with their unpredictability and their propensity for exploring all probabilities. Even your atomic structure, then, is poised between probabilities. If this is true, then obviously "you" are aware of only one small probable portion of yourself—and this portion you protect as your identity (underlined). If you think of it as simply a focus taken by "your" greater identity, then you will be able to follow what I am saying without feeling puny by contrast, or lost.[6] The focus that you have is indeed inviolate.

I have often said that even in your lifetimes, all probable variations of any one event occur, but I never went much further. With your focus, it seems that you have a line of identity from birth to death. Looking back at any point, you are sure that the "self" of ten years ago is the self of today, though perhaps changed in certain respects.

There is, of course, no single-line kind of development at all. In the first place, as you know, your life is at once, though you experience, practically, a life-to-death sequence—Ruburt's living area in *Adventures*.[7] Every probable event that could happen to you, happens. I gave you one or two small examples of your mother's probable existences. Think in physical terms of the generations going out from one seed into the ages.

Now: Your self-reality in any given moment is like that seed, following probable generations that appear in other dimensions as well as this one. In each now-moment, you draw from the vast bank of unpredictable actions certain ones that are "significant" to you; and your private idea of significance will result in what then seems to be predictable action.

(10:36.) Propensity is a selection of significance, an inclination toward the formation of selected experience. This applies on all levels—atomic and psychological—and to biological stimulus and mental intent.

These basic units move toward organizations then of a selective nature. Having an unpredictable field to draw from, they select activity according to those significances. Period. Various kinds of significances are the result of the units' individual natures. The body that you have is a probable body. It is the result of one line of "development" that could be taken by your particular earth personality in flesh. All of the other possible lines of development also occur, however. They occur at once, but each one simultaneously affects every other. There is actually far greater interaction here than you realize, because you are not used to looking for it. The harder you work to maintain the official accepted idea of the self in conventional terms, the more of course you block out any kind of unpredictability.

Because of the great organizing nature of these basic units, there are also psychological structures that are quite capable of holding their own identities while being aware of any given number of probable selves. Life after death has great meaning in your reality, because death is a part of it. Your greater reality obviously transcends both your births and your deaths. The idea of one universe alone is basically nonsensical. Your reality must be seen in its relationship to others.[8] Otherwise you are always caught in questions like "How did the universe begin?" or "When will it end?" All systems are constantly being created.

Only in a context of probabilities can immortality make any sense. Heredity springs from the great inherent unpredictability that is then broken down to specifications inside the chromosomes,[9] no two of which are alike. What you think of as daily life is then a focus upon certain probable events above others, a choosing of significances, a selection of pattern. Other portions of the self follow different selections.

Now you may take your break.

(10:55. Jane was quickly out of another good trance; once again it had been a long one. Her delivery had been fast at times. "I knew what I was saying when I said it, but I've forgotten it all now . . ." She paused, then continued in a way I thought somewhat unusual for her: "We're doing the best we can with what abilities we've got. You wonder what this material's application is—what good does it do to know it?"

("Well," I said, "once it's incorporated into your consciousness you'll put it to use like you would any other information. It's certainly enlarged my own ideas of what human beings are all about, for instance—their motivations, their behavior—"

(Jane wondered how tonight's material applied to my mother, [who had died three months ago]: ". . . to Mom Butts herself—not just the theory of it . . . Is she in another probability now?"

("I'd say the part of her that was close to us is. But that part may be resting there, too." For reasons too personal to go into here, we haven't yet tried to "tune into" my mother in her new environment. I suggested that the rest of the session be devoted to Jane herself, but Seth had other ideas. Resume at 11:15.)

Now: Because your greater identity is aware of its probable existences, you are in matter and out of it at the same time—in time and out of it.

You have a greater identity outside of your context, yet a part of it is inside your context, as you. Your youness is your significance, a focus of awareness, conscious of itself, that seeks out and views experience with its own unique propensities. The existence of probable realities and probable selves in no way denies the validity of your own experience or individuality. That rides secure, choosing from unpredictable fields of actuality those that suit its own particular nature.

(With gestures, emphatically:) That selfhood jumps in leapfrog fashion over events that it does not want to actualize *(pause),* and does not admit such experience into its selfhood.

Other portions of your greater identity, however, do accept those same events rejected by you, and form their own selfhoods.

Now some of you might choose some of the same events, and there probabilities will merge. Such points of inter-section are highly charged and creative. These intersections can happen in individual and mass terms. One historical event may be simultaneously accepted in several probable realities, for exam-ple, while others may occur in one and not in an alternate history.

(Long pause at 11:29.) While words are difficult to use here, again, what I am saying applies, in different ways perhaps, to the behavior of worlds, atoms, and psychological structures. Give us a moment . . . In the life that you know, as given in *Personal Reality*, your beliefs act to specify the particular probable events that will become "real."[10] Because you are a probable self, an understanding of your own nature will show you some of the abilities, not used here, but present, that you can indeed choose to actualize. You can draw then from your own bank of probable abilities, for there will be traces of them in you. They are being developed in another reality; therefore in this one thay can be utilized far easier than you might suppose. When you exercise your right arm, your left arm benefits. When you develop abil-ities in one system, to some extent they are easier to develop in another. (To me:) In deciding to do some writing (for the Seth books, as an example), you are also drawing upon abilities that you have worked on in another system, and through your intent you are to a certain extent blending probabilities.[11]

Even a simple understanding of this would help people realize that no existence is dead-ended.

Now give us a moment for our friend.

(Pause at 11:36. Seth came through with a page or so of material for Jane, then wound up the session at 11:48 P.M.

(I'd say that Seth's information after 11:29 implies at least a partial answer to the questions Jane asked at break. And tonight, just as she had following last Monday's session, Jane realized that she was actively delivering material on probabilities both in the sleep state and while partially awake.)

NOTES: Session 682

1. Seth finished dictating *Personal Reality* in July, 1973, but it took me until November to complete my notes for it and type the finished

manuscript. Prentice-Hall will publish it in July, 1974. Jane and I still have
to correct page proofs for the book, however; they're due from the printer
next month.

    2. See Note 5 for Session 680.

    3. A note added later: Of course, as soon as Seth mentioned
units of consciousness in *"Unknown" Reality* I thought of the electromagnetic energy units (EE units, as he called them) that he'd discussed in
1969 and 1971. See sessions 504 through 506 in the Appendix of *The Seth
Material*, and the 581st session in Chapter 20 of *Seth Speaks*, respectively.
In the latter material he used several evocative analogies to describe his EE
units: ". . . basically animations rising from consciousness . . . the invisible
breath of consciousness . . . The emanations are actually emotional
tones . . . The units are just beneath the range of physical matter."

    However, nowhere in tonight's 682nd session does Seth refer to
EE units by name—and for a reason, as will be seen late in the next session.
In his earlier material he left himself plenty of room to add to his data on
such units of consciousness. "They are <u>one form</u> [my emphasis] that emotional energy takes," he told us in the 504th session. And in the 581st
session: "There are many ranges and great varieties of such EE units, all
existing beyond your perceivable reach. To lump them together in such a
way, however, is misleading, for within all of this there is great order."

    4. Again, see the 581st session in Chapter 20 of *Seth Speaks* for
material on EE units and postulated faster-than-light particles like the tach-
yon. (It's been stated in theory, incidentally, that although tachyons themselves travel faster than light, their radiation doesn't. This radiation, then,
the carrier of all of the information we could gather about tachyons [or
similar particles], would be observable by us.)

    Many physicists now think it untenable to consider that each
condition or event in the universe embodies the same kind of time. Physicists and parapsychologists have suggested various sorts of minute and undis-
covered entities (mindons, psychons, psitrons, and so forth) that can move
backward in time relative to our conscious conception of what time is, or
that are at least free of our idea of a time that flows inevitably forward. Or
consider the positron, which is a positively charged electron, a bit of anti-
matter that's said to be temporarily moving backward in time. ("Regular"
electrons, as we think of them in our world, are negatively charged.)

    The electron is one of the wave-particles in motion adjacent to
the atom's nucleus. It would be very large when compared to Seth's basic
unit of consciousness, but because an electron can "move" from the orbit of
one nucleus to that of another without traversing the space between, the
electron can still furnish a crude analogy to the ability of those units of
consciousness to "appear in several places at once, and without going
through space."

    5. See notes 1 and 5 for the 681st session.

    6. For the second time in the session, Seth referred to the

chance that the individual might feel insignificant within the enormous reaches of the inner universe. He also mentioned such a possibility in the 681st session at 10:00 (See Note 2 for that session as well.)

I find Seth's discussions about probabilities most intriguing, and sense no physical or emotional threat. Jane feels the same way. "My concern, when I'm aware of it, is for the readers," she told me after the session. "I don't want any of them to feel swept away."

7. See Note 5 for Session 680.

8. It may not be so easy to see our reality in relation to others, though. See Note 1 for Appendix 3.

9. Chromosomes are microscopic bodies into which the protoplasmic substance of a cell nucleus separates during cell division. They carry the genes, the factors or units—"blueprints"—that determine hereditary characteristics.

10. Much of *Personal Reality* contains material on beliefs, of course; see chapters 14 and 15, among others. Seth's information on "the point of power," given in the 657th session in Chapter 15, is especially appropriate here.

11. Seth's description of how I'm blending two probable selves reminded me of his material on the way Jane is doing the same thing. See the 680th session at 11:02. It can hardly be coincidental that Jane and I are using our individual writing abilities as the cohesive—the "glue"—to unite our respective sets of probable selves.

Session 683
February 18, 1974
9:39 P.M. Monday

(*In Note 6 for the last session I wrote quite easily that Jane and I felt "no physical or emotional threat" as we considered the vastness of the inner universe described by Seth. While we talked after supper tonight, however, I discovered to my surprise that Jane did entertain some doubtful thoughts on our places within this great organization of things. She also questioned the emotional value of the material on probabilities. But then, she added, her feelings stemmed from her being blue today.*

(*Actually, Jane continued, she found the material on probabilities intellectually stimulating, while wondering about its emotional connotations—the inferences that she was but one of countless billions of creatures, "blinking on and off like lights in all of those probable worlds . . ." What value was there to the tiny individual? she asked herself.*

(*In an effort to reassure her, I looked up what Seth*

said in Chapter 9 of Personal Reality, *and showed it to her. See the 637th session: ".... think now of the life of the self as one message leaping across the nerve cells of a multidimensional structure—again, as real as your body—and consider it also as a greater 'moment of reflection' on the part of such a many-sided personality... I am aware that [these analogies] can make you feel small or fear for your identity. You are more than a message, say, passing through the vast reaches of a superself. You are not lost in the universe."*

(I also had a few questions—suspicions, really—that I wanted to discuss with Jane and/or Seth sometime during the session. I'd kept them to myself so far.

("Well," Jane said at 9:33, after we'd been sitting for the session for some 15 minutes, "at least I feel Seth vaguely around...." Finally:)

Now: Good evening.

("Good evening, Seth.")

(Slowly:) Give us a moment... Through these units consciousness makes its mark, and not one scribble is ever annihilated.

The experience of any given unit, constantly changing, affects all other units... Give us time... It is difficult to explain because your concepts of selfhood are so limited... These units contain within themselves, in your terms, all "latent" identities, but not in a predetermined fashion. Selves may be quite independent within the framework of their own reality, while still being a part of a larger reality in which their independence works not only for their own benefit, but for the sake of a greater structure.

Within these units there is, again, a propensity for growth and organization. Within a literally infinite field of activity, meaningful order arose out of the propensity for significance. Briefly, certain units would settle upon various kinds of organization, find these significant, then build upon them and attract others of the same nature. So were various systems of reality formed. *(Pause.)* The particular kind of significance settled upon would act both as a directive for experience and as a method of erecting effective boundaries, within which the selected kind of behavior would continue. The units can and do intermix, yet because of the propensity for selectivity and significance, whole groups of them will "repel" other whole groups, thus providing a protective inner system of interaction.

The units form themselves into the various systems that they have themselves initiated. They transform themselves, therefore, into the structured reality that they then become. Ruburt is quite correct in his supposition of what he calls "multi-personhood" in *Adventures.*[1]

You think of one I-self *(spelled)* as the primary and ultimate end of evolution. Yet there are, of course, other identities with many such I-selves, each as aware and independent as your own, while also being aware of the existence of a greater identity in which they have their being. Consciousness fulfills itself by knowing itself. The knowledge changes it, in your terms, into a greater gestalt that then tries to fulfill and know itself, and so forth. There have been experiments upon your earth *(by consciousness)* with both men and animals at a different level than just mentioned, but with that in mind—herds of animals, for example, with each animal quite aware of the joint knowledge of the herd, the dangers to be encountered in any individual territory, and a psychological structure in which the mass consciousness of the herd recognized the individual consciousness of each animal, and protected it.

There was a constant give-and-take between the individual animal and the mass herd consciousness, so we are not speaking of a condition in which the individual animal was controlled.

The same thing with variations happened with your own race, and for that matter is happening. In the past as you think of it historically, several groups experimented along those lines. At those times the individual consciousness became so entranced with its own experiences, however, that the clear-cut, steady, and conscious communication with the mass consciousness went underground, so to speak. It became available to those who looked for it, but the same kinds of psychological organization did not result on those occasions.[2]

(Pause.) Other kinds of psychological gestalts have been and are being tried—some that would appear quite inconceivable to you; and yet now and then versions of them appear within your system.

It is quite possible, for example, for several selves to occupy a body, and were this the norm it would be easily accepted. That implies another kind of multipersonhood, however, one actually allowing for the fulfillment of many abilities of various natures usually left unexpressed. It also implies a freedom and organization of consciousness that is unusual in your system of reality, and was not chosen there.

("Some people are going to hook up all of this with possession, aren't they?" I asked.

(10:11.) Not when I am finished. Most individuals, for example, develop intellectually or emotionally or physically, ignoring to a large degree the body's and the mind's full potential. The limited I-structure that you presently identify with selfhood is simply not capable of fully using all of those characteristics.

The I-structure arises from the inner self, formed about various interests, abilities, and drives. Selections are made as to the areas of concentration. You rarely find a person who is a great intellect, a great athlete, and also a person of deep emotional and spiritual understanding—an ideal prototype of what it seems mankind could produce.

In some systems of physical existence, a multiperson-hood is established in which three or four "persons" emerge from the same inner self, each one utilizing to the best of its abilities those characteristics of its own. This presupposes a gestalt of awareness, however, in which each knows of the activities of the others, and participates; and you have a different version of mass consciousness. Do you see the correlation?

("Yes.")

In the systems in which evolution of consciousness has worked in that fashion, all faculties of body and mind in one "lifetime" are beautifully utilized. Nor is there any ambiguity about identity. The individual would say, for example, "I am Joe, and Jane, and Jim, and Bob." There are physical variations of a sexual nature, so that on all levels identity includes the male and female. Shadows of all such probabilities appear within your own system, as oddities. Anything apparent to whatever degree in your system is developed in another.

The point of all this is that these units are unpredictable, and fulfill all probabilities of consciousness. Any concepts of gods or other beings that are based upon limited ideas of personhood will ultimately be futile. You view the fantastic variety of physical life—its animals, insects, birds, fish, man and all his works—with hardly a qualm; yet you must understand that the nature of consciousness itself is far more varied, and you must learn to think of an inner reality that is as infinite as the exterior one. These concepts alone do alter your present consciousness, and change it in degree. The present idea of the soul, you see, is a "primitive" idea that can scarcely begin to explain the creativity or reality from which mankind's being comes. You are multipersons (intently). You exist in many times and places at once. You exist as one person, simultaneously. This does not deny the independence of the persons, but your inner reality straddles their reality, while it also serves as a psychic world in which they can grow.³

I do not want to get involved in a discussion of "levels," in which progression is supposed to occur from one to the other. All such discussions are based upon your idea of one-personhood, consecutive time, and limited versions of the soul. There are red, yellow, and violet flowers. One is not more progressed than the others, but each is different.

These units combine into various kinds of gestalts of consciousness. Basically, it is not correct to say that one is more progressed than another. The petal of a flower, for example, is not more developed than the root. An ant on the ground may see that the petal is way above the root and stem, but ants are too wise to think that the petal must be better than the root.

Now: Consciousness flowers out in all directions—

(We were interrupted by a long-distance telephone call at 10:37. A television producer wanted Jane to appear on his show. I asked him to write us. When I hung up, Jane said, "I'm still half in." She sat quietly for a few moments, then resumed the session.)

All directions taken by the flower of consciousness are good. The flower knows it is alive in the bulb, but it takes "time" for the bulb to let the stem and leaves and flower emerge. The flower is not better than the bulb. It is not even more progressed than the bulb. It is the bulb in one of its manifestations. So in your terms, it may seem as if there are progressions, or consecutive steps of development, in which more mature comprehensive selves will emerge. You are a part of those selves now, as the petals are of the bulb. Only in your system is that time period meaningful.

Your idea of one soul, one self, forms a significance and a selectivity that blinds you to these other realities that are as much "here and now" as your present self. The units of consciousness that compose your physical being alone are aware of those greater significances, to which your limited ideas make you opaque.

The concepts in such a system as this can help break those barriers. There are, then, stratas of consciousness existing at once. The ones you are not aware of yet seem more progressed, developed than your own. You are a part of them now. You can know them as you begin to stretch your concepts of personhood and awareness. In terms of time you have many bodies, as you are born and reborn in earth experience. Your consciousness straddles those existences, and even the atoms and molecules within your present body contain the coded knowledge of those other (really simultaneous) forms. These units of consciousness are within all physical matter, containing their own memories. Both biologically and psychically, then, you are aware of your multipersonhood.

(10:45.) Now: Your system does not include the kind of experience mentioned earlier *(in this session),* where the body is able to contain in one lifetime the experience of many selves. It uses a time context instead, with each self given a body and a time; but a knowledge of the ideas of multipersonhood could help you realize that you have available many abilities not being used, latent to you but still important in your entire identity, and significant enough to you personally to be developed.

(With emphasis:) Reincarnation simply represents probabilities in a time context (underlined)—portions of the self that are materialized in historical contexts. Period. All kinds of time—backward and forward—emerge from the basic unpredictable nature of consciousness, and are due to "series" of significances. Each self born in time will then pursue its own probable realities from that standpoint. Again, each such self is immediate.

(Long pause, one of many.) All consciousness, in all of its forms, exists at once. It is difficult, without appearing to contradict myself, to explain. Go back to our bulb and flower. In basic terms they exist at once. In your terms, however, it is as if the flower-to-be, from its "future" calls back to the bulb and tells it how to make the flower. Memory operates backward and forward in time. The flower—calling back to the bulb, urging it "ahead" and reminding it of its (probable future) development—is like a future self in your terms, or a more highly advanced self, who has the answers and can indeed be quite

practically relied upon. The gods can be seen in the same light, only on a larger scale; and understood in that context, they can be relied upon. It is almost a natural tendency to personify the gods while you are caught up in limited ideas of personhood. Larger concepts of personhood will indeed lead you to some glimpse of the truly remarkable gestalts of consciousness from which you constantly emerge.

These are emotional and psychological beings of such richness that your concepts of selfhood force you to dilute them to a degree that you can understand.[4] Each of your persons is a part of that greater personhood. Again, these ideas alone can help you, so that to some degree you can emotionally and intellectually sense that greater godhood out of which personhood emerges.

(11:10. *Long pause during a strong delivery.)* That godhood is formed from the eternal yet ever-new emergence and growth of those basic units of consciousness. The reality of the godhood straddles the reality of each unit, and the mass reality of all units.

Take your break.

(11:13. Jane had been really under during another long delivery. She seemed to come out of her trance easily enough, but her eyes rolled up a few times. Her rocker had crept three feet to her left.

("I've got a few questions," I said after she'd rested a bit. "I was going to ask them during the delivery, but I'm afraid to hear the answers—at least to the first two." I was only half joking. I'd had the first question in mind since Seth had come through with the 679th session two weeks ago:

(1. "Are these recent sessions supposed to be the beginning of a new book?"

("I don't know," Jane said. "The material doesn't seem like *a book, but when I started getting stuff in my sleep after the last two sessions, I did wonder . . ."* I had to laugh: She hadn't mentioned her own suspicions to me. At the same time I thought she might be putting up barriers to the idea of another Seth book so soon, since we still have editorial work to do for the last one, Personal Reality *[see Note 1 for the 682nd session].* "Maybe these sessions are for your own writing," Jane speculated. "I love them, though—but another *book? Now?"*

(2. "Are these units of consciousness that Seth started

*talking about in the last session the same as the EE units he
described in* Seth Speaks, *a development of that original idea, or
what?" [See Note 3 for Session 682.]*

(*Jane paused. "I think Seth will clear that one up
soon."*

(3. *"It would be nice if Seth would say something
about the dream I had the night before last, in which I think I
contacted my [deceased] mother for the second time." Yesterday I wrote an account of the experience for use in the book I've
started on my own:* Through My Eyes. *Seth broached the idea of*
Through My Eyes *in Chapter 6 of* Personal Reality. *I enjoy
working on the project, and have had particularly strong urges to
do so since the death of my mother three months ago. In writing
about my parents, I discovered that I wrote about my own childhood. See the notes preceding the 679th session; the questions I
asked then helped initiate this series of sessions.*

(*Resume at 11:30.*)

Now: (*Louder and deeper:*) "The 'Unknown' Reality
(*colon*): A Seth Book." And put "Unknown" in quotes.

It is two things: A book of mine, and a source book
for you. Do you follow me?

(*"Yes . . . You mean I can use your book in connection with my own writing."*)

I do indeed. Now: We will call the basic units of consciousness "CU"—the letter "C," the letter "U"—consciousness
units. From them EE units are formed, and the first roots sent
out into the world of physical matter. Period.

(*Pause, eyes wide, staring at me.*) Now for your dream.
You are of course making contact with your mother. She is
beginning to stir, as you surmised. Ruburt's (*written*) comments
about the dream are also pertinent, showing your own caution.
None of these encounters have been normally emotional ones,
for example, but glimpses in which there was no communication
in ordinary terms.

It may interest you to know that your athletic tendencies are somewhat involved in your out-of-body travel, in that it
seems to you that the body must be poised and balanced, and
have support—hence the hallucinations you use. You can use
those tendencies to help you, however, if you think in terms of a
completely free body, able to move unsupported in space,
capable of manipulations in the dream state that are denied it in

physical reality. The "inner" body can perform in ways that the physical body cannot, and you can use that as a challenge. Find out what you can do with your inner body; experiment.

You have the assurance that your mother continues to exist. As far as a relationship is concerned, however, you are looking at her from a distance. She is still wondering—that is, she is able to identify with other portions of you than she was during life. She does not want to frighten you, now, with an emotional display, so distance is being used on both of your parts.[5]

(Pause at 11:44.) Give us a moment . . .

(Seth delivered half a page of material on another matter. Then:)

I bid you both a fond good evening.

("Thank you. The same to you.")

This book will progress at your convenience.

("All right. Good night, Seth." 11:50 P.M. Then a minute later, as we talked about "Unknown" Reality, Jane briefly dipped back into trance:)

Keep it free and uncontracted for, for now.

("Okay."

("It sure doesn't start out like a book to me," Jane said. "It doesn't seem to be simple, like the others. Maybe this time he's going to go ahead and do it his own way . . . I can honestly say that the title was completely unknown to me." She smiled at her unwitting pun on "Unknown" Reality. "Are you ready to start a new book, Rob?"

("Well . . ."

("I remember Seth mentioned it as a source book for you—"

("If it's a source book for me, it can be for others, too." I added that I didn't care how "tough" or difficult a book it might be—if such was needed to get Seth's ideas across, then okay. Again, I had to laugh at Jane. It was obvious that she was pleased with this new project, that the successes of Seth Speaks *and* Personal Reality *had given her a strong confidence in Seth's and her own abilities; yet she was starting right in with questions:*

("What the hell's going to be in it?" she demanded. "Really—where can he go, considering where he started? Oh, forget it. As I came out with that, I got something over here"— she gestured to her right, indicating one of the channels of information available from Seth—"about the unpredictability of

consciousness, and precognition and heredity: the cell's soul and the soul's cell . . ."
        As I did when she began delivering each of the other Seth books, I suggested to Jane that she relax about the whole thing and just let Seth do his work. We quit for the night at 12:03 A.M.)

NOTES: Session 683

        1. Jane uses "multipersonhood" on the last page of Chapter 11 in her *Adventures in Consciousness: An Introduction to Aspect Psychology.* "But really," she said, "the whole chapter builds up toward that definition, or idea." In her view, the quality called multipersonhood encompasses all of the inner personifications, or Aspects, of the source self, which she defines in the Glossary of *Adventures* as "the 'unknown' self, soul, or psyche; the fountainhead of our physical being." In her own case, then, Seth would be a personification of an Aspect of her source self; but he would also have an existence of his own at other levels of reality.
        See also Note 5 for the 680th session.
        2. In connection with Seth's discussion of animals and men here, see his excellent material in Chapter 12 of *Personal Reality.* Summarizing parts of that chapter very simply: In Session 647 Seth goes into the challenges early man faced as he contended with his own burgeoning consciousness. In Session 648 he discusses animal instinct, health, illness, and suicide, and the eras during which men and animals *mixed.* For the same session Jane contributed impressions of her own on animal medicine men.
        3. A note added later: I found most of the material Seth had delivered since 10:11, but especially at this point, to be strongly reminiscent of a passage in the 657th session in Chapter 15 of *Personal Reality.* I've put together these excerpts from that session: "Each of your reincarnational selves has its own 'points of power,' or successive moments, in which it materializes daily existence in a linear manner from all the probabilities available to it. In a way that will be explained in another book, there is a kind of coincidence with all of these present points of power that exists between you and your 'reincarnational' selves. There is a constant interaction in this multidimensional point of power, therefore, so that in your terms, one incarnated self draws from all of the others what abilities it wants. These selves are different <u>counterparts</u> [my emphasis] of yourself in creaturehood, experiencing bodily reality; but at the same time your organism shuts out the simultaneous nature of experience."
        Jane and I placed no particular emphasis upon this information when Seth came through with it, but in retrospect we realized that it contains two significant points: Seth's reference to "another book," which we

think is *"Unknown" Reality*, and his use of the word "counterparts." In its ordinary dictionary sense, the term has appeared a few times in the sessions, but Seth's use of it in the passage quoted above has a special implication, I think; one that Jane and I missed at the time of its reception. For in Volume 2 of *"Unknown" Reality*, Seth's concept of counterparts certainly takes on its own unique meaning within his study of personhood. (Although not bringing up his ideas of reincarnation or points of power in the 683rd session, Seth implied both of those qualities in many parts of that material.)

As I write this note, I'm struck by a curious connection I feel but find almost impossible to explain in words, let alone simply—that while Seth's mention of "another book" in Session 657 may refer to *"Unknown" Reality*, it's also echoed in the first question I asked Jane at break in tonight's session. Yet how can this be, I wonder, since when the 683rd session was held I didn't have Session 657 in mind; and when the 657th was delivered I had no ordinary way of knowing I'd have the question to ask in the 683rd. I'm unwilling to ascribe the "conventional" notions of precognition or retrocognition to such a tenuous relationship between the two sessions. Such odd connections have arisen before in the Seth material. Usually I simply recognize their existence and my inability to think clearly about them, and go on from there.

4. See Note 2 for the 681st session.

5. This "margin of safety" between my mother and me is beautifully illustrated in my dream of two nights ago. And as if to further reassure my conscious mind, I saw my mother with people who were still "living"; this has been the case in other recent dream experiences I've had with her. Here's the relevant portion of the description I wrote for *Through My Eyes*: "Then I saw my mother [Stella] between my brother Linden and his wife, all separated each from the other a little bit, all walking obliquely toward me across a featureless plain. Everything was in brilliant color. The three figures were cut off at their waists, as though I saw them on a screen. My mother didn't speak to me or look directly at me; like the others, she faced just past my left shoulder.

"Linden and his wife were close to their present physical ages in the dream, a year or so younger than I am, at 54, but Stella looked to be a few years younger than she should have been [she died at 81]. I know I created my dream image of her to make our communication understandable to me—yet I felt that she was *alive*, in our terms and in hers. My mother was obviously in control of her faculties, even though she appeared to be a little distraught . . . The fact that she looked past me speaks of some sort of barrier, or distance, between us even in the dream state. This could be for my own protection, I think. . . ."

As for my out-of-body journeys, I do often hallucinate a support of some kind in such ventures: the crossbar on a telephone pole, the fragile, topmost branch of a dead tree . . .

Session 684
February 20, 1974
9:42 P.M. Wednesday

(Last night, Jane told her students in ESP class that Seth had started a new book. Seth had a few things to say about the book, too. From the transcript of the class tape [received a week later]: "Now, reality has no beginning and no end. Hopefully—hopefully—hopefully, in your terms of time, you may get a glimpse of what I mean. There is indeed an expanding universe, and it is formed in the eternal present. In my book I will go as far as I can into those precepts, yet some [of you] will not follow. You create your own reality. That works, and is true, whether or not you follow, or care to follow, into these other realms . . .

("For those of you who do accompany me, I promise you an adventure, a creative alteration of consciousness, and experiences beyond those that you have known in your terms. You look at the world around you and are amazed at its richness and variety. Do you think that the inner world is not as rich,

*even more rich, more valid? Do you think there is but one kind
of consciousness?*

("Your world is formed out of the vast unpredictability of consciousness. From it you form your own ideas of
significance and of yourself... You must stop thinking in terms
of ordinary progression. It is bad enough when you worry about
keeping up with the Joneses. It is something else, however, when
you start worrying about which kind of self [or consciousness] is
superior to another kind."

(A note: Jane telephoned Tam Mossman, her editor,
today—and learned that Tam already felt that Seth might have
begun another book: he'd wondered about it several times in
recent days.

(As we waited for the session to begin at 9:30, Jane
said, "I'm getting ready—waiting for that certain clear focus—the
one clearest place in consciousness for the material to come
through...")

Good Evening.

("Good evening, Seth.")

Now: These units of consciousness (CU's) move faster
than the speed of light, then—but that statement itself is
meaningless in a way, since the units exist outside as well as
inside the framework in which light itself has meaning.

(Pause.) As these units approach physical structure,
however, they do slow down in your terms. Electrons, for
example, are slow dullards in comparison with EE units.[1] It goes
without saying that the units of consciousness are "mental," or if
you prefer, disembodied, though from their inner organization all
physical forms emerge. Certain intensities are built up of unit
organization even before the smallest physical particle, or even
invisible "physical" particle, exists. These units form what you
think of as the mind, around which the structure of the brain is
formulated. The units permeate the brain.

The great communication system within the body
itself is dependent, then, upon the constant inner flux and flow
of these units. On one level the body's very survival is largely
determined by the units' propensities for selectivity and significance. Also, however, the body's physical reality is a <u>seeming</u>
constant in a seemingly constant physical existence.

(Slowly:) Only because these units have their source
outside of space and time is the present corporal reality a

triumph of probabilities. Period. Your present image, for example, seems to be the only one possible for you, permanently yours for your lifetime at least; and what happens to it appears almost inevitable. If you become ill, say, you may wonder why, and yet once illness has happened it becomes part of the body's reality, and seems almost like an inevitable part of its experience.

Yet the units of consciousness, being independent of space and time, form your cellular structure, and that structure deals in a most basic manner with the nature of probabilities. Although the body appears permanent and in existence from one moment to the next, basically it constantly rises out of the bed of probabilities, hovering at your now-point of perception and experience, and its apparent stability is dependent upon the knowledge of "future" probabilities as well as "past" ones.

Your present is the result of your own poised consciousness, choosing its perception and the nature of its life from a field that is at all predictable only because of the greater area of organization available to it.

(Slower at 10:07:) Your body's condition at any time is not so much the result of its own comprehension of its "past history" as it is the result of its own comprehension of future probabilities. The cells precognate. This is being simplified for now. I will make it clearer later in the book.[2] But your limited ideas of time cause conceptual barriers that operate even when you consider the structure of physical biological life.

For example: It is truer to say that heredity operates from the future backward into the past, than it is to say that it operates from the past into the present. Neither statement would be precisely correct in any case, because your present is a poised balance affected as much by the probable future as the probable past.

At no time, as a rule, is your body not here to you. Your experience seems centered within it, with the rest of the world safely outside. However, the particular selectivity of your kind of consciousness rides over lapses that you do not recognize. In a manner of speaking, your bodies blink off and on like lights. Their reality fluctuates, from your standpoint. For that matter, so does the physical universe.[3]

You can understand what is meant by saying that your consciousness fluctuates—for each individual is aware of various intensities and concentrations. You are more alert, or, in your terms, more conscious on some occasions than others. Now the same applies to these units of consciousness—and to atoms, molecules, electrons, and other such phenomena. The world literally blinks off and on. This reality of fluctuation in no way bothers your own feeling of consistency, however. The "holes *(spelled)* of nonexistence" are plugged up by the process of selectivity. This process chooses significances then, again, around which experience is built, and around which "life" is felt. The very sensations of one kind of life then automatically set up barriers against other such "world-schemes" (hyphen) that do not correlate with their own.

It is impossible for you to examine an atom, a cell, or anything else except in your now. Period. Because your sense experience follows a time pattern that you can understand, then you take it for granted that a cell, for example, is the result of its past, and that its present condition arises from the past.[4] The fetus grows into an adult, not because it is programmed from the past, but because it is to some extent precognitively aware of its probabilities, and from the "future" then imprints this information into the past structure.

From your viewpoint, however, an examination of a cell will not show you that, but only its present condition. It should appear obvious from what I am saying that neither future nor past is predetermined. From your platform of poised now-experience, you alter both the past and the future, and that alteration, that change, that action, causes your point of immediate sense life.[5]

(Long pause.) The precious privacy of your existence, and indeed of your universe, is all the more miraculous, so to speak, precisely because its probable reality emerges from an infinite field of probabilities, each forever inviolate. *(Long pause.)* It is important that these ideas be considered.

Take your break.

(10:35. Jane's pace had been slow often, but emphatic throughout. Resume in the same manner at 10:49.)

Now: Give us a moment . . .

You cannot separate your beliefs about reality from the reality that you experience. That is, your beliefs about reality form it. Your ideas about what is possible and what is not possible are reflected in all areas.

It is almost impossible to begin with concepts of one

isolated universe, one self at the mercy of its past, one time sequence, and end up with any acceptable theory of a multi-dimensional soul or godhead that is anything else but a glorified personified concept of what you think man is.[6]

Not only do your metaphysics and sciences suffer, but your daily experience as a human being is far less than it could be. There are, then, probabilities quite present, and for that matter biologically practical, that would allow for a change in individual consciousness so great as literally to propel the race into another level of experience entirely. As in your terms the cavemen ventured out into the daylight of the earth, so there is a time for man to venture out into a greater knowledge of his subjective reality, comma, to explore the dimensions of selfhood and go beyond the small areas of himself in which he has thus far found shelter.

(11:11.) In terms of history as you understand it, man felt safe and secure as a prime species under one sun, imagining that all else revolved about his being. This provided, in that framework, a stability that was dispensed with as man allowed his consciousness other freedoms. So he must now come to realize that he himself chooses from a myriad of probabilities the one that he now encounters.

The one self that he recognizes is the only part of himself of which he is presently aware. Other facets of consciousness available to him, and a part of his greater nature, appear foreign, or "not-self," or "beyond self," because of the focus of selectivity as it now operates.

This obviously does not mean that there are not entities whose selfhood is completely apart from your own. It does mean that your concepts force you to misinterpret and distort any "intrusive" information, or experience, that is part of portions of your own being that you do not recognize as your official self.

(A one-minute pause at 11:22.) Such behavior even causes a certain corporal dishonesty, for the cells' freedom from time means that on certain levels the cellular structure is aware of probable future events, as mentioned (just before break). The body, therefore, is reacting to future and past activity as well, in order to maintain its present corporal balance.

The body's innate knowledge, then, will try to translate itself often into psychological activity that may result in hunches, premonitions, and so forth. The senses may be utilized to clarify the message. You might hear a voice mentally, for example, or see a flashing image. According to your beliefs, you may interpret such data in any of many ways, but because such experiences are not an accepted part of recognized, <u>official</u> activity, they can appear frightening. Period. You may assign them to "spirits" or disembodied personalities, but in such a way that these are thrown together in a confusing mass of dogma or superstition.

If you understood to begin with that <u>you</u> are a spirit, and therefore free of space and time yourself, then you could at least consider the possibility that some such messages were coming to you from other portions of your own reality. Such messages are often ways of allowing you to avoid certain probable actions.

Give us a moment—a good one—

(Jane paused at 11:33, still in trance, and lit a ciga-rette. Since starting the series of sessions that make up "Unknown" Reality, *it's becoming something of a custom for her to deliver a little material on other subjects after book dicta-tion; she did so again now, and finished the session at 11:51 P.M.*

(Following the last session, Jane began thinking about chapter divisions and headings for the new book. Seth hasn't given any, of course. I told her that the book might not have chapters, that Seth might have something else planned. [And added later: The eventual resolution of this little dilemma is given early in my Introductory Notes.])

NOTES: Session 684

1. See Note 4 for the 682nd session.

2. A note added later: Seth does add to his material on cellular precognition in a number of later sessions in *The "Unknown" Reality.* Among others in Volume 1, see sessions 690-91 in Section 2.

3. In Note 1 for Session 681 I dealt very briefly with fluctu-ations of consciousness, or reality, and referred the reader to the 567th session in Chapter 16 of *Seth Speaks.* For additional material on the same subject in the same book, also see the 535th session in Chapter 9 and the 576th in Chapter 19.

And in connection with Seth's statement tonight that "... your bodies blink off and on like lights," see Jane's comments on her own feelings about related ideas in the notes at the beginning of the last session.

4. In earlier days, Jane and I only thought of the cell as a result of its past, too. Yet at the same time, Jane in her poetry was trying to see through that pervasive belief. The few lines below are from *Pathétique,* a long poem she wrote in 1959. She was 30 years old, and her development of the Seth material lay five years in the future.

> *These cells remember*
> *Their past deaths and all past deaths,*
> *And bear, within their atoms' yellow whisper*
> *The chill, the first frost and the final frost . . .*
> *Miraculous beyond all knowing,*
> *The fire within is blowing.*
> *If I must die, why then*
> *Once these atoms upright walked*
> *And knew themselves and spoke my name,*
> *And singing are eternal.*

5. See Seth's material in *Personal Reality* on reprogramming the past: sessions 654 and 657 in chapters 14 and 15, respectively. Some of his earlier information on the fetus can be found in sessions 503-4 in the Appendix of *The Seth Material.*

6. Seth discusses a multidimensional god in Chapter 14 of *Seth Speaks,* and Jane does so from her viewpoint in Chapter 17 of *Adventures in Consciousness.*

Session 685
February 25, 1974
9:51 P.M. Monday

(When Jane lay down for a nap late this afternoon she had quite an unusual experience. From her notes: "Just before I went to sleep, I had a sort of mental projection that seemed to be into the past, my past. I was a baby in my hometown, Saratoga Springs, N. Y. The time was about 1931 to start with. Everything was misty, gray, without color. First, 'I' looked down on 'myself' in my carriage. Then, I moved through the streets easily enough as I got 'older' during the projection. Wait—just now as I wrote this I picked up something [from a part of my consciousness other than Ruburt or Seth], to the effect that the projection environment is as focused as mine is, really, but that it's a probability of mine. Biologically I wasn't keyed into it in my 'now'; I was in it and not in it, between focused realities . . . traveling in or through these fluctuations of consciousness Seth talked about in the last session. He mentioned probable kinds of consciousness

in that session, too. Was I trying to develop one of those here in
my own physical reality? But this was definitely a waking event,
taking place just before my nap. I described the whole thing to
Rob as soon as I got up . . ."
        (We'd waited for tonight's session since 9:26. As we sat
talking desultorily, Jane grew more and more impatient. Once
again, as she had before the 684th session and on other occa-
sions, she said that now "something was different" in the ses-
sions: For this book she had to "get a certain clear focus . . .")
        Good evening.
        ("Good evening, Seth.")
        Now: Give us a moment . . . Body is also pattern.
Period. While the material that composes it changes constantly,
the pattern maintains its own integrity. The form is etched in
space and time, and yet the pattern itself exists outside of that
framework also—the body is a projection, therefore, into the
three-dimensional field.
        The consciousnesses of the cells within it, however, are
eternal. The physical framework, then, is itself composed of
immortal stuff. The projection in time and space may disappear,
in your terms, wither and die. The main identity continues to
exist, even as the consciousnesses of millions of cells still exist
that at one time were part of the body.
        (A one-minute pause at 9:59.)
        While inhabited by the usual human consciousness, the
living body operates as an intense focus point. The conglomeration of consciousnesses within it on all levels focuses its own
network of communication. This private network is connected to
all others like it. There are levels of interaction then simply
between all bodies, electromagnetically and biologically. The network is more far-reaching than that, however. Not only can all
cells respond to each other, but their mass activity triggers even
higher centers of consciousness to respond to a given set of world
conditions, rather than to other quite-as-legitimate world conditions that do not fit the accepted pattern. Probabilities to some
extent, then, are determined along cellular lines. This should be
obvious.
        (A long pause, one of many, at 10:07.) The body's
very structure will in itself set patterns for the kinds of probabilities that can be practically experienced. The source-reality
out of which all else springs is never predetermined—that is,

predestined, or even set. The universe in any terms is always being created. Period.

When consciousness is being specified, it always sees itself at the center of its world. All specifications of consciousness and all phenomenal appearances occur when the basic units of consciousness, the CU's, emerge into EE units, and hence into the dimensions of actuality in your terms. Your mainly accepted normal consciousness is within the matter of your body, and through it—the body—you view your world. There is nothing to prevent you from viewing your body from a standpoint outside of it, except that you have been taught that consciousness is imprisoned within the flesh.

The body is a sending and receiving organism; your home station, so to speak, and the focus for your activity. You can, however, quite consciously leap from it—and you do often, when for a while, particularly in the dream state, you view the world from another perspective.

Give us a moment . . . In some adventures you do visit other probable realities in which you have a body structure quite as real as "your own." Your own psychological makeup, for that matter, achieves its marvelous complexity because it draws from the rich bank of your greater probable existences. Even a small understanding of these ideas can help you glimpse how limiting previous concepts of psychology have been.

(A one-minute pause at 10:25.) The self that you know and recognize carries within it hints and traces of all of your probable characteristics that can be actualized within your system of reality. Your body is equipped to bring any of these to fulfillment. Now, because of the selectivity mentioned earlier,[1] certain directions may be easier than others, and some may appear impossible. Yet within the psychological and biological structure of your species, the roads of probabilities have more intersections than you know.

The conscious mind as you normally think of it directs your overall action, and its ideas determine the kind of selectivity you use. It is for this reason that I am trying to expand your conscious ideas, so that you become better equipped to choose your line of physical experience from all those probable ones open to you.

Now take your break.

(10:32. I thought Jane's trance had been a good one,

even though she'd used many pauses, but she told me that she hadn't been at her best. Nor had she been aware of her slow delivery. She also felt that we'd eaten supper [at 7:30] too close to session time.

(I discussed with Jane the questions I'd thought of when Seth had commented, above, on ". . . how limiting previous concepts of psychology have been.": As a discipline, why was psychology so narrowly developed? Why hadn't it continued expanding until it encompassed ideas like those Jane was delivering tonight, for instance? Her work was unique in that it was coming through her individual personality, I added—yet, why wasn't the theory of probabilities, or its equivalent, say, common knowledge, or at least considered, in psychology today? I asked if Seth cared to comment.

(After we talked for a few more minutes, Jane said, "I've got the feeling you're going to get answers to your questions about psychology—but they'll be presented as the Preface to this book." We hadn't given the idea of a preface a thought. Making a joke, I asked Jane what was coming up next in the session. I meant generally, but she replied, "The Preface." Even then, I don't think either of us expected Seth to carry out such a project tonight. But as he came through at 10:57:)

Now: Preface: There is an "unknown" reality, in quotes as given. I am part of it and so are you . . .

(Seth finished at midnight. Jovially:) <u>End of Preface.</u>
("Okay.")
End of session.

("All right. Thank you, Seth. Good night," I said at 12:01 A.M., and Seth was gone almost at once. See the Preface at the beginning of this book. Jane said that although Seth hadn't actually considered my specific questions about psychology after all, they had served as an impetus for the Preface. She felt good. I read the Preface to her—and she felt even better.

(Although the session ostensibly ended here, there were actually several succeeding—and continuing—effects that grew out of it. Jane's Saratoga experience is involved, too. All of the relevant material is given in detail in Appendix 4.)

NOTES: Session 685

1. Seth discusses selectivity in the 682nd session at 10:36.

Session 686
February 27, 1974
9:45 P.M. Wednesday

(The effects continued to flow out of last Monday night's session. Jane was very intrigued by the material she produced "on her own" after the session, both in the sleep state that night and in the statements she wrote the next day. See Appendix 4. As we made ready for tonight's session at 9:10, and discussed the information she'd received, she began to feel a continuation of the experience. This time, however, it came through verbally, as dictation, although Seth wasn't involved. I made notes on most of what she had to say; it's presented as Appendix 5, and I suggest that the reader review it before continuing with this session.

(It was 9:40 by the time Jane finished her dictation. She sat quietly for a few moments. "Now I'm just waiting for Seth," she told me. Then: "It's as though I feel a lot of concepts around me right now, and I'm letting him get them organized for me . . . But now I think I'm about ready. . . .")

(Softly:) Good evening.

("Good evening, Seth.")

Now: Basically, the cell's comprehension straddles time as you think of it. Period.

Mankind's consciousness, however, experimented along time-specific lines. As he developed along those lines, various biological and mental methods of selectivity and discrimination were utilized. When in historic terms mankind became aware of memory, and recalled his past as a past in your terms, it was possible for him to confuse past and present. Vivid memories, out of context but given immediate neurological validity, could compete with the brilliant focus necessary in his present.[1]

Though the past is actually quite as immediate, alive, and creative as the present is, man made certain adjustments, on several layers, that would focus definite distinctions and set past and present experience apart. While your particular kind of consciousness was developing, it began to intensify selectivity, to concentrate specifically in a small area of activity while blocking out other data. This was necessary because the particular kind of physical manipulation of corporal existence required instant physical response to immediately present stimuli.

(9:55.) Such selectivity and specialization therefore represented a pertinent method, as consciousness familiarized itself with earthly experience. Hunters had to respond at once to the present situation. In time terms, the "present" animal had to be killed for food—not the "past" animal. That animal—the past one—existed as surely as the one presently perceived, yet in man's context, physical action had to be directed to a highly specific area, for physical survival depended upon it.

(Pause, and slowly:) The cells' basic innocence of time discrimination had to be bypassed. At deeply unconscious levels the neurological structure is more highly adaptable than it appears. Adjustments were made, therefore. Basically, the neurological structure responds to both past and future data. Biologically, then, such activity is built-in. The specialized "new" kind of consciousness in one body had to respond pinpoint fast. Therefore it focused upon only one series of neurological messages.

(As Seth, Jane was enunciating the material very carefully, almost syllable by syllable, as though to give me time to write it down without error. Her diction in trance is usually

*excellent, though; it's not often that I have to ask her to repeat a
word or phrase.)*

These became more and more biologically prominent,
so that man's consciousness rode them, or leaped upon them.
These particular pulses or messages became the biologically and
mentally accepted ones. They were clued into sense perception,
then. These pulses or messages became the only official data that,
translated into sense perception, formed physical reality. This
selectivity gave an understandable line of reference from interior
to exterior existence.

(10:10. Deliberately but intently:) Other quite-as-valid
messages were ignored. They became, while present, biologically
invisible. The cells still reacted to these otherwise neglected
pulses, as they needed data from both the past and future to
maintain the body's balance in "the present." The necessity for
immediate conscious exterior action at a "definite" point of
intersection with events was left to the emerging ego
consciousness.

While the cells required future and past data, and used
it to form from that invisible tension the body's present corporal
reality, the same kind of information could be a threat then to
the ego consciousness, which could be overwhelmed. Within the
corporal structure, however, there are indeed messages that leap
too quickly or too slowly[2] from your viewpoint to allow for any
physical response. In that way cellular comprehension is allowed
its free flow; but the selectivity mentioned *(in sessions 682-3)*
bypasses such information, so that it does not conflict with
present sense data requiring physical action in time.

Other pulses, carrying messages, are quite as valid as
those that you perceive and physically react to. Again, the cells
respond to those constantly. The body, as mentioned *(in the
685th session)* is an electromagnetic pattern, poised in a web of
probabilities, experienced as corporal at an intersection point in
space and time.

When man, speaking in your terms of history, began to
experiment with memory, there were innumerable instances
where the emerging ego consciousness did not distinguish clearly
enough between the past and present, as you understand them.

The past, in the present, would appear so brilliantly
that man could not react adequately in circumstances of time
that he had himself created. The future was blocked, practically

speaking *(long pause)*, to preserve freedom of action and to encourage physical exploration, curiosity, and creativity. With memory, however, mental projections into the future were of course also possible so that man could plan his activities in time, and forsee probable results: "Ghost images" of the future probabilities always acted as mental stimuli for physical explorations in all areas, and of all kinds.

("Do you mean in all areas of the planet, for instance?")

These ghost images provided stimuli for mental, spiritual, and physical experience. That answers your question, I believe.

("Yes.")

The race was dealing with the creation of a new world of physical experience. To do this particular kind of experiment, it was necessary that physical manipulation be concentrated upon. Ghost images from the future were one thing, inspiring mankind. Had such data instantly appeared before him, however, man would have been deprived of the physical joys, endeavors, and challenges that were so basic to the experiment itself. Do you want to rest your hand?

(I shook my head, no. Jane had been speaking for Seth for three-quarters of an hour, and showed no real inclination to stop. As in the other sessions of this book, I was aware of an extra charge or impetus, an added determination on Seth-Jane's part. Now in trance, Jane was going through these complicated sentences without trouble, even indicating punctuation.)

It would have been quite possible for you as a race to have chosen any other "series" of neurological pulses, or messages, as the "real" ones, and to structure your experience along different lines. The biological structure and the mental consciousness together, however, chose the most comfortable sequence in which a present area of activity, brought about by neurological recognition, would be backed up by unconscious mental knowledge and other biologically invisible neurological connections.

The psyche knows itself and is aware of its parts. When ego consciousness reached a certain point of biological and mental competence, when experience in the present became extensive enough, then ego consciousness would be at the stage where it could begin to accept greater data. Indeed, it is now at that stage.

(Pause at 10:37.) Its focus in the present is now secure. That focus finally brought about, in your terms, an expansion of consciousness, and one that early man did not have to handle. In your terms, time now includes more space, and hence more experience and stimuli. Again speaking historically, in the past the private person in any given hour was aware at once only of those events happening in his immediate environment. He could respond instantly. Events were, to that extent now, manageable. And rest your hand if you want to.

(I felt all right, but Jane, still in trance, held up her empty cigarette pack. She waited quietly while I got her a fresh one.)

The ego specialized in expansions of space and its physical manipulation. It specialized with objects. As a result, now, a person in any given hour is aware of events happening at the other end of the world. No immediate physical response he or she can make seems adequate or pertinent on many occasions. Bodily physical action, then, to that extent, loses its immaculate precision in time. You cannot kick an "enemy" who does not live in your village or country; an enemy, furthermore, whom you do not even know personally. *(Intently:)* Again, to that extent instant physical action in time is not the same kind of life-and-death factor that it was when a man was faced with an enraged animal, or enemy, in close combat.

("Can I ask a question?" As Seth, Jane nodded. "Will you give us a definition of what you mean by early man? I think readers would be interested." I'd been hoping Seth would go into this. Still in trance, Jane nodded again when I had finished—and I had the distinct impression that I shouldn't have interrupted her delivery.)

Now: In the past in the same way, love could be immediately expressed. In historic terms, early man, using here your theories about the race—early man—was in intimate contact with his family, clan, or tribe. With the developing expansion of space, however, loved ones often dwell far apart, and sudden bodily response cannot be expressed at once, at a particular point of immediate contact.

(10:57.) These developments, with others, are already triggering changes in man's behavior, and inspiring him toward further alterations of consciousness. He now needs a more expansive viewpoint of past and future in order to help him deal

with the ramifications of the present as it has evolved through experience.

Recognized concepts of the self are the ego's interpretation of selfhood. They are projected into concepts of God and the universe. They meet with a certain biological validity because of the selectivity earlier mentioned, whereby only one series of neurological pulses is accepted—and upon these rides the reality of the egotistical self. At one "time" a god interpreted in those terms served as a model for the egotistical behavior of one self toward another self.

(*I read the last paragraph back to Seth to check it. I had it down all right; I hadn't lost my way after all.*

(*Slowly:*) In a world in which individuals were confined in space in a tribe or clan (*a one-minute pause*), action was immediate. The environment presented a framework in which consciousness learned to deal with stimuli in a direct fashion. It learned how to focus. The necessary specialization meant that only so much data could be handled at once, emotionally or otherwise. The formation of different tribes allowed man to behave cooperatively, in small numbers. This meant that those on the outside were selectively ignored, considered strangers.

(*Intently:*) At that point, consciousness in those terms could not handle focused concentration, the emergence of ego consciousness, and simultaneously experience powerful feelings of oneness with other large groups. It was struggling for individuation.

Individuation, however, was dependent upon the cooperation of individuals. As the ego learned to feel more secure, the cooperative tendencies broadened so that the growth of nations was possible. It was inevitable, however, that ego consciousness would produce a reality in which it would finally need, in those terms, to accept other data and information that in the beginning it had to ignore.

I am speaking so far in historic terms, as you understand them. History, however, is but your official line of accepted stimuli. Later in the book that will be made clear.

New paragraph (*and more rapidly*): As egotistical consciousness expands to include hereto largely neglected data, then it will experience, practically speaking, a new kind of identity; knowing itself differently. Its concepts of godhood will significantly alter, as will the dimensions of emotion. Your heritage includes vastly richer veins of love, yet your concepts of self and godhood have severely limited these. You often seem to hate those with different beliefs than your own, for example, and you have perpetrated cruelties upon others in the name of religion and in the name of science, because your limited ideas about the nature of the self led you to fear your emotions. Often you are afraid that love will overwhelm you, for instance.

(A one-minute pause at 11:20.) While you were so concerned with protecting what you thought of as the boundaries and integrity of one selfhood, as a race you actually arrived at a point where you were beginning to deny your own greater reality. But all of this is part of the experiment upon which the race embarked in <u>your probability</u>.

Where your physical survival, in those terms, once depended upon a narrowed focus while you learned physical manipulation, now the success of that manipulation necessitates a broadening of focus—a new awakening into the larger existence of the selfhood, with what will be a corresponding rerecognition of neurological activity that is now only briefly sensed by some *(like Jane)*, but present in the heritage of your corporal structure.

(Louder:) Now I do not think you can reasonably be expected to take any more notes without a break, and so I give you one.

("Okay. Thank you.")

(11:26. Actually, this was one of those times when it seemed that I could have continued note-taking indefinitely. Seth-Jane certainly appeared able to keep going. Jane had been in trance for an hour and forty-one minutes, but even so she was out of it rapidly. "The trances have changed since he started this book, though," she said. "Once I get on the right track, Seth just keeps going, and I don't want to change it or get off . . . I think it's a great development. But you know: If you think you're on to something no one else has, you're afraid you'll be called batty by the rest of the world . . . Seth is a great organizer, though. It's like there's a tremendous amount of work being done behind the sessions, so I can get the data—but this isn't like the channels from Seth [as described in the 616th session in Chapter 2 of Personal Reality]."

(Jane said that I might better ask questions only during break, at least for now. My inquiry about early man hadn't "seriously" disturbed her; but I'd been correct in feeling that I

shouldn't have interrupted her then. She also talked about possible confusions or conflicts between Seth doing "Unknown" Reality *while she was writing her own* Adventures in Consciousness. *She's had no trouble, however, and is still enthusiastic about her book; she's putting Chapter 4 into final form.* Adventures *is due at her publishers, Prentice-Hall, Inc., in September 1974.*

(*Resume in a quiet manner at 11:48.*)

Now: Here, and throughout this book there will be sections dealing with Practice Elements—in capitals—where to some extent you can see how certain of these concepts can be practically experienced, and receive at least a hint of their application.

Centered (*with gestures*):

PRACTICE ELEMENT 1

In a waking state, Ruburt found himself in Saratoga Springs, N. Y., where he grew up, in what seemed to be a kind of mental projection. (*See Jane's notes at the beginning of the last session.*) Everything was gray. The immediate nature of full-blast sense data was missing. Vision was clear but spotty, highly selective. Motion was, however, the strongest sense element. Ruburt was bodiless on the one hand, and on the other he perceived some of the experience through the eyes of an infant in a carriage.

Quite sharply he perceived a <u>particular</u> curb at the corner of a definite intersection (*York Avenue and Warren Street*), and his attention was caught by the focus: a curb, a slope of dirt, and then the sidewalk; and the motion of the carriage as it was wheeled up.

The child was himself in the past on the one hand, and yet he was a <u>probable</u> future self in that past. (*Pause.*) From the standpoint of Ruburt's official mental focus, and from the standpoint of the neurologically accepted present, that past environment had to remain off-center, or blurred. He could experience it only by sidestepping officially accepted neurological activity. He visited a store that is not at that location "anymore," and here the sense data were somewhat clearer. He had no conscious memories of the store's interior, yet it was instantly apparent to him—the dark oiled floor, spread with sawdust. Even the odors were present.

He toured his (*public*) grade school where he attended

kindergarten to third grade,³ saw the children come out for
recess, and felt himself one of them—while during the entire
experience he knew himself as an adult, embarked upon that
adventure.

He went from place to place, floating bodiless—a tour
of consciousness. That same environment exists now, alternately
with Ruburt's present, and as vividly as his present does. It was,
however, from his viewpoint, a probable past.⁴

The infant with whom he momentarily identified as
the self he is now only opaquely and indirectly shared common
experience. This was not simple regression, then. That child grew
up in that probability, and Ruburt grew up in this one. (Pause.)
He touched upon certain coordinates that were neurologically
shared, however, by both: He and the child were familiar with
the carriage and the curb, the mother who pushed the carriage,
and the house into which Ruburt felt himself, as the child, being
carried.

He sensed the house interior and the stairway vividly.
He knew that the mother then went down the stairs to bring in
the carriage, but when he tried to perceive this, the motion became too fast. The mother's figure blurred so completely that he
could not follow it. He felt confused, and found himself entering
the store around the corner, and then consciously circled the
block and went into the school.

The school and the store were not in the infant's
experience, for in that probability the family moved away. The
blur of activity earlier was the result of neurological confusion,
and Ruburt switched over unknowingly to an environment still in
the same physical block that was meaningful to him, but not
shared by the future experience of that infant. You must understand that your own past exists as vitally as does your present—
but your probable pasts and presents exist in the same manner.
You simply do not accept them in the strands of experience that
"you" recognize.⁵

(Pause.) Skip several spaces.

As part of the work on this book, Ruburt is just
beginning to experiment with the conscious recognition of probable material, and the conscious acceptance of kinds of experience
usually tabooed according to the selectivity already mentioned.

(12:19.) In the sleep state after our last session, then, he allowed his consciousness to expand enough so that it became aware of information and experience usually censored automatically through mental and neurological habit. In *Adventures* Ruburt uses the term "prejudiced perception"—an excellent one—that is applicable here. For you have prejudiced yourself spiritually, mentally, and physically in those terms. In the sleep state Ruburt became unprejudiced, at least to some degree, so that he encountered information that seemed alien or out of context with usual experience.

Your theories of time are connected with your usual neurological pulses. It is one thing to play with concepts of multidimensionality, or probabilities, and quite another to be practically presented with them, even briefly, when your thought patterns and neurological habits tell you that they cannot be translated. So Ruburt felt frustrated, and he told me in no uncertain terms *(see Appendix 4)* that his consciousness could not contain the information he was receiving.

Like a good teacher *(humorously)*, I took his protests into consideration. Later he wrote a statement that came to him. This was his conscious interpretation of the information he had received the night before, translated as best he could in linear terms.

I have my own existence, that is quite different from Ruburt's, and yet I also have a reality that is connected to his psyche.[6] Each of you also have the same kind of connection with other "more knowledgeable" portions of yourself, or your greater identity, that are independently themselves and yet also alive in your psyches. They are portions of the "unknown" reality.

Now I am able to obtain information that Ruburt, in his terms, does not have. In other terms he does have it, and so do you, but you have been mentally, spiritually, and biologically prejudiced against it. As a race, you are ready to become more aware of your greater reality, however, and to explore its "unknown" aspects. Period. Hence this book.

You may experience some irritability with some of the concepts in it, simply because you have so schooled yourselves to ignore them. You should also experience an acceleration of consciousness, however, and as you read it, a growing sense of familiarity. The framework of the book itself will lead you, if you allow it, into other strata of your own greater knowledge.

(Loudly:) Period. End of session. I will have some personal recommendations next time. Ruburt's favorite television programs are good for him, and allow his mind to rest. They are his mental play, and for that reason, important.

(12:37 A.M. "Good night, Seth. Thank you very much."

(Jane's trance had been very deep. Now she was bleary-eyed: "I feel as though I don't want to think for two weeks . . ." Seth hadn't said so during the session, but Jane told me she'd "picked up from him" that she should eat an extra meal a day for a while—usually late at night, as, say, after a session. Also, she should take extra exercise each day, moving as rapidly as she could. She wasn't under any additional strain while producing "Unknown" Reality, she added, since she wanted to do it, but those simple actions would help refresh her. Her use of energy since starting the book has been lavish. Jane's comments before tonight's session about possible instructions from Seth are given in Appendix 5.

(After finishing Personal Reality *in July, 1973, Jane and I took quite a bit of time off from our usual Monday-Wednesday session routine while we prepared that book for publication. We developed the habit of watching certain television programs on Wednesday evening, but since we've gone back to holding sessions regularly, we haven't been able to see them. I suggested to Jane that we shift Wednesday night's session to Thursday night.*

(And once more: Many times during the night after this session, Jane discovered herself involved with dictation for "Unknown" Reality, both in the sleep state and out of it.)

NOTES: Session 686

1. Once again (I suggested the same reference in Note 2 for Session 683), see sessions 647-48 in Chapter 12 of *Personal Reality.*

2. See Jane's own material in Appendix 5. However, while studying Seth in this session—as well as the notes presented during break at 11:26—it's a good idea for the reader to keep both appendixes 4 and 5 in mind.

3. See the 679th session at[4], as well as Note 4 itself.

4. In *Seth Speaks* alone there is much material on probabilities

that I could cite in connection with this session. One of my favorite sessions, however, is the 566th in Chapter 16, where Seth discusses the "profound psychological interconnections" involving probable pasts and futures, dreams, telepathy, present abilities, suggestion, and related subjects. He also produces lines like, "As you sit reading this book in your present moment of time, you are positioned in the center of a cosmic web of probabilities that is affected by your slightest mental or emotional act."

5. A note added within the week: The specific exercise connected with this first Practice Element appears in the next, 687th, session.

6. A note added later: We're still acquiring information about the psychic connections between Jane and Seth, of course. Even now, more than 10 years after Jane began speaking for Seth, one might say that each session we hold represents another step in this learning process; we fully expect it to continue as long as the sessions do.

Session 687
March 4, 1974
9:42 P.M. Monday

(See Appendix 6 for the material on parallel man, alternate man, and probable man that Jane began dictating to me shortly after last midnight.

(In chapters 3 and 12 of Personal Reality, *I inserted notes describing how Jane and I had seen geese during their migrations south, then north, respectively, in 1972 and 1973. Now that truly sublime and mysterious phenomenon was upon us again—and if anything we found it more meaningful than ever. For myself, I made intuitive connections between the regular travels of the geese and our own work rhythms in producing the Seth books.*

(There were welcome similarities between our sighting of today and that of last March: Again, the weather was very warm for this time of year; again, a fine rain was falling. I threw open a kitchen window when Jane called my attention to that

familiar honking sound. The geese came in low over the river half
a block away, flying beneath the clouds and in the rain—a great
wide "V" of them, heading north.

(I'd never seen so many in one flock, or gaggle, before.
A certain number of birds shuttled back and forth within the
formation at any one moment, changing their positions for
reasons unknown to us, "talking" all the while. Once again, I
found great reassurance in watching the spectacle of their flight.
Those birds, I thought, knew *where they were going—they* knew
what they were doing, in ways man could barely comprehend. I
followed the formation until it disappeared in the mists and trees
on the horizon.

(We'd waited for the session to begin since 9:20. At
9:37 Jane said impatiently, "Come on, Seth . . . Hmm; I've done
this a lot lately, haven't I?" Then: "I feel him vaguely
around . . ." And Seth continued his material on Practice Ele-
ment 1.)

Good evening.

("Good evening, Seth.")

Now: Such experiences as Ruburt's Saratoga episode
are valuable because they begin a process in which other neurological pulses are to some degree recognized.

Over a period of time, this can bring about some conscious experience with probable realities. In the beginning the
glimpses may be very brief, and the sense experience misty.
Nevertheless, new patterns and cognitive endeavors are being set
up between the neurological structure and the consciousness that
you know.

An excellent preliminary exercise is the following:

Take any remembered scene from your own past.
Experience it as clearly as possible imaginatively, but with the
idea of its probable extensions. Sometime, immediately or after a
few tries, a particular portion of the scene will become gray or
shadowy. It is not a part of the past that you know, but an intersection point where that past served as an offshoot into a series
of probabilities that you did not follow.

Instead of a shadowy element, you yourself may feel
unsubstantial—"ghostly," as Ruburt did. Period. Instead of any
of those things, the imagined dialogue—if there is any—may
suddenly change from the dialogue that you remember; or the
entire scene and action may quickly alter. Any of these

occurrences can be hints that you are beginning to glimpse the probable variations of the particular scene or action. It is, however, the subjective feeling that is the important clue here, and once you experience it there will be no doubt in your mind.

Some people will have little trouble with the exercise, and others will need to exert persistence before finding any success at all. *(Pause.)* This method is even more effective if you choose from your past a scene in which a choice was involved that was important to you.

In such a case, begin imaginatively, following through with the other decision or decisions that you might have made. At one point a shadowy effect—grayness, or other characteristics just mentioned—will occur. One or several of these may be involved, but again, your subjective feeling is the most important clue. Imagination may bring you a clear picture, for example, that may then become fuzzy, and in that case the blurred quality would be your hint of probable action.

Until you have tried the exercise and become fully acquainted with it, you will not understand its effectiveness. You will know, for instance, when the remembered event and imagination intersect with another probability. Whether or not you have any great success, the exercise will begin a neurological reorientation that will be most important if you hope to glimpse realities that are outside of your present neurologically accepted sense-reality.

(Pause at 10:01.) This exercise is a mental and biological doorway that can expand both your concepts of yourself and reality. There may be instances in which it seems that little progress is made during the exercise itself. During the day, however, having made an important decision in one direction, you may begin to feel the reality of the opposite decision and its ramifications. The exercise may also result in a different kind of a dream, one that is recognized within the dream state, at least, as an introduction to a probable reality. You deal directly with future probabilities in the dream state in any case. *(Pause.)* For example, in a series of dreams you may try out various solutions to a given problem, and choose one of these.[1] That choice becomes your physical reality.

According to the intensity of the situation, now, another also desirable solution may be worked out in a probable reality. On an unconscious level you are aware of your probable

selves, and they of you. You share the same psychic roots, and
your joint yet separate dreams are available to "all of you." This
does not mean that you are dreaming someone else's dream, any
more than it means that twins, for example, do. It does mean
that your probable selves and you share in a body of symbolism,
background, and ability. The multistructured nature of the
dream state allows for dream dramas in which probable selves do
appear. They may appear as symbolically representing strong
characteristics upon which they have focused, though you have
ignored them.

(Slowly:) The dream state, however, does operate as a
rich web of communication between probable selves and probable existences. All probabilities spring from inner reality, from
the psyche's own inner activity and structure. (Long pause.) The
consciousness that you know can indeed now emerge into even
greater realization of itself, but not by obsessively defending its
old position. Instead it must recognize its power as the director
of probable action, and no longer inhibit its own greater
capacities.

In your terms, until now your consciousness has specialized in neurological patterning. As mentioned (in Session
682), this was extremely important while it learned the art of
specialized focus. Now, however, it must begin to recognize that
it can indeed expand, and bring into its awareness other quite
legitimate realities. The nature of probabilities must be understood, for the time has come in the world as you experience it
where the greatest wisdom and discrimination are needed. Your
consciousness and neurological prejudice blind you to the full
dimension of physical activity. The true implications of physical
action are not as yet apparent to you.

(A one-minute pause at 10:23.) You are beginning to
understand the reality of your planet. You cannot plunder it, for
example—something you are only beginning to learn. Opening
up your consciousness to previously denied messages would bring
you in direct contact with other life-forms on your planet in a
way that you have formerly denied yourselves. Your cellular
knowledge of past and future probabilities alone would teach
you a spiritual and corporal courtesy.

(Another one-minute pause.) Give us a moment . . .
The "unknown" reality sustains you and the web of life as you
understand it. Your conscious concepts must enlarge so that the

conscious self can understand its true nature. As you think of it, consciousness is barely—barely—half developed. It has learned to identify with one small group of neurologically accepted responses. Portions of the brain not used lie latent, waiting for the recognition that will trigger them into activity *(intently)*. When this happens, the mind will become aware of the rich bed of probabilities upon which the ego now rides so blindly.

The great latent-but-always-sensed dimensions of spiritualized creaturehood will then begin to flower. A few great men have glimpsed those abilities, comma, and their love of the race and their integrity had caused them to trigger the unused portions of the brain.[2] In their way they sensed the great probable future and its ramifications.

In centuries past they saw your present, though through their own vision, and so it was only partially the present as you know it. Your emotional reality truly leaps into its own only now and then, for your very concepts of yourselves deny the multidimensional aspects of your being. The need and the yearning to love and to know are both biologically present within you. They are present within the animals, and within a blade of grass.

The concepts of God that you have, have gone hand-in-hand with the development of your consciousness. The ego, emerging, needed to feel its dominance and control, and so it imagined a dominant god apart from nature. Often nations acted as group egos—each with its own god-picturing, its own concepts of power. Whenever a tribe or a group or a nation decided to embark upon a war, it always used the concept of its god to lead it on.

(Faster at 10:45:) The god concept then was an aid, and an important one, to man's emerging ego. To develop its sense of specialization, the ego forgot the great cooperative venture of the earth. If a hunter literally knows his relationship with an animal, he cannot kill it. On deeper levels both animal and man understand the connections. Biologically the man knows he has come from the earth. Some of his cells have been the cells of animals, and the animal knows he will look out through a man's eyes.[3] The earth venture is cooperative. The slain beast is tomorrow's hunter. In terms of ego consciousness, however, there were stages of growth; and the god concepts that spoke of oneness with nature were not those that served the ego's

purposes in the line of development as you understand it (deliberately).

For a while such techniques worked. Always, however, there was the undeniable inner self in the background: man's dreams, his biological and spiritual integrity, and these in one way or another were always before him.

In your probability you did allow the inner self some freedom. Therefore, the so-called egotistical consciousness was not given complete sway. It remained flexible enough so that even hidden in its god concepts[4] there were symbols of greater reality. Your system deals with physical manipulability, again, and the translation of creativity into physical form. An exterior separation had to occur for a while, in which consciousness forgot, egotistically speaking, that it was a part of nature, and pretended to be apart.

It was known, however—and unconsciously written in the cells and mind and heart—that this procedure would only go so far. When man's consciousness was sure of itself it would not need to be so narrowly focused. Then the true flowering of humanity's consciousness could begin. Then the ego could expand and become aware of realities it had "earlier" ignored. Period.

(*Jane, in trance, sat with a hand to her closed eyes as she rocked back and forth.*)

A brief break.

(*10:59 to 11:07.*)

You have put yourselves in a position where your consciousness must now become aware of the probable pasts and probable futures, in order to form for yourselves a sane, fulfilling, and creative present.

Ego consciousness must now be familiarized with its roots, or it will turn into something else. You are in a position where your private experience of yourself does not correlate with what you are told by your societies, churches, sciences, archaeologies, or other disciplines. Man's "unconscious" knowledge is becoming more and more consciously apparent. This will be done under and with the direction of an enlightened and expanding egotistical awareness (*much louder*), that can organize the hereto neglected knowledge—or it will be done at the expense of the reasoning intellect (*again louder*), leading to a rebirth of superstition, chaos, and the unnecessary war between reason and intuitive knowledge.

(*Pause.*) When, at this point now, of mankind's development, his emerging unconscious knowledge is denied by his institutions, then it will rise up despite those institutions, and annihilate them. (*Pause.*) Cult after cult will emerge, each unrestrained by the use of reason, because reason will have denied the existence of rampant unconscious knowledge, disorganized and feeling only its own ancient force.

If this happens, all kinds of old and new religious denominations will war, and all kinds of ideologies surface. This need not take place, for the conscious mind—basically, now—having learned to focus in physical terms, is meant to expand, to accept unconscious intuitions and knowledge, and to organize these deeply creative principles into cultural patterns.

The great emotion of love has been thus far poorly used, yet it represents even the biological impetus of your being. Your religions in a large measure have taught you to hate yourselves and physical existence. They have told you to love God, but rarely taught you to experience the gods in yourselves.

Now: In one way or another religions have always followed, again, the development of your consciousness, and so they have served its purposes and yours; and they have always reflected, though distorted, those greater inner realities of your being. In historic terms, as you understand them, the "progression" of religion gives you a perfect picture of the development of human consciousness, the differentiation of peoples and nations, and the growth of the ideas of the "individual."

There is nothing wrong with the concept of an egotistically based individual being, colon: I am not suggesting, therefore, that your individuality is something to be lost, thrown aside, or superseded. Nor am I saying that it should be buried, submerged, or dissolved in a superself. I am not suggesting that its edges be blurred by a powerful unconscious.

(*Intently:*) I am saying that the individual self must become consciously aware of far more reality; that it must allow its recognition of identity to expand so that it includes previously unconscious knowledge. To do this you must understand, again, that man must move beyond the concepts of one god, one self, one body, one world, as these ideas are currently understood.[5] You are now poised, in your terms, upon a threshold from which the race can go many ways. There are species of consciousness. Your species is in a time of change. There are potentials within the body's mechanisms, in your terms, not as yet used. Developed, they can immeasurably enrich the race, and bring it to levels of spiritual and psychic and physical fulfillment. If some changes are not made, the race as such will not endure.

(11:26.) This does not mean that you will not endure, or that in another probability the race will not—but that in your terms of historical sequence, the race will not endure.

(Pause.) Speaking now in those historic terms that you understand, let me say that there was no single-line development from animal to man, but parallel lines, in which for centuries animal-man and man-animal coexisted cooperatively. In the same way now, unknown amongst you, many species of what you may call probable man[6] dwell in embryo form.

Because of the ego's particular line of development, you have experimented with artificial drugs and chemicals, both in foods and for medicinal purposes, as well as for "religious" enlightenment. Some of the effects of LSD[7] and other artificial psychedelic drugs give you a hint of other probable directions your consciousness might have followed, or might still follow. As the experiments are conducted, however, and in the ignorance of the framework, the conscious mind takes a subordinate position. Instead, using methods other than drugs, it could be taught to expand its knowledge far more safely, to organize it in ways that could be most advantageous. Still, some of the experiments do give hints of certain aspects of one of the species' probable developments.

Give us a moment. Rest your hand . . .

(Very intently:) You cannot do anything, literally, that is not natural. Nevertheless, over a period of time "artificial" chemicals taken with food into the body will form a new kind of nature, in your terms. Your bodies are beautifully equipped, and will turn almost anything to their advantage. According to many schools of thought, artificial drugs, so-called, or chemicals, are considered in a very negative light, cutting you off from nature. Yet such experiments represent a strong line of probability only in its "infancy," in which man could sustain himself without draining the earth, live without killing animals, and literally form a new kind of physical structure connected to the earth, while not depleting its substance.

This does not mean that some biological confusion might not result in the meantime. It does mean that even in those

terms, <u>and</u> consciously <u>unknowing</u>, mankind is experimenting
with a probable species and working out quite spiritual issues.
Your probable futures and your probable pasts, in larger terms,
exist at once. I will begin by explaining your history to you, at
least to some extent, in the historical terms you recognize. To
that degree, I hope to make your unknown reality consciously
known.

Now—that is the end of Section 1, to be composed of
the sessions as given, except with the Preface first. Section 1
should be entitled "You and the 'Unknown' Reality," with
"Unknown" in quotes. Give us a moment. . .

(*Pause at 11:58.*) As I describe some of early man's
past in historic terms, I will also show how that "heritage" is
alive in your daily experience with the world as you know it.
Period.

The archaeology of the soul and the blood is not
buried, but alive in your experience. A photograph is no more a
relic than a fossil is. Each is filled with the energy of being.
Neither is buried in a past beyond your knowing. A photograph
lives in the present of your psyche, and a fossil in the living
vitality of your cells (*spelled*).

Section 2

**PARALLEL MAN, ALTERNATE MAN,
AND PROBABLE MAN:
THE REFLECTION OF THESE
IN THE PRESENT, PRIVATE PSYCHE.**

**YOUR MULTIDIMENSIONAL REALITY
IN THE NOW OF YOUR BEING**

Session 687

March 4, 1974
(continued)

(12:01.) Now: Section 2: "Parallel Man, Alternate Man, and Probable Man," colon: "The Reflection of These in the Present, Private Psyche." That is the heading.

(Pause.) Separated from that—that is one heading—the next heading: "Your Multidimensional Reality in the Now of Your Being."

(Louder:) <u>End of session—</u>

("All right—")

—and my heartiest regards to you both. Ruburt is regenerating. I will have more to say to him shortly. I like him to get some of his goodies *(on this book)* first.

("Thank you, Seth. Good night."

(12:04 A.M. Jane was soon out of her trance, but it had been a very good one nevertheless. Sitting in her rocker, she began to rapidly pound her feet on the floor. I felt the vibrations.

119

"These trances are so deep that I want to do something when I come out of them," she said. She continued to thump away. "They're different, there's no two ways about it . . ."

(The next morning Jane told me that once again she'd done "a lot of book dictation" after she went to bed. But this time, she thought, she'd been alert: When she realized that the material was "running through her," as she often puts it [meaning she isn't aware of Seth's presence], she sat up, turned on a night light, and began to record the data on the pad she keeps on her bedside table. I wasn't disturbed as I slept beside her. "Aha," Jane told herself at last, when the information stopped flowing, "this time I got it all down." She lay back in bed—and woke up. She had dreamed the recording part of the experience.)

NOTES: Session 687

1. Seth's material here about dream solutions reminded me of a few lines—just about all that were saved—from a poem Jane wrote when she was 17 years old:

I have found dreams and followed them
And lost them.
I have found speckled pebbles by the seashore
And saved them,
But the dreams were what I wanted.

Jane's first published material on dreams (precognitive and otherwise) can be found in chapters 4 and 5 of *The Coming of Seth* (original title: *How to Develop Your ESP Power*).

She quotes Seth on dreams in Chapter 14 of *The Seth Material*, and to some extent he discusses them directly in *Seth Speaks* and *Personal Reality*. However, we've accumulated quite a bit of unpublished Seth material on dreams, and I'll start looking for chances to insert some of those data in the rest of *"Unknown" Reality*.

2. I'd say that when he talks about the "unused portions of the brain," that physical organ, Seth means qualities of nonphysical mind as well. We still have much to learn about the brain (let alone the mind); even though by now all sections of the brain have been probed down to the molecular level, no trace or imprint of a thought has ever been found within its tissue. As an analogy, the innate knowledge of probabilities that Seth postulates here may be related to the brain in the same way that memory evidently "happens" throughout its parts, instead of being localized in just one of them.

For material on mental and psychic expansions in old age, and the hemispheres of the brain, see the 650th session in Chapter 13 of *Personal Reality*. And in Chapter 21 of *Seth Speaks*, Seth briefly mentions the eventual activation of "new areas" in the brain to "physically take care of" past-life memories. See the 586th session at 11:02.

3. Speaking literally, because of their dissolution upon the death of their host, the man's cells won't become part of the animal's structure—but at least some of the long-lived molecular components of those cells could do so, and with all their memories intact. I think there's more to the idea than such a "tight" interpretation as this, however; with possibly the transference of cellular memory (or some equivalent quality) from creature to creature being involved. We haven't asked Seth to go into this yet.

Jane treated similar concepts poetically in 1965:

Illumination

Speechless as a stone
I felt myself
Within me, mute.
Comprehension ate my foot
And gobbled up my arm.

The wind lifted
Layers off my skin.
My heart and giblets lay
All drying in the sun,
Unpackaged and exposed.

Wrens came, hawks and worms,
Innocent communicants
To a sacramental feast.
Delicious anatomy—
Piece by piece carried off.

I saw from a wren's tipped wing
Myself in the hawk descend
From the blameless sky,
And in the worm I felt the smooth
Sides of the earth give way.

I was unsectioned,
Distributed among the stars,
Scattered, melted, frozen.
My cells blew loose
In the skulls of frogs.

"Who am I?" cried the worm and the hawk,
The frog, the star, the rock.
My heart and giblets sang out,
Answering in multitudinous
Voices.

4. For material on probabilities, the god concept, and religion, see chapters 14-17 and 21 in *Seth Speaks*, and Chapter 17 in *Adventures in Consciousness*.

5. Much of Seth's material in the Preface and the 683rd session applies here.

6. See Appendix 6.

7. In *Personal Reality*, see Session 638, bridging chapters 9 and 10, then Session 639. The latter contains excerpts from Jane's *Dialogues*. These in turn illustrate some of her own "trips"—but without drugs.

Session 688
March 6, 1974
9:47 P.M. Wednesday

(Today I showed Jane the finished version of my "ghost image" portrait of her as a male in another probability. The painting represented a new approach in art for me, and had caused me a good deal of puzzlement at first. I began it early in February. I won't take the space to describe the series of mistaken efforts I went through in producing the work, except to say that finally I came to the rather simple conscious understanding that I was trying to paint a probable Jane. All at once, as I watched her delivering the 684th session on February 20, I saw strong resemblances between my painting and certain poses she repeatedly took while in trance.

(Then came Jane's projection-probability experience involving her home town of Saratoga Springs; she described this episode in her notes preceding the 685th session, in Section 1, and Seth elaborated upon it considerably in the next session. The

ghostly qualities in that event fit in with what I was trying to do
in the painting: By leaving the thick gray and white under-
painting of my "portrait" of "Jane" without color, I realized, I
could express not only a probable interpretation of her, but the
colorless qualities of the Saratoga experience itself. Once I made
those conscious connections I was able to finish the painting very
easily. I intend to do more work in this manner.

(A rather humorous note: Jane has decided that she
prefers to continue with the scheduled Wednesday sessions, in-
stead of switching them to Thursday night. Television on Wed-
nesday night doesn't offer that many attractions after all.
Besides, she said, tonight she "felt stuff around, about cells and
prayer, and things like that"; she announced that she wanted to
hold the session.

("And now that I'm sitting here," she said, patting the
arms of her rocker, "I can feel the material getting organized. It's
a great help . . .")

Good evening.

("Good evening, Seth.")

Now: The beginning of Section 2. You already have
the heading. Give us a moment . . .

The CU's, or units of consciousness,[1] are literally in
every place and time at once. They possess the greatest adaptability, and a profound "inborn" propensity for organization of
all kinds. They act as individuals, and yet each carries within it a
knowledge of all other kinds of activity that is happening in any
other given unit or group of units.

Coming together, the units actually form the systems
of reality in which they have their experience. In your system,
for example, they are within the phenomenal world. They will
always come under the guise of any particular pattern of reality,
then. In your terms they can move forward or backward in time,
but they also possess another kind of interior mobility within
time as you know it.

As there are insides to apples, so think of the ordinary
moment as an apple. In usual experience, you hold that apple in
your hand, or eat it. Using this analogy, however, the apple itself
(as the moment) would contain infinite variations of itself <u>within</u>
itself. These CU's therefore can operate even within time, as you
understand it, in ways that are most difficult to explain. Time
not only goes backward and forward, but <u>inward and outward.</u> I

am still using your idea of time here to some degree. *(Pause.)* Later in this book I hope to lead you beyond it entirely. But in the terms in which I am speaking, it is the inward and outward directions of time that give you a universe that seems to be fairly permanent, and yet is also being created.

This inward and outward thrust allows for several important conditions that are necessary for the establishment of "relatively" separate, stable universe systems. Such a system may seem like a closed one[2] from any viewpoint within itself. Yet this inward and outward thrusting condition effectively sets up the boundaries and uniqueness of each universal system, while allowing for a constant give-and-take of energy among them.

(10:04.) No energy is ever lost. It may seem to disappear from one system, but if so, it will emerge in another. The inward and outward thrust that is not perceived is largely responsible for what you think of as ordinary consecutive time. *(Pause.*[3]*)* It is of the utmost and supreme importance, of course, that these CU's are literally indestructible. They can take any form, organize themselves in any kind of time-behavior, hyphen, and seem to form a reality that is completely dependent upon its apparent form and structure. Yet, disappearing through one of the physicists' black holes,[4] for example, though structure and form would seem to be annihilated and time drastically altered, there would be an emergence at the other end, where the whole "package of a universe," having been closed in the black hole, would be reopened.

There is the constant surge into your universe of new energy through infinite minute sources. The sources are the CU's themselves. In their own way, and using an analogy, now, in certain respects at least the CU's operate as minute but extremely potent black holes and white holes, as they are presently understood by your physicists. Give us a moment . . .

The CU's, following that analogy, serve as source points or "holes" through which energy falls into your system, or is attracted to it—and in so doing, forms it. The experience of forward time and the appearance of physical matter in space and time, and all the phenomenal world, results. As CU's leave your system, time is broken down. Its effects are no longer experienced as consecutive, and matter becomes more and more plastic until its mental elements become apparent. New CU's enter and leave your system constantly, then. Within the system *en masse,* however, through their great and small organizational structures, the CU's are aware of everything happening—not only on the top of the moment *(gesturing)*, but within it in all of its probabilities.

Now: This means that biologically the cell is aware of all of its probable variations, while in your time and structures it holds its unique position as a part, say, of any given organ in your body. *(Pause.)* In greater terms the cell is a huge physical universe, orbiting an invisible CU; and in your terms the CU will always be invisible—beyond the smallest phenomenon that you can perceive with any kind of instrument. To some extent, however, its activity can be indirectly apprehended through its effect upon the phenomenon that you can perceive.

(Pause at 10:26. I got Jane a beer while she sat waiting in trance.)

The EE units mentioned earlier[5] represent the stage of emergence, the threshold point that practically activates the CU's, in your terms. We will have more to say about these later.

It is vital that you understand this inward and outward thrust of "time," however, and realize that from this flows the consecutive appearance of the moment. The thrusting gives dimensions to time that so far you have not even begun to realize. Again, you live on the surface of the moments, with no understanding of the unrecognized and unofficial realities that lie beneath. All of this, once more, is tied in with your accepted neurological recognition of certain messages over others, your mental prejudice that effectively blinds you to other quite valid biological communications that are indeed present all of the "time."

(Intently:) I am trying to tell you something about the greater reality of your species, yet to do so with any justice, I must divest you, if possible, of certain concepts about the beginning of time, or "man's early history."

To start with, however, we will for a while lean on the old terminology, while hoping to gradually leave it behind. Give us a moment and rest your hand . . .

(I had to smile. After about 30 seconds Jane, as Seth, was already waiting to continue.)

The CU's form all systems simultaneously. Having formed yours, and from their energy diversifying themselves into physical forms, they were aware of all of the probable variations from any given biological strain. There was never any straight line of development as, say, from reptiles to mammal, ape, and man. Instead there were great, still-continuing, infinitely rich parallel explosions of life forms and patterns in as many directions as possible. There were animal-men and man-animals, using your terms, that shared both time and space for many centuries.[6] This is, as you all well know, a physical system in time. Here cells die and are replaced. Knowing their own indestructibility, the CU's within them simply change form, retaining however the identity of all the cells that they have been. *(Intently:)* While the cell dies physically, its inviolate nature is not betrayed. It is simply no longer physical.

That kind of "death" is, then, natural in one way or another within your system. I will be speaking here from many viewpoints, and later I will discuss in full your ideas of mortality. Here, however, let me state that all life is cooperative. It also knows it exists beyond its form.

The experience of your species involves a certain kind of consciousness development, highly vital. *(Pause.)* This necessitated a certain kind of specialization, a certain "long-term" identification with form. Cellular structure maintains brilliant effectiveness in the body's present reality, but knows itself free of it. Man's particular kind of consciousness fiercely identified with the body. This was a necessity to focus energy toward physical manipulation. To some important extent the same applies to the animals. The cell might gladly "die," but the specifically oriented man-and-animal consciousness would not so willingly let go.

The cell is individual, and struggles for rightful survival. Yet its time is limited, and the body's survival is dependent upon the cell's innate wisdom: The cell must die finally for the body to survive, and only by dying can the cell further its own development, and therefore insure its own greater survival. So the cell knows that to die is to live.

(10:59. Jane delivered all of this material in a most forceful manner.)

Man's consciousness, and to some extent that of the animals, is more specifically identified with form, however. In order to develop his own kind of individualized awareness, man had to consciously ignore for a while his own place within the structure of the earth. His experience of time would seem to be the experience of his identity. His consciousness would not seem to flow into his body before birth, and out of it after death. He would "forget" there was a time to die. He would forget that death meant new life. A natural message had to replace the old knowledge.

Give us a moment . . . In the body certain cells "kill" others, and in so doing the body's living integrity is maintained. The cells do each other that service *(with gestures)*. In the exterior world certain animals "kill" others. You had for centuries, then, speaking in your limited terms, a situation in which men and animals were both hunters and prey. In those misty eras[7] —from your standpoint—these activities were carried on with the deepest, most sacred comprehension. Again, the slain animal knew that it would "later" look out through its slayer's eyes[8] —attaining a newer, different kind of consciousness. The man, the slayer, understood the great sense of harmony that existed even in the slaying, and knew that in turn the physical material of his body would be used by the earth to replenish the vegetable and animal kingdoms.

Even when you lost sight—as you knew you would—of those deep connections, they would continue to operate until, in its own way, man's consciousness could rediscover the knowledge and put it to use—deliberately and willfully, thereby bringing that consciousness to flower. In your terms this would represent a great leap, for the egotistically aware individual would fully comprehend unconscious knowledge and act on his own, out of choice. He would become a conscious co-creator. Obviously, this has not as yet occurred.

I told you *(after 10:26 in this session)* that you presently perceive only the surface of the moment; so you also perceive but one line of the species' development. Yet even within your system, there are hints of the other probable realities that also coexist. The dolphins are a case in point.[9] In your line of probability they are oddities, yet even now you recognize their great brain capacity, and to some dim extent glimpse the range of their own communication.

At one time on your earth, in the way you look at time, there were many such species: water dwellers, with brain capacities as good as and better than your own. Your legends of mermaids, for example, though highly romanticized, do indeed hint of one such species' development. There were several species smaller than the dolphins, but generally the same structurally.

Their intelligence was indisputable, and old myths of sea gods arose from such species. There is even now an extremely rich emotional life on the part of the dolphins, to which you are relatively blind; and more than this, on their part a greater recognition of other species than you yourselves have.

(A one-minute pause at 11:24. Then at a slower pace:)
The dolphins possess a strong sense of personal loyalty, and an intimate family pattern, along with a highly developed individual and group recognition and behavior. They cooperate with each other, in other words. They go out of their way to help other species, and yet they do not take pets *(softly, staring at me)*. There were also, however, many varieties of water-dwelling mammals—some combining the human with the fish, though roughly along the lines of a combination chimpanzee-fish type, hyphen. These were small creatures who moved with amazing rapidity, and could emerge onto the land for days at a time.

In other probabilities, water-dwelling mammals predominate. They farm the land as you farm the water, and are only now learning how to operate upon the land for any amount of time, as you are only now learning how to manipulate below the water.

The physical universe serves then as a threshold for probabilities, and all possible species find their greatest fulfillment within that system, each of them neurologically tuned into their own reality and their own "time." So the body itself, as it presently exists, is innately equipped with other neurological responses that to you would seem to be biologically invisible. Nevertheless, your consciousness and your beliefs are what direct this neurological recognition. At birth, and before structured learning processes begin, you are far freer in that regard.

You could (underlined twice) walk into "yesterday" as well as tomorrow at that point of birth—if you could walk—and indeed your perception brings you events both in and out of time sequence. Responses to out-of-time events do not bring the infant recognition, approval, or action, however. It immediately begins to learn to accept certain neurological pulses which bring results, and not others, and so neurological patterns are early learned. This can be a frightening process, though it is accompanied by reassurances. The infant sees, out of context, both present and future without discrimination, and *(intently)* I am speaking of images physically perceived.

Nightmares on the part of children often operate as biological and psychic releases, during which buried out-of-time perceptions emerge explosively—events perceived that cannot be reacted to effectively in the face of parental conditioning. The body, then, is indeed a far more wondrous living mechanism than you realize. It is the body's own precognition[10] that allows the child to develop, to speak and walk and grow.

In the same manner, the species as you think of it is at one level aware of its own probabilities and "future" lines of development. The child learning to walk may fall and hurt itself, yet it does learn. In the same way the race makes errors—and yet in response to its own greater knowledge it continues to seek out those areas of its own probable fulfillment.

(Louder, smiling:) Either break, or end of session.

("Well, we'll take the break and see what happens.")

(11:50. Jane's trance had been profound. She was amazed to learn that it had lasted for over two hours; actually, she had run through the whole session without a break. "It's still a different kind of trance," she said, "and once you're in it, it's better to stay there. But it's exhilarating in ways that I can't explain.

("It's wild," she continued, "but I know that all of this is leading up to alternate man, probable man, and parallel man. [See Appendix 6.] I thought you were tired tonight, but I decided I wanted the session instead of looking at reruns on TV . . especially after I got that stuff while I was doing the dishes tonight, on cells and biological prayer."

(Jane decided to "wait a second" at 11:55, to see if she should resume the session. Then we declared an end to it at 12:05 A.M. Actually, I was the one who was bleary. Jane felt fine; she told me that she could cheerfully continue the session for another two hours. I was tempted, but . . .)

NOTES: Session 688

1. See Section 1, sessions 682-84.

2. In general, given the nature of the CU's—Seth's postulated "basic" units of consciousness that make up all realities—closed systems cannot exist. From Session 581 in Chapter 20 of *Seth Speaks*: "Basically, however, no system is closed. Energy flows freely from one to another, or rather permeates each. It is only the camouflage [physical] structure that

gives the impression of closed systems, and the law of inertia does not apply. It appears to be a reality only within your own framework and because of your limited focus."

Then, for some early quotes from Seth about his own ability to move among certain systems of reality, see Note 4 for the 680th session in this volume.

(Seth, in the 512th session in Chapter 1 of *Seth Speaks*: "Now at times I will be using the term 'camouflage,' referring to the physical world to which the outer ego relates, for physical form is one of the camouflages that reality adopts.")

3. This little note fits in here for two reasons: Jane's pause, and Seth's discussion of our kind of time. Here's what I wrote at 9:55 in the 24th session for February 10, 1964: "Jane reports that when she pauses for Seth during a delivery, she can sense the whole concept of the subject being discussed. Subjectively, it appears to 'hang over her.' Since on those occasions it's too much to handle at once, however, she feels Seth withdrawing it, to release it to her a little at a time in the form of connected words."

And added later: Also in that session, Seth describes how he must "disentangle concepts" from their patterns in order to relate them through Jane. His material on this will be given in an appendix for Session 711, in Volume 2 of *"Unknown" Reality*. In that appendix I assemble from various sessions information on the complex relationships involving Jane-Ruburt-Seth (and also Rob-Joseph).

4. A typical black hole, according to predictions made by Einstein in his theory of gravity, is thought to be the collapsed remnants of a giant star that's used up all of its nuclear energy. Its density is unimaginably great, its gravity so powerful that not even light can escape from it. Hence, such an object is invisible, forming a "hole" in space.

(Yet, it has been proposed that some light radiation might escape from the "event horizon" just above, or surrounding, the black hole, and that eventually this radiation may be detected with more advanced satellite equipment. Seth hasn't commented one way or the other on such theoretical attributes of black holes.)

See the 593rd session in the Appendix of *Seth Speaks*, where Seth briefly discusses both black holes and their suggested counterparts, white holes.

5. See Note 3 for Session 682, and the 683rd session just after 11:30.

6. See Appendix 6.

7. Just a week ago, in the 686th session, I asked Seth to comment on our ancient origins, but without getting an answer. At this writing, then, we still don't know what period in our past he's referring to. Evidently it's a very long time ago; even in conventional paleontological terms, recent discoveries in East Africa place a toolmaking man in action 3 million years ago, with a lineage possibly going back 14 million years. Now we plan to ask

Seth to develop his man-animal material soon, adding more specifics and including the probabilities involved.

A note added later: Unfortunately, we never did receive the kind of information we wanted here, especially that on human origins, before Seth finished *"Unknown" Reality.* The main reason? I became so occupied with the succeeding sessions of this manuscript that I forgot to make the request.

8. See Session 687 at 10:45, as well as Note 3.

9. At once Seth's material reminded me of a novel about dolphins that Jane worked on in 1963. Her first book-length fiction, *The Rebellers,* had been published (as a paperback) that summer, and she was experimenting with several new ideas. A couple of months before these sessions began in late November of that year, she wrote an outline and five chapters for a novel about the development of communications between mankind and cetaceans, and called it *To Hear A Dolphin.* We hadn't realized it at the time, of course, but it embodied some of the ideas Seth was to enlarge upon in his own material. Jane had time to show her manuscript to one publisher—who rejected it—before the Seth material got under way. *To Hear A Dolphin* was then laid aside, evidently for good. We still talk about it every so often; we still think its basic premises are good ones. Yet were she to do the book now, Jane says, she'd have to rewrite it completely.

10. Concerning such bodily precognition, in Section 1 see the beginning of the 679th session, and the 684th session at 10:07.

Session 689
March 18, 1974
9:55 P.M. Monday

(See Appendix 7 for an account of Jane's accomplishment of a week ago Sunday, when, in an altered state of consciousness, she received the outline for a potential new book, The Way Toward Health.

(We held just one session last week, and it did not involve work on either "Unknown" Reality or the book on health. The rest of the time we were busy with ESP class, a television show, correspondence, and other matters. Jane's rate of delivery this evening was rather slow.)

Good evening.

("Good evening, Seth.")

Dictation: Now: To some extent the development of consciousness as you understand it follows the development of the gods through the ages; and in those stories appear the guises that man might have taken, as well as those that he did.

All animal gods hint of various experiments and species in which consciousness took different forms, in which the birth of egotistical awareness as you know it tried several areas of exploration. There were, for example, different versions of man-animal comprehension and activity.

(*Long pause.*) From approximately 50 million to 30 million years ago[1] there were innumerable species that would now seem to you to be mutated forms. The distinction between man-animal and animal-man was not as clear as it is in your time. In some ways consciousness was more mobile, less centered, and more experimental. That early rapport, that early mixture, would later be remembered in myths of gods in animal form. Such a variety existed long before your paleontologists realize that it did. There were many toolmaking animal species, some predating man's toolmaking facility. Consciousness knows all of the probabilities of fulfillment open to it. Each species carries in its individual and mass psyche the blueprints of such probable actualities. These blueprints are biologically valid—that is, they allow the cells precognitive knowledge, upon which present behavior is based. This applies not only individually, so that the cell knows its future pattern, for example; but in the same way, an entire species will unconsciously have the knowledge of its own "ideal" fulfillment in its overall world environment.

As specified,[2] ego consciousness grew. These inner patterns, native to the psyche of any species, turned into concepts, mental images—intuitive projections that were all meant to give conscious direction. The gods served, then, as stimulators of development. Seemingly outside of the self, they were meant to lead the self into its greatest area of fulfillment. The god images would change as consciousness did. The various god concepts that have fallen by the wayside, so to speak, represent areas of development that were not chosen, in your terms, but they are still latent. The totem pole, for example, is a remnant from an era where there was much greater communication between man and the animals—when, in fact, men went to the animals to learn, and from them first acquired knowledge of herbs and corrective medicinal behavior.[3]

(*Long pause.*) Historically, it seems to you that mankind was born from an animal's undifferentiated kind of consciousness into egotistical self-awareness. Instead, many types of consciousness existed in the period of which I am speaking. The animals chose to develop their own kind of consciousness, as you chose your own. Animal awareness may seem undifferentiated to you. It is however highly specific, poised in the moment, but so completely that in your terms past and future are largely meaningless.

The specific concentration, however, results in an exquisite focus. Ego consciousness lost part of that focus in comparison. The totem poles date back to the time when men and animals understood each other, before that point of departure. Physical species that existed and flourished in those epochs then became probable to you, for they did not develop in your system but became extinct. Their living relics exist in the god concepts that embodied them. Give us a moment . . .

(A one-minute pause at 10:28.) In one way or another all mythology contains descriptions of other species existing on the earth in various forms. This includes stories of fairies and giants, for example. Mythology tells you about the archaeology of your race psychically as well as physically. There were, then, smaller and larger species of men,[4] with varying conscious connections with the rest of nature. The larger experiments involved the production of a species that would be a part of the earth, and yet become aware co-creators of it. There were innumerable considerations, innumerable experiments, with size, brain capacity, neurological structure, and with a kind of consciousness flexible enough to change with its environment, and also vigorous enough to explore and alter that environment. Do you have that?

("Yes.")

The emerging consciousness had to have, latently at least, the capacity to become aware of world conditions. When man knew no more than a simple tribal life, his brain already had the capacity to learn anything it must, for one day it would be responsible for the life of a planet.

Such leeway left room for many probabilities and for many "errors," but the developing consciousness had to be free to make its own judgments. It would not be programmed any more than necessary by "instinct." It was, however, biologically locked into earthly existence, and so meant to understand its natural heritage. It could not separate itself too much, then, or become overly arrogant. Its survival was so linked to the rest of nature that it would of necessity always have to return to that base. It responds to an inborn impetus for its own greatest fulfillment, and will automatically change directions in answer to its own experiments and experiences. There are great sweeping changes in religious concepts abroad in your times, and these represent man's innate knowledge. His consciousness—his psyche—is projecting greater images of his own probable fulfillment, and these are seen in his changing concepts of God.

You may take your break.

(10:47 P.M. Jane's trance had been excellent. She was quite willing to continue the session, but I was tiring; we decided not to go on.)

NOTES: Session 689

1. Seth is letting his material automatically answer my question about early man; see Appendix 6, as well as Note 7 for Session 688. According to our dictionary, the geologic time span he indicates in tonight's session falls within the Tertiary Period of the Cenozoic Era. This period is further broken down into epochs. The important thing here (the dictionary notes) is that many kinds of mammals were about in those far days—including "manlike apes."

2. See Jane's first delivery for Session 686, in Section 1.

3. Check (once again) the 648th session in Chapter 12 of *Personal Reality*—especially Jane's own material there at 11:30.

4. Many readers of the Bible will remember the famous statement in Genesis 6:4, that "There were giants in the earth in those days." In connection with Seth's material here, however: In the United States alone there have been many discoveries of human (and/or humanlike) tracks, both large and small, in very ancient rock formations. These have been found in Pennsylvania, Kentucky, Missouri, Texas, New Mexico, California, and other states, and range back an incredible 300 million years to the Carboniferous Period. In Texas, very clear giant-sized human tracks, dating from the Cretaceous Period of 140 million years ago, have been found intermixed in rock with those of several kinds of great dinosaurs—a discovery completely at odds with current scientific ideas that man is at most but a few million years old. (See Appendix 6 for Session 687, and Note 7 for Session 688.)

Certainly theories of evolution (Darwinism) forbid the notion that dinosaurs and man, or *any* kind of man, were contemporary! Generally speaking, science chooses not to accept the discoveries mentioned here, for were any of them to be officially recognized then several learned disciplines—among them geology and biology—would be shown to be very much in error in important ways.

How does the human data from such very ancient times fit in with the comparatively modest dates—of "only" 50 million to 30 million years ago—that Seth cites for his mutated forms at the beginning of this session? We don't know. Jane has been aware of the information in this note for several years, without paying much attention to it. In time terms, however, both of us are interested in questions of origins. We think Seth can help put it together to at least some degree, should we ever ask him to try.

Session 690
March 21, 1974
9:32 P.M. Thursday

(Jane had "no idea at all" of the material in the last session. She tried reading my notes for it now, since I had only one page typed from them, but couldn't decipher my homemade shorthand. She hadn't particularly felt like having a session last night so we ran errands instead. Tonight, Jane said, she'd try letting Seth come through, although she didn't think she was at her best. By 9:28, she sat "waiting to just get it clear.")

Now, good evening—

("Good evening, Seth.")

—and dictation . . . To be effective within your system of reality, consciousness must of course deal with specializations.

Beneath these, so to speak, the CU's (or units of consciousness) are aware of the different kinds of consciousness of which they are part. By their nature certain kinds of organization, behavior, and experimentation exclude other quite-as-valid but different approaches. The CU's, in their freewheeling nature beneath all matter, are acquainted with all such organizations, so that some of the lessons learned by one species are indeed transferred to another.

(*Long pause.*) One particular experiment in consciousness may be pursued by one species, for example, and that knowledge given to another, or transferred to another, where it appears as "instinct." Here it will be used as a basis for a different kind of behavior, exploration, or experiment. I have said that evolution does not exist as you think of it, in any kind of one-line, ape-to-man time sequence.[1] No other species developed in that manner, either. Instead there are parallel developments. Your time perception shows you but one slice of the whole cake, for instance.

In thinking in terms of consecutive time, however, evolution does not march from the past into the future. Instead, the species is precognitively aware of those changes it wants to make, and from the "future" it alters the "present" state of the chromosomes and genes[2] to bring about in the probable future the specific changes it desires. Both above and below your usual conscious focus, then, time is experienced in an entirely different fashion, and is constantly manipulated,[3] as physically you manipulate matter.

The CU's, forming the structure later in its entirety, form all the atoms, molecules, cells, and organs that make up your world. Land changes and alterations of species are conditions brought about in line with overall patterns that involve all species, or land and water masses, at any given "time." There is a great organization of consciousness involved on such occasions—sometimes creative cataclysms, in which, again from its own precognitive information, nature brings about those situations best suited to its needs. Such biological precognition is firmly based in the chromosomes and genes, and reflected in the cells. As mentioned earlier (*in the 684th session*), the present corporal structure of any physical body of any kind is maintained only because of the cells' innate precognitive abilities. To the self the future, of course, is not experienced as future. It is simply one of the emerging conditions of an experienced Now (you had better capitalize that). The cells' practically felt "Now" includes, then, what you would think of as past and future, as simple conditions of Nowness. They maintain the body's structure in your poised time only by manipulating themselves in a rich medium of probabilities. There is a constant give-and-take of communication between the cell as you know it in present time, and the cell as it "was" in the past, or "will be."

The cell's comprehension leaps its present form. The reality, the physical reality of a given cell, is the focused result of its existence before and after itself in time; and from its knowledge of past and future it receives its present structure.

(*Long pause.*) In a larger sense the same applies to any given species. You are your selves in time, then, because of the selves that exist before and after you in time. On a cellular basis this is true. In psychic terms it is also true. Your thoughts and feelings are quite as real as your cells. They also form organizations. Your desires go out from you in time, but in all directions. On the one hand as a species your present forms your future, but in even deeper terms your precognitive awareness of your own possibilities from the future helps to form the present that will then make that probable future your reality.

In physical terms you may want a new city, so now you begin urban renewal, colon: Architects draw plans that first were dreams, of course; inside their minds, preparations are begun, buildings torn down. In very simple terms the architect's dream can be called a precognitive event, inserted from a probable future into the present. The physical planning carried out is in line with the envisioned future, and brings it about. In greater terms the race has plans for itself; only these are based on a much vaster comprehension of the probable issues, abilities, and conditions involved. (*Pause.*) A people's recognized god represents such a psychic plan, projected out as an ideal. It will be followed by physical organizations, structures meant on a different level to help achieve such a "spiritual" evolution.

Because you dwell in time, however, the god image will also reflect the state of your consciousness as it "is," as well as point toward the future state desired. The god concept will operate as a psychic and spiritual blueprint just like the architect's plan, only at a different level. Each species has within it such blueprints to varying degrees, and these are important, for they carry within them the idealized probabilities. They are valid, again, psychically and biologically. They will serve as biological patterns to the cells, as well as psychic stimuli in terms of consciousness.

Rest your hand a moment, and open our friend some beer.

(10:16. Jane lit a cigarette while I performed the necessary actions. She was still in trance.)

The spiritual and the biological cannot be separated. Their purposes and reality merge. Give us a moment . . . *(Long pause at 10:19.)* I will have much more to say concerning this later in the book. For now simply let me mention that any gods appearing among you must always be of your time, while expressing ideas and concepts that must shoot beyond your time into the future, and serve as psychic stimuli strong enough to effect future changes. When, in historic terms, the race was in the process of adopting a necessary artificial separation of itself from the rest of nature; when it needed to be assured of its abilities to do so; when it took upon itself the task of a particular kind of specialization and individual focus, it needed a religion that would assure it of its abilities.

The male-female tendencies at that time became psychically alienated from each other.* The differences were exaggerated. The ancient mother-goddess concept became "unconscious"; the male, purposely forgetting the great natural aggressive thrust of birth, took physical aggression and force as his prerogative—for this came to represent the quality of ego consciousness in its need to physically manipulate its environment.

While it *(ego consciousness)* recognized its deep oneness with the earth and all creatures, it could not at the same time develop those abilities of specialization and its own particular unique focus. The growth of separate tribal cultures, for example, and later of nations, could emerge only through a sense of separation, and a certain kind of alienation. This, however, allowed for a diversity that could not otherwise be achieved under the accepted conditions. *(Pause.)* The seemingly local Jewish god *(Yahweh/Jehovah)* ended up in one way or another by destroying the Roman Empire, and in so doing brought about a complete reorganization of planetary culture.

Give us a moment, and rest your hand . . .

(10:35. Once again, Jane remained in trance during a short break. A little over an hour had passed.)

Christ, as he is known historically, psychically

*See Appendix 9.

represented man's probabilities. His theories and teachings could be interpreted in many ways; they stood for kernels that man could sow as he wished. Because of Christ, there was an England—and an Industrial Revolution. The male aspects of Christ were the ones that Western civilization emphasized. Other portions of his teachings did not follow the main line of Christian thought, and were buried.

The church ignored Christ's physical birth, for example, and made his mother an immaculate virgin, which meant that the consciousness of the species would for a longer time ignore its relationship with nature and its feminine aspects. I am speaking now of mainline Western civilization. God the Father would be recognized and the Earth Goddess forgotten. There would be feudal lords, therefore, not seeresses. Period. Man would believe he did indeed have dominion over the earth as a separate species, for God the Father had given it to him.

Rising ego consciousness then would have its religious reasons for domination and control. The pope became God the Father personified, but that god had indeed changed from the old Jewish Jehovah. Christ, historically speaking, had altered that concept enough so that at least God the Father was not quite as capricious as Jehovah. (Pause.) Some mercy came to the forefront. Growing ego consciousness could not run rampant over nature. On the other hand, holy wars and ignorance would keep the population down. The church, however—the Roman Catholic Church— still held a repository of religious ideas and concepts that served as a bank of probabilities from which the race could draw. The religious ideas served as social organization, much needed, and many of the monks managed to preserve old manuscripts and knowledge underground. Those who were allied with religious principles, now, mainly survived, and brought forth communities and descendants who were protected. Psychic and religious ideas, then, despite many drawbacks, served as a method of species organization. They are far more important in terms of "evolution" than is recognized. Religious concepts from the beginning kept tribes together, provided social structures, and insured physical survival and the protection that made descendants most probable.

Take your break (louder), or end the session as you prefer.

("We'll take the break, then."

(10:55. Jane's trance had indeed been deep, her pace

usually good. Now she felt very much better. The material had been clear, she said, coming from that "certain necessary level" that she had to reach in order to do this book.

(She said the "buried" material about Christ and main-line Christian thought had to do with occult [meaning hidden] teachings and the Essenes, who were one of the four major Jewish sects known to exist in the Holy Land early in the first century, A.D. [see chapters 21 and 22 in Seth Speaks.] *Jane added that she might have read speculative matter involving Christ, the occult, and the Essenes; and probably, we thought, many "secret teachings" have been attributed to Christ.*

(Then we wondered whether Seth had referred to aspects of Christ's philosophy that were truly buried—quite unknown today. Almost always I refrain from interrupting the flow of session material with questions, but now I wished I'd asked Seth about that. Jane and I also liked the idea that from their earliest times, religious forces had been operating in the development of the species; this seemed to be a very sensible concept—and quite obvious once it was mentioned.

(Resume at 11:25.)

Now: Realize that for now I am emphasizing your Western civilization.

American democracy arises directly from the birth of Protestantism, for example, and a new kind of venture. Luther[4] is as much responsible for the United States of America as George Washington is.

(Long pause.) Other democratic societies had existed in the past, but in them democracy was still based on one religious precept, though it might be expressed in different ways—as, for example, in the Greek city-states *(in the sixth and fifth centuries B.C.).* The Holy Roman Empire united a civilization under one religious idea, but the true brotherhood of man can be expressed only by allowing the freedom of man's thought under the banner of cooperation; and only this will result in the fulfillment of the species, with developments of consciousness that in your terms were latent from the beginning.

(11:29.) I am telling you that so-called evolution and religion are closely connected. Further developments in your concepts will lead to greater activation in portions of the brain now not nearly utilized,[5] and these in turn will trigger expansions in both psychic and biological terms.

The growth of ideas space-wise was a prerequisite. Men on one side of the planet had to know what men were thinking on the other side. All of this presupposed spatial manipulation. Religious incentives always served to stimulate man's <u>spatial</u> curiosity *(intently).*[6]

Many of the species that share your world bear within themselves latent abilities that are even now developing. Men and animals will again meet upon the earth, with the old understanding in yet a new situation.[7] There are no closed systems, and in deep biological orders each species knows what another is doing, and its place in the overall scheme that has been chosen by each. You <u>are</u> perceived in one way or another by all those inhabitants of earth you may consider beneath you. Probable man is emerging now, but also in relationship with his entire natural environment, in which cooperation is a main force. You are cooperating with nature whether or not you realize it, for you <u>are</u> a part of it.

End of dictation.

(Pause at 11:42.) Give us a moment . . .

(Seth now delivered a paragraph of material for Jane and me.)

End of session, and my heartiest regards. A fond good evening.

("Thank you, Seth. Good night." 11:44 P.M. Jane had been really out.)

NOTES: Session 690

1. In the 582nd session in Chapter 20 of *Seth Speaks,* I quoted Seth during a 1971 ESP class: "All consciousness does, indeed, exist at once, and therefore it did not evolve in those terms . . . the theory of evolution is as beautiful a tale as the theory of Biblical creation . . . both might seem to exist within their own systems, and yet, in larger respects they cannot be realities. . . ."

See Note 4 for the 689th session (as well as the session itself), and Appendix 8 for this session.

2. See Note 9 for Session 682.

3. And Seth joins in the action. As early as the 14th session, for January 8, 1964, he told us: "To me, time can be manipulated, used at leisure and examined. It is a vehicle . . . it is therefore still a reality of some kind to me. . . ."

Jane dealt with some of her own concepts of time—one of them being, for instance, that the past has its *own* past, present, and future—in her novel, *The Education of Oversoul 7*, published by Prentice-Hall, in 1973.

4. Martin Luther, the German theologian and translator of the Bible, lived from 1483 to 1546. He was a monk as a young man but, eventually rebelling against the Catholic Church, became the leader of the Protestant Reformation in Germany.

5. See Note 2 for the 687th session.

6. See Session 686 from 10:37 to 11:26.

7. Refer to Appendix 6 for the 687th session, as well as the 689th session itself.

Session 691

March 25, 1974
9:35 P.M. Monday

(*Neither Jane nor I could remember what last Thursday's session was about, and I had but one page of it typed from my notes—a situation quite similar to that prevailing before the last session. We were ready this evening by 9:20. At 9:30 Jane said she was starting to get "bleed-throughs" about Seth's material for tonight.*)

Good evening.

(*"Good evening, Seth."*)

Now: Dictation—and can't you do something about this?

(*Seth indicated Jane's bangs, which were close to hanging over her eyes. I'd been meaning to trim them.*

(*"Yes."*

(*Amused:*) A word to the wise . . .

Your particular society has set up such an artificial

division between intuitional and intellectual knowledge that only the intellectually apparent is given credence. With all of their dire faults and distortions, religions have at least kept alive the idea of unseen, valid worlds, and given some affirmation to concepts that are literally known by the cells. Period.

The conscious mind has always been aware of the cells'—

(At 9:39, the telephone began to ring insistently. I answered it while Jane came out of trance. The call was a follow-up to a long-distance one she'd taken shortly after supper tonight, and concerned a missing person and a government agency. No other details need be given here, except to say that the case was a complex one.

(Although she doesn't usually do such work because of the time required, as well as her own emotional attitudes, Jane had given impressions during the earlier call. She was told now that those impressions had checked out very well, so, in an exchange that lasted for three-quarters of an hour, she gave more such information. She finished with the tentative understanding that by midnight she'd receive another call, after there had been time to check her second set of impressions. Jane laughingly told me that if the new data "wasn't good enough," she'd probably never again hear from the people involved—but at this time we didn't realize what was to follow.

(I read her the material Seth had given so far this evening; at 10:30 she resumed the session as though there hadn't been any interruption at all:)

—comprehension, period. The invisible reality within the cell is what gives it its structure. The remarkable organization of the body in terms of its learning abilities, and adaptability, will never be understood unless the cells' precognitive comprehension is taken into consideration.[1]

This *(precognitive ability)* steers the cell through mazes of probabilities, while allowing it to retain knowledge of its own greatest fulfillment—the idea of itself, which is always alive in any given period of your time. On a different kind of scale, then, each individual has the same sort of idealized version of the self, and so does each species. Here I mean each species, and I am not simply referring to mankind. Obviously these are not apparent to the physical senses, yet they are strong energy centers that to some degree do stimulate the physical senses toward activity. To that degree, then, there are indeed "tree gods," gods of the forest, and "gods of being" connected with each person.

Angels have been represented in just this fashion.

At one time there were also species of birds, however, with high intelligence—this before the period mentioned earlier.[2] They were not humanoid; not, for example, people with wings. They were large birds, with the capacity for dealing with concepts. They were social, could swim well *(pause),* and for some time could live on the water. They had songs of great beauty, and a most extensive vocabulary. They had talons. *(Her eyes wide and dark, Jane held up her hands, fingers bent as though ready to grasp—or claw.)* When he was a cave dweller,[3] man saw these birds often, particularly in cliffs by water. Many times the birds saved children from falling. Man identified with their easy flight up the cliffsides, and followed the sounds of their songs to safe clearings. These memories turned into the angel images. In each case in those times there was the greatest cooperation, on a global scale, between species. The inner impetus toward development, however, came from the innate comprehension of future probabilities. In that picture all species alive at any time joined. This included plants and fauna. Those who cooperated survived, but they did not think in terms of the survival of their own species alone—but, in time terms, of a greater living picture, or world inviolate, in which all survived.

There are various orders of existence even within your system itself. You merely focus upon the one to which you are oriented. There are, then, "spirits" of all natural things—but unfortunately, even when you consider such possibilities you project your own religious ideas of good and evil upon them. You may simply dismiss such concepts as silly, for they seem intellectually scandalous to many. If you do entertain such ideas yourself, you must often personify such spirits, projecting upon them your own ideas of personhood. Instead, you should think of them as different kinds or orders of species that are connected with all natural living things.

They certainly have a reality in energy, and they aid in the conversion of energy into physical terms. They are active rather than passive, then. You see about you physical forces and think nothing of them. For example: You feel the wind and its effects, but you cannot see it. The wind itself is invisible. So these other forces are also invisible. In basic terms they are no more good or evil than the wind is. I say this because you usually imagine that if something is good, there must be a countering force that is evil. Such is not the case. In greater terms these forces are <u>good</u>. They are protective. They nourish every living thing. They have been the impetus for what you <u>think of as</u> evolution. They are biological in that they are to some extent composed of mass cellular knowledge—basically free of time, but <u>directing</u> physical activity in time, and thereby maintaining physical equilibrium.

There is great cooperation, again, between such forces. In such a way one tree in a forest knows of the entire environment and its relationship in it. Its <u>treeness</u> can merge with soilness, for example.

(11:02. Again the telephone began to ring. It was the expected, if somewhat early, third call in the series already described. While Jane was coming out of trance once more, the caller told me about being "impressed" by her abilities—and, I thought privately, considerably surprised. When Jane came to the phone, she was informed that insofar as it was possible to verify her earlier data, practically all of it had been correct. Encouraged, she now gave additional impressions; these were more specific and personal. By the time she was finished it was 11:38.

(I suggested that she end the session, but she decided to sit for it again to "see what happens." So, a minute later:)

Now: A bit more dictation.

(Pause.) Because you are people, you personify what you perceive—"peopleize" it. You imagine such "spirits" to be small people, endowed with your own kind of characteristics. Instead there are simply <u>species of consciousness,</u> entirely different from your own, not usually perceived physically under most conditions. They are indeed connected with flora and fauna, but also with the animals and yourselves, and they are the "earth gods" that Ruburt imagined as a young person.

You each have your own earth god. The term may not be the best, but it is meant to express that portion of you that is as yet unexpressed in your terms—the idealized <u>earth version</u> of yourself, which you are becoming. The idealized earth version is not meant to mean a perfect self in flesh at all; instead, it represents a psychic reality in which your own abilities fulfill themselves in relationship with your earthly environment to the fullest extent possible, within the time and place you have already chosen.

That earth-god portion of yourself attempts to direct
you through probabilities. Again, on deep biological levels beneath normal consciousness, and on psychic levels above normal
consciousness, you are aware of the integrity of your being—but
also of your great connection, while living in flesh, with the
natural environment of time and space. The earth-god concept
can be consciously used, but only to your greatest advantage if
you understand the purposes of your conscious mind and its
relationship with your biological nature.

Your conscious mind tells you where you are in time
and space, and directs your activity in a world of human action.
That world has its own kind of rich complication, that is as
unknown to the animals as is much of their acute realization
unknown to you. Because you have a conscious mind, then,
other portions of your being rely upon it to give them an adequate picture of your situation, and to give the conscious orders
for action. These orders will then be carried out. To do this, you
must use that mind as completely as possible. The picture of
reality in time and space that you give to your cells must be
accurate. They must act on a minute-to-minute, second-
to-second, microsecond-to-microsecond basis, even though their
own orientation is not familiar with your time concept.

End of dictation (heartily). Short break. Then a few
remarks, if you are up to it.

("Okay."

(12:18. Jane's trance had been excellent, her delivery
strong and sure. And since we decided that we were up to it, Seth
returned in a quarter of an hour with better than two pages of
material for Jane and me. The session was finally over, then, at
12:50 A.M.)

NOTES: Session 691

1. "The cells precognate." See the 684th session (with its
Note 2) in Section 1.

2. The time span Seth referred to here existed 30 million to 50
million years ago, he told us in the 689th session, and fell within the
Tertiary Period. How long before that period had the intelligent birds lived?
I wasn't quick enough to ask him; I didn't remember the details in the
689th session well enough . . .

3. Nor was I quick enough to ask Seth if the material Jane

delivered for him tonight constituted any kind of contradiction with that of the 689th session; for in that session he discussed man-animal and animal-man as existing within the Tertiary Period. Presumably these "mutated forms" had implied the beginnings of man, in ordinary terms, yet now Seth spoke of cave-dwelling humans as coexistent with large birds at an earlier time. Had Jane distorted information in one session or the other? Was it possible that during the complicated rhythms of history, man could have been *man* (at least approximately as we know him) even before the Tertiary Period, then moved into a long cycle of animal-man forms before returning to being man again? In tonight's session had Jane tuned into data on a parallel (or probable) reality, for example? Too involved to determine, these questions, on too little material.

(And just as I added much later to Note 7 for Session 688: Even though we were interested in questions of human origins, in those terms, we never resolved them before Seth finished *"Unknown" Reality*.)

Session 692
April 24, 1974
10:03 P.M. Wednesday

(See Appendix 10 for a summary of Jane's psychic work in connection with "the affair of the missing person," as we came to call it. She first encountered the event on the evening the last session, the 691st, was held. I've added a few quotes from Jane and Seth to the appendix material.

(On Wednesday, March 27, we received from Jane's publisher the page proofs for Seth's second book, The Nature of Personal Reality: A Seth Book.[1] No session was held that night. Actually, correcting the proofs—carefully scrutinizing well over 500 printed pages word by word, checking and rechecking notes, spelling, punctuation, and so forth—kept us so busy that we suspended the next eight scheduled sessions, covering a period of 26 days. Ordinarily Seth would have used those sessions to deliver work on "Unknown" Reality. We disliked interrupting our creative rhythms in that fashion, although in the meantime Jane kept

152

ESP class going as usual, coming through as Seth and as Sumari within that context. And we told ourselves that Seth was perfectly capable of resuming work on "Unknown" Reality whenever we were ready to do so, whether the time lapse involved one week or six months.

(Such was the case, of course. And once again, Seth used a "fresh" event—a dream experience of mine that transpired on the third night following the last session—as a basis for his book dictation tonight.

(On Friday morning, March 29, I told Jane that sometime during the previous night I had awakened with the certain knowledge that I'd just finished having two dreams at once. I retained conscious memory of one of them for just a moment before it irrevocably faded. Neither Jane nor I remembered hearing of, or experiencing, what I'll call double dreaming. I wrote an account of the phenomenon while wondering if I'd distorted some quite ordinary dream happening—and while knowing at the same time that I hadn't. I decided to ask Seth to discuss the two dreams when we went back to having sessions again, then forgot about them until I got around to rereading my first rough version of these notes last week. [When Seth discusses my "dreams" in this session, however, it turns out that from his perspective he's able to be more accurate about labeling them than I was.]

(Before finishing the notes I thought of asking a few other people if they had either heard of double dreaming, or had experienced it. The first person I talked to was our friend Sue Watkins, who has attended ESP class almost from the time Jane started it in 1967. I was more than a little surprised when Sue said that she'd enjoyed such events several times. Jane and I have known Sue since 1965, yet as far as any of us could remember [and for whatever reasons], the subject of double dreaming had never been discussed among us.

(But not only had she done it more than once, Sue said: She could recall portions of the simultaneous dreams she'd had on some of those occasions, which was a lot more than I could claim. Grinning, she proceeded to confound me further by describing the double dreams of another class member—since, obviously, the individual in question had also had certain dream adventures that Jane and I didn't know about. I ended up thinking that my own little experience hadn't amounted to so much after all; but still, it had made Jane and me aware of another

facet of dream life. See Note 2 for any other information on double dreams that I may assemble, as well as for an excerpt from the description Sue wrote [at my request] of a multiple-dream happening of her own.

(Dreaming two at once led me to write down a second question for Seth. I wanted him to enlarge upon the statement he'd made at 11:29 in the 690th session: "Further developments in your concepts will lead to greater activation in portions of the brain now not nearly utilized, and these in turn will trigger expansions in both psychic and biological terms." I wondered what connection, if any, might exist between the capacity to have [and/or to remember] more than one dream at a time, and those "portions of the brain now not nearly utilized."

(I read my two questions to Jane as we waited for tonight's session to begin. She listened carefully, then said that "there's something there on the dreams"—meaning that Seth was around, was aware of our conversation, and would probably comment. Actually, Jane had grown very relaxed since suppertime; so much so that she'd considered skipping the session. She decided not to because of the time we'd missed lately. We waited. Jane sipped from a glass of wine. Then, taking off her glasses, she was in trance.)

Good evening.

("Good evening, Seth.")

Now, to begin with your dream: The entity is aware of the experiences of all of its personalities. Give us a moment . . .

To the entity, your own consciousness could be likened to one stream of consciousness, in your terms. The greater part of your own identity, then, is completely aware of all of your conscious and unconscious living material. It is also aware of the same kind of data from all of (its and your) parts.

Because you identify your experience with the regular line of consciousness with which you are familiar, you are rarely able to "bring in" any "other-self" material and hold it while retaining your own sense of identity. Such material may at times bleed or intrude into your own thought, where it blends and is not recognized. In such cases, it takes on the coloration of your own thought patterns. It adds to the overall atmosphere of your being. Without understanding or training, you would have to "lose" your own consciousness in order to perceive the "other-consciousness."

There is a correlation here with something Ruburt said in [ESP] class last evening. He said that writing can be, first, a method of standing apart from life to some extent—in order to capture life, and preserve the unutterable uniqueness of any given day. But, he said, you can then discover that the writing itself becomes the day's experience. You are then "lost" in the writing as much as you feared being lost in normal living, with no way to step aside and view the experience. My addition, now, to those remarks is this: You would need the creation then of another "self," who stood aside from the writing self in order to preserve the original intent.

Now: In the same way you could not, practically speaking, experience such other-consciousness (with a hyphen) unless you learned to stand somewhat aside, like the writer in Ruburt's remarks. Period. But even if you did, the very experience of other-consciousness itself would supersede your living space. You would need another self, able to hold both lines of consciousness at once, lost in neither but maintaining footing in each. This would be a very difficult achievement in normal life in any sustained fashion.

Now: In the dream state your specialized focus need not be as precise or time-oriented as in the waking state.

(10:20.) In your case, you did perform an excellent accomplishment. You were aware of the simultaneous dreams, each being experienced in alternate realities. You could not at this point remember both dreams, because the physical brain apparatus could not handle the simultaneous data. This has reference to portions of the brain not used, as mentioned in this book.[3]

At certain levels the brain can handle simultaneous material, of course, even though you may be conscious of only a smattering of it. The body is aware of multitudinous simultaneous stimuli that consciously escape you, and is able to act on the information. This includes all kinds of sense data that are not consciously pertinent. *(Intently:)* Because of the particular kind of ego-orientation that the race decided upon, however, many probabilities of development inherent in the species have been latent. Inherently the physical brain is capable of dealing with more than one main line of consciousness. This does not mean the development of dual personality, by the way. It means the further expansion of the concept of identity: "You" would not only be aware of the you that you have always known, in the same way that you are now, but a deeper sense of identity would also arise.

That identity would contain the you that you have always known, and in no way threaten it. The new you would simply be more than you are now. You would just have another expansion of consciousness, another self-who-is-aware-of-being in the same way that—using an analogy, granted—the writer is aware of the self who lives, in those terms; is the self who lives while being in a position of some apartness, able to comment upon the life being lived.

Now in a very small way, admittedly, that analogy hints at the kind of deeper events that occur as selves are born out of selves to operate in various levels of activity. In the case of entities, each such self dwells entirely in its own dimension or system of reality.

(To me:) You are, in a rudimentary fashion, beginning to open up those unused areas of the brain, or you would not have even been aware of the fact of two simultaneous dreams. Language and your verbal thought patterns make such translations highly difficult, however, even in the best of circumstances. A multilingual individual, in that regard at least, might have some idea of how concepts are structured through verbal pattern, and hence possess some additional freedom in such translations—provided of course that he or she was aware of the possibilities to begin with.

Now: One experience was a dream of your own, in usual terms. The other "dream" experienced simultaneously was, instead, your muddled interpretation of vital experienced reality on the part of another portion of yourself, in another reality entirely; a dimensional bleed-through. Once you are aware of such experience, most likely you will also have others in "your" dream state.

Now: Take a break or end the session as you prefer.

("Let's take a break, then."

(10:43. Jane took a few moments to come out of a deep trance. Her delivery had been steady, almost fast. "I have a pretty good idea of what was said," she told me. "And just before the session, I knew what Seth would say about your dream experience. Not that I could tell you now what he did say—but still I contained that knowledge somehow . . ." She also *knew that the dream event tied in with my question about the "unused" portions of the brain.*

(Jane was still very relaxed, so I asked her again if she wanted Seth to say something about her state. She decided to see what developed. Her head kept dipping down; she yawned, blinking; her hands, she said, felt "like water." At times such signs have marked the beginning of a pronounced altered state of consciousness for her, but she added that she wasn't going into "a psychedelic experience" now.

(Resume at 10:59.)

Now *(quietly)*: In the waking state you would find such an experience highly threatening without some suitable preparation—and I must be very cautious in my treatment of your concepts of the self and your ideas of one-personhood.[4]

I am not speaking of you personally, Joseph, so much as I am emphasizing that the race at present identifies its individual being with highly limited concepts of the self. Those ideas are vigorously protected, and indeed must be understood and given honor even while attempts are made to expand them. Period. Certainly the quality of consciousness has changed through the centuries in many different ways, and sometimes in what would appear to be contradictory ones; but in your present you have nothing against which to compare your current consciousness of experience.

To a very limited extent, the different civilizations and cultures with which you are historically familiar represent a dim glimmering of the various qualities of consciousness and their varieties of experience. But as there are physical species, so there are what you may call species of consciousness also *(intently).*[5]

(11:08.) There are even now in your species a number of different kinds of consciousness; different in that the physical life-situation is qualitatively experienced in ways that are not native to you in your culture; different in that the entire fabric of meaning, interpretation, experience, and life itself is "alien" to the kind of experience with which you are familiar. This does not mean that such differences occur as the result of cultural backgrounds or situations, for some such individuals exist within your own culture, and some with your kind of consciousness exist in cultures where they are a minority. I am simply saying that on your earth now there are species of consciousness, though that is probably not the best term. You have been so obsessed with

exterior differences, especially of color and nationality, that you
have completely ignored these other far more important variations in the form that consciousness takes in relation to physical
life within your race—the race of man.

(Pause at 11:15.) In terms of your personal experience,
the Sumari[6] is a case in point. The members of each "species"—
and you had better put that in quotes—of consciousness relate to
physical experience in their characteristic ways, even viewing time,
space, and action differently. They orient to their bodies in their
own particular manners. Each group does possess a different relationship with the body, with nature, and with the world in general.

Give us a moment . . . (Still in trance, Jane lit a cigarette.) Your stratified concepts of one-personhood overlook all
such inherent differences, however, and you have a tendency to
transpose your own concepts whenever you come in contact with
those whose ideas you cannot understand. Even now in some
"tribal societies," for example, the self is experienced far differently; so that, while so-called individuality as you understand it is
maintained, each self is also experienced as a part of others in the
tribe, and the natural environment. To some, this seems to mean
that individuality is stillborn or undeveloped. You protect your
ideas of selfhood at all costs—even against the evidence of nature,
which shows you that all are related.

Uniqueness, private experience, and individuality attain
their dimensions of being and their true grandeur only when the
inherent relationships among all elements of being are understood. You fight against your own greater individuality, and the
spacious dimensions of your own being, when you overprotect
your ideas of selfhood by limiting the experience of the self.

Now: That is the end of the session. My heartiest regards
to you both.

("Okay. Good night, Seth."

(11:29 P.M. Jane had really been under. "Boy, I was
getting that stuff through clear as a bell," she said finally. "But
then it stopped and the session was over, all at once . . ." Her
very enjoyable state of relaxation continued.)

NOTES: Session 692

1. See Note 1 for Session 682.

2. A note added a month later: My surprise over the

double-dream phenomenon continues, for by now I know of nine people (including Sue Watkins and myself), who have experienced either the same thing or closely related versions of it. Six people on the list attend ESP class; one is a close personal friend of Jane's and mine; and two are strangers. Actually, we've heard of the strangers but haven't met them. Both are professional writers, and their experiences with double dreams were relayed to me by Tam Mossman, Jane's editor.

Already it seems that without too much difficulty an investigator could acquire enough material on double dreaming for a most interesting study. The variations mentioned above are intriguing in themselves, and range from an account of an "overlapping double dream"—that is, the individual's second dream began in the middle of the first one, and extended beyond the end of the first dream—to one in which the dreamer told me, "I knew I'd been having *two* dreams at once, but I remembered them almost as *one* dream."

Sue Watkins is gifted psychically and as a writer. (See the material she wrote for the 594th session, in the Appendix of *Seth Speaks*. She also appears in Chapter 5 of Jane's *Adventures*.) In the opening notes for this session I mentioned a multiple dream experience of Sue's, and promised to present something here from her description of it. Rather than material on the dreams themselves, I chose the first paragraphs in which Sue outlines the subjective framework of the whole dream event:

"As a dream self I'm sitting in my living room with a friend, Stephen, when suddenly self-knowledge, connections among events, symbols, and the inner logic and fabric of my life and experience became crystal clear. They begin piling up in a strange way, like cell on cell, or lines of freight cars crashing into each other just outside my awareness. It's as though my dream self can handle only so much at once, and the stuff heaps up, and I get up and walk to the kitchen. 'What's going on?' Stephen asks me, but all I can say is that I'm on the edge of a *bursting*. I don't have time to explain further.

"As I walk into the kitchen the head of my dream self fills with vivid scenes, like other dreams, interpretations of each cell of this new awareness. I project all of this outward around me into literally *hundreds* of brilliant scenes; expressions, I knew, of probabilities, 'past' and 'future' events, sideways events I can't even understand . . . all happening at once, with perfect comprehension of that by the 'anchor' dream self. I feel that while all of this is still coming from this anchor self, the selves in these dreams are equally as focused—each of them being dream selves, existing in their universes, and with each of their own connections expanding outwards in much the same way that mine do. I literally become the experience of being myself contained in all of these selves, while being these selves contained by me. In at least one of these selves, the knowledge of this entire event comes to consciousness like a half-recalled dream of its own, and the experience of recalling and being recalled is like liquid electricity in me, the anchor self.

"Upon waking, I can remember clearly but three of these dreams, yet the feeling of containing experiences simultaneously in this manner stays with me . . ."

One of the writers mentioned in the first paragraph of this note is Lee R. Gandee. Tam Mossman edited Lee's autobiography, *Strange Experience*, which was published in 1971 by Prentice-Hall. In Chapter 9 of his book Lee describes a double dream experience of his that also contained strong precognitive elements. Here's the capsule version of the event that he sent to Tam after I'd asked Tam if he knew of anyone who remembered having such dreams:

"As for double dreams, yes, I do dream two at once sometimes. If you'll go to page 144 of *Strange Experience*, you'll find my account of two simultaneous dreams. In one of them I'm on a troop train [in World War II] traveling to Karachi, India, and in the other I'm asleep in a cold *barrack*. I wrote in the book that 'I was conscious of every movement, sound, and odor on the train, yet conscious that I was in a barrack that was very chilly. I was also aware that both the train and the barrack were dreams, and that my body was in the chilly tent at Leesburg, Florida.'

"Then, later, as in one of the dreams I got off the train, then went back inside looking for myself, in the other dream I got up, dumped coal in the stove and spread my overcoat over the blankets on the bunk in the *barrack*—and woke up in the *tent*. So I do have those double dreams, and the Karachi dream was a *true* dream. The men aboard the train in the dream were Air Corps men I knew in waking life, and they were sent there [within the month]."

And this is the place to mention one of those happy analogies that I'm able to make occasionally (even though in this case it took me several months after I'd had my own little double dream to come up with the very obvious association)—for in our reality, the double or multiple dream happening offers at least a pale insight into the numerous lives that, according to Seth, our entity or whole self experiences simultaneously.

I wrote in the Introductory Notes that I thought Jane's speed in producing the Seth material was "a close physical approach to, or translation of, Seth's idea that basically all exists at once—that really there is no time . . ." I'll add here that the phenomenon of double dreaming can be another way of approximating the idea of simultaneous time (or lives), about which we as physical creatures always have so many questions.

3. Refer to the second of my questions in the opening notes for this session, and Note 2 for Session 687.

4. See the 683rd session up to the first break.

5. Seth's first use of "species of consciousness" came after 11:38 in the last session. And added later: He comes up with another evocative phrase, "civilizations of the psyche," in the 715th session in Volume 2 of *"Unknown" Reality*. Much of that session can be taken as an extension of his material here on the qualities of consciousness that have

existed on the earth. In the 715th session, Seth also lets fall some rather humorous comments on Jane's own mixed reactions when she first encountered such hints of the "multidimensionality of your beings."

6. See Appendix 9, with its notes 2 and 3.

Session 693

April 29, 1974

9:45 P.M. Monday

(Just before she went into trance, Jane said to me: "I've got something fascinating for you . . .")

Good evening.

("Good evening, Seth.")

Now, give us a moment . . . In one way or another throughout this book, we will be dealing with history as you know it and as you do not know it. We will be discussing it in terms of the "past" of your species.

In many ways history is your built-in past, the obvious events that are significant. All of the different variations that can be played upon human consciousness, all of the racial probabilities, are in one way occurring in ages past—but they are also happening in what you think of as your present. As mentioned earlier *(in sessions 680-82)*, your consciousness seizes upon certain events over others and brings these into significance, and therefore into the official reality that you know.

New paragraph: Even in your private lives, however, there are clues as to other kinds of sequences in which events can occur—and do. You are usually unaware of the significance of such hints. They pass beneath your notice simply because they do not fit the ordered sequence with which you are familiar. In your idea of reality such clues appear insignificant. They make no sense, particularly in the ordered scheme of reality generally recognized.

Your cellular structure is innately able to follow such sequences. Believing such clues to be meaningless, the conscious mind does not perceive them, or calls them coincidences. Such clues in your intimate daily life, however, looked at in a different way, can tell you much about the potentials of the species, and give you glimpses of other systems of reality in which human consciousness can respond. I am here using an incident from the experience of Ruburt and Joseph, but the reader can make his or her own correlations, and discover like events from which the same conclusions can be drawn.

New paragraph. Driving through Sayre,[1] Pennsylvania, one Sunday afternoon, Joseph noticed a house for sale in a neighborhood he knew—and remembered that it had belonged, in his memory, to a man of whom his mother had been fond. On impulse, Joseph had Ruburt call the real estate firm whose sign was on the house. The house was still owned by the man in question. Joseph only remembered his mother speaking of this gentleman in the past. In the recognized reality shared by the Butts family there had been no intimate contact between Joseph's mother and Mr. Markle (as I'll call him). Joseph's mother had been greatly struck by the man, however, and was convinced that she could have married him instead of the husband she had chosen. Through the years she fantasized such a situation. Mr. Markle was, and is, wealthy. Now of course he is an old man, unable to tend to his home any longer. He is now in a home for the aged, but well cared for.

Joseph felt strong leanings toward Mr. Markle's home. Though the price was quite high, Ruburt and Joseph thought about buying it, and were taken through the home by the real estate people. A coincidence—a mere trick of fate that Joseph could be walking through the old man's home,[2] and that Mr.

Markle would be spending his last time in a nursing home, as had Joseph's mother—meaningless but evocative that this house was for sale, and that the old man was insisting upon a price higher than the house is worth, just as Joseph's mother insisted upon a high price for her own home, and determined to get it.[3] Period. That is how it looked from the outside. It appeared to be one of life's curious incidents.

(10:12.) Instead you have a rich interweaving of probabilities; for in one probability the two were indeed married, and that Stella [Butts] saw the house go to the eldest son *(myself).* In this probability, this Joseph instead comes upon the house of a relative stranger, finds it for sale, and can or cannot purchase it according to the new set of probabilities then emerging. There is a cross-blending of "effects." In this probability Joseph's mother left little in financial terms, relatively speaking, and her house was sold. The family did not get it.

(Humorously:) Now, all probabilities are related. Joseph's mother is dead, in your terms, and aware to some extent of the nature of her own reality beyond the physical. She is able, again to some extent, to follow through with her own probable existences: That is, she is conscious of her own being outside of the official framework.[4]

Her own psychology and characteristic methods of behavior are still hers, however, and operate, so that "she" "tunes into" those areas of probabilities that concern her own desires and interests. In this system she wanted Joseph to have her own house *(see Note 1),* but for many reasons that did not develop.

(Pause.) It was, then, at her behest to some strong degree that Joseph happened upon the *(Markle)* house in question, felt that he did indeed want it, and took the steps that he did in his reality.

(Her eyes dark, Jane held up her empty glass.)
Keep him in trance . . .
(She had been sipping beer. Now she sat quietly waiting while I got another bottle from the refrigerator.)
Do you want to rest your fingers?
("No.")
If your mother did not get the man and the wealth, then—to her way of thinking, now—you can still get the house that she fantasized was her own during her life.

(I had to laugh a bit, for Seth's description of my mother's thinking processes was so very characteristic of her.)

She often dreamed of living in it. On a mental level and an emotional one, she used that probability in this life to enrich her own hours through daydreaming—but without, of course, any realization that those daydreams had their own reality.

Even now she wants Joseph to have a finer home than either of his brothers has—*(emphatically and amused:)* you can cut that if you want.

New paragraph: This is, however, a clear case of the interweaving of probabilities. In this one Joseph can choose whether to buy or not, so there is no coercion *(by Stella Butts),* for example. Joseph and Ruburt were also shown a second house in Sayre—one a good deal cheaper, but generally much like the one in which Joseph's mother lived in this life. They saw both houses on the same day. The second, like the first, was for sale because of age: An elderly couple recently moved from the second house to a home for the aged. Again, the "official" mind says, "Coincidence. All of this is quite natural: Many homes are for sale because the elderly can care for them no longer."

(Pause at 10:33.) The second house had no garage, and was not in as fashionable a neighborhood, but it had its own elegance. It made Ruburt, now, laugh, with its odd nooks and crannies. Give us a moment . . . That house did not have the weight of Stella's intent upon it, yet it was also a house that she had noticed, thinking it more grand than her own—one in which she could have been happy. It was her second choice.[5]

The real estate couple *(the Johnsons)* were also connected. Again, the official mind says that it was a coincidence that this couple were, in their way, artistically inclined, enjoyed painting and writing, free-lanced, and still lived in an apartment after some years of marriage—and that the man was relatively quiet in contrast to the woman *(with amusement).* Yet again probabilities merge, for the woman could well have been a writer, the man an artist; and seeing Ruburt and Joseph, they related with other probabilities inherent in their own natures.

The intent [that] Joseph's mother had lives beyond the grave, in those terms. She still wants Joseph to have a house, and one that will be more fashionable and wealthy than her own. Now Mr. Markle, a wealthy businessman, also had strong artistic abilities. He was a dealer in precious stones and fine antiques.

These qualities attracted Joseph's mother, Stella, and with the situation as she set it up in that life she was impressed, knowing that the man's talents would bring him wealth. His artistic leanings caused him to choose real estate people who had latent artistic abilities of their own.

Give us a moment . . . *(Jane, as Seth, took the time to light a cigarette.)*

As the two couples talked, it turned out that there were other "coincidences": Ruburt and Joseph had recently thought of taking a weekend vacation at a particular resort motel, within the general area but not especially close by. This real estate couple had been forced to spend a night at the same resort due to poor weather, at a time when a psychic was featured as an entertainer.

This psychic startled the couple by correctly identifying some specific elements of their experiences, so there was some kind of psychic connection also. Again, of course, coincidence. So says the officially organized mind. The rich interweavings of probabilities are apparent in all of your lives if only you stop organizing your perceptions and experience in prepackaged ways *(emphatically)*.

The many directions possible for the species exist now. Joseph reacted on a cellular level in one respect. The cells recognized the probable reality involved,[6] and he, Joseph, felt that he was "at home" *(in the Markle place)*, and yet consciously could not explain the feeling. In certain terms his mother will feel vindicated if Joseph buys that house, but the choice is still his and Ruburt's. If you pay more attention to what you think of as coincidences, you will discover another kind of order that underlies the recognized order you follow. This has all kinds of implications biologically as far as the species is concerned; you can perhaps understand, then, that there are also probable histories beneath your lives, individually and *en masse*.

The neurologically unrecognized orders <u>can</u> show themselves once you recognize their reality. Then your sense data will begin to confirm what has not been confirmed thus far.

Take your break. *(Smiling:)* I have mercy on your fingers.

(10:58. "I feel funny," Jane said. Her trance had been very deep, her delivery rather fast for the most part. She inhaled repeatedly now, as though taking in extra air. "I was really out—

be could have kept me under for four hours . . ." She explained
that just before the session began she'd received glimmerings of
the material to come, but hadn't had time to tell me about it.
Certainly neither of us had expected Seth to go into the affair
involving the two houses in Sayre.

(We haven't talked a great deal about the probable
ramifications inherent in the whole house episode—rather, we
expected such concepts to operate if the Seth material has any
validity. Our ways of thinking have changed considerably since
these sessions began over a decade ago. Every so often Jane and I
remind ourselves of just how much of a change there has been for
each of us; this helps us relate our individual worlds to those of
others. Neither of us believes in chance or coincidence in usual
terms, for instance—nor have we since Seth began discussing the
elements behind such qualities some years ago. We always assign
reasons, even if they're hidden at times, for any action. [And
often, we've discovered, further observation will bear out those
reasons.] This way of thinking led to our taking the chain of
circumstances involving the two houses almost for granted; each
unfolding had seemed to fall so effortlessly into place that deep
questioning hadn't been called for: "Oh, of course—things would
work out that way. . ."

(As of now we think it unlikely that we'll buy either of
the houses. We haven't asked Seth what to do, and do not plan
to. There are more "coincidences" involved than those Seth de-
scribed tonight, none of them consciously known to Jane and me
before the Sayre adventure: Mr. Markle is in a nursing home but
a few miles from where we live in Elmira, and my mother spent
her last days in a similar home less than 15 miles away; one of
Mr. Markle's children lives in Elmira, and is connected with a
store Jane and I have visited; Mr. Johnson, of the real estate
couple that conducted us about in Sayre, did sign painting and
truck lettering as a younger man, as I did; he and I had several
mutual acquaintances in Sayre, among them an older artist of
some reputation—and now deceased—that we had known in our
high school days; and so forth.

(Then Seth went into another "house connection"
after break ended at 11:24:)

Give us a moment . . . The apartment house in which
Ruburt and Joseph presently reside has a shared driveway.

In certain terms it is the connection, the symbol,

between the two probability systems, for Mr. Markle's house also has a shared drive. Ruburt and Joseph live in double apartments, in a large old mansion redone into such quarters. The driveway is shared with a very wealthy family next door, in which the same size house is a home to one family. Joseph's mother wanted Joseph to be very wealthy. The drive symbolically connects the two realities, and is a point where the two merge.

Give us a moment . . .

(Pause at 11:28. This was the end of book dictation. As we had requested that he do just before the session, Seth directed his final delivery to some other material for Jane and me. He finished at exactly midnight.

(A note: Since the next session was held before I was through typing this one from my notes, I can add that in the 694th session Seth deals with some of the obvious questions we had about my mother's role in our house affairs.)

NOTES: Session 693

1. Jane and I took our drive three weeks ago, on April 7. The town of Sayre is only 18 miles from Elmira, N. Y., where we live now, and it sits in the beautiful Pennsylvania hills between two smaller communities— Athens to the south, and Waverly to the north in New York State. Locally the three are known as "The Valley." We visit Sayre occasionally. Although it's close by as far as miles go, for me important aspects of it are far away in terms of years.

It's an old, predominantly lower-middle-class railroad town that used to derive much of its importance from being a junction point for several major lines; yet it's also the site of a well-known hospital and clinic that has continued to grow. Sayre's population was probably less than 6,500 when my two brothers and I were growing up there, and it isn't much more today. My family lived in the neighborhood Seth describes from 1922 (when I was 3 years old) to 1931 (when I was 12), then moved to the opposite end of town. I remember quite well that I was most reluctant to move; the young boy didn't want to leave his friends and the surroundings he loved. My parents' motives for moving were meaningless to me at the time. They bought the "new" house, however, and it remained in the family until 1972—a year after my father's death, a year before my mother was to die.

For related material see Note 9 for Session 679, and notes 2 and 3 for Session 680.

2. The "real estate people" who showed Jane and me through the

Markle place last Thursday, April 25, are a husband-and-wife team who operate a small real estate and insurance agency in Sayre. We liked the Johnsons (although that isn't their real name) at once. Going through Mr. Markle's house was quite an experience—certainly I hadn't expected to find myself doing so now, some 43 years after the last time I'd been in it. Jane wasn't attracted to it as much as I was, of course, so that knowledge helped keep my own enthusiasm in check. From my grade-school days I thought I remembered the house's large living room especially; for the Markles had raised two children who were contemporary with my next youngest brother and me; sometimes the four of us met at the house, then went to school together.

The house the Butts family had occupied at that time is situated just around the corner, a block away—almost visible from the front porch of the Markle place. (Later I found several old photographs of it in one of our family albums, and was reminded that in those days the streets had no curbs.) Even today I can recall most of the families, and their children, who'd lived in the immediate area. Those few blocks largely made up my childhood world.

Now when Jane and I drive over those modest streets, I feel a sense of familiarity and strangeness that's hard to describe. Curbs or no, the neighborhood has changed remarkably little considering the number of years involved. I tell myself that all of the trees are much taller and thicker now, and I experience an odd wonder that the wooden houses are still standing. I also tell myself that many others must have similar feelings about environments that were once important to them—and that, indeed, still are. But since becoming acquainted with Seth's ideas of time, I'm more than ever conscious that when we journey there's much more involved than a trip through space.

3. Not only did my mother insist "upon a high price for her own home," but to the surprise of everyone involved in the sale—family members, real estate agents, and others—she succeeded in getting it.

4. In his Preface, Seth discusses the relationship between my mother's death and his beginning *"Unknown" Reality*; in sessions 679-80, some of my mother's probable lives; and in Session 683, my contacts with her in the dream state. See the appropriate notes for each session.

5. I'd say that Seth's statement here, "It was *her* second choice," calls for careful interpretation. Its possible implications escaped me during the session; otherwise I could have asked for some clarification then. Since I neglected to do so, I ended up rewriting this note a year later.

At the time of the session I understood Seth to mean that the second house Jane and I looked at on April 25 was also my mother's second choice *of the day* for us. Sometime later we began to wonder whether he might have meant that this second house had been Stella Butts's next best choice for *herself* over the years, after Mr. Markle's. We took the conservative approach; we decided this wasn't likely. For not only would

both houses have to be for sale at the same time, and not only would Jane
and I have to inspect them on the same day—but of the hundreds of houses
in Sayre, it would be necessary that these two had ranked first and second
in my mother's preference for many years. The odds against this last point
coinciding with the first two points would be very great. We thought that
the two houses were already involved in a remarkable-enough series of
"coincidences."

And yet—tiny possibilities existed in spite of all this logic. My
mother *could* have had some emotional connection to this second house.

The place in question is located within a few blocks of the neighborhood to which my family moved in 1931, as described in Note 1. Since
it sits on one of the main streets of Sayre, at a busy corner, I know that I
must have passed by it many times in subsequent years; yet I'd never
noticed the house as an individual entity until Jane and I walked up to its
front door with the Johnsons. When the Johnsons told us who the owners
were, I could only reply that I'd heard the name while living in Sayre; the
old couple would be contemporary with my mother. Although I couldn't
remember my mother mentioning them, it was at least possible that she'd
known them. There could have been links through mutual friends. To some
small extent, then, Jane and I could toy with inferences drawn from Seth's
comment that that particular house had represented my mother's second
choice. I could hardly ask her, since she'd died five months ago, but Stella
Butts *could* have known the owners, and been in their home; she *could* have
liked it inordinately . . .

6. See sessions 684-85 in Section 1.

Session 694
May 1, 1974
9:29 P.M. Wednesday

("Well," Jane said, indicating two points in front of her as we sat waiting for the session to begin, "there's book stuff there [to the left], and stuff on me there [to the right]. But that's funny: I don't think of Seth being over there—just the information. It's as though I wait for the material to fall into a slot; then Seth, who's here"—she touched her belly—"deals with it.

("I can sense the information outside of me, say, but I can't get it in my regular state of consciousness. When Seth comes through he's at the same level the material's at, and he—or I—can then pull it in ... It's as though there's a store of information there, but I have to go through a door of consciousness to reach it."

(Jane's delivery was rather slow as the session started.)
Good evening.

171

("Good evening, Seth.")

Now: Dictation *(whispering, eyes closed).* Give us a moment . . .

The relatively insignificant example of probable events and their interaction just given *(in the last session)* provides a few important clues to the nature of probabilities in general. An organization is definitely present, but it is not the kind of order you are used to recognizing. This small private experience is repeated endlessly with different variations in all areas of daily living—that is, probable events constantly interact, and *(intently)* through their interaction you end up with one recognized series of episodes that you accept, called physical reality.

Underneath this recognized order of events, however, there is actually a vast field of ever-occurring action. These fields of probabilities are action sources for your reality; but your world-action is also a source for these other probabilities.

This applies at all levels, mental and biological. Probabilities involve the atoms and molecules, therefore, and the cells. They involve thoughts also, as well as more obviously physical events. Your bodies are probable-constructs (hyphenate that if you want to), in that they exist only because of the atoms' appearance at certain points of probability. At other levels the atoms do not exist at those same points, and your bodies there *(Jane leaned forward for emphasis)* are not the same physical constructs. They do not, then, exist there.

Scientifically, with all of your instruments, you are thus far able to perceive the atom's presence only in the field of your own system of probability. Since you perceive physically through the body, which is atomically structured, then of course your sense perceptions lead you to block out recognition of other probable stimuli or reactions. In his book *Adventures in Consciousness,* Ruburt mentions what he calls "prejudiced perception."[1] It is an excellent term in this regard.

(Long pause.) Give us a moment . . . *(Another long pause.)*

Some of this is difficult to verbalize. The EE units[2] within matter, within the atoms and molecules, are aware of the probable fields of action that are possible. While the body's integrity must lie in a constant reiteration in one probability, and maintain within that probable system a certain "constant," and while physically perception is largely directed there, the basic integrity of the body system and consciousness comes from outside the system into it. Period.

(Seth-Jane finished the last sentence on a note of triumph, after indicating all of its punctuation.)

The atoms, while behaving properly within the system, and seeming to adhere to its rules and assumptions, nevertheless actually straddle probabilities. Your time structures, then, are intimately connected with probable action and fields of actuality. In your terms, for example, it would seem as if Joseph could not have seen that house for sale until after a given series of events had occurred. It would seem as if all of this was dependent upon earlier events: his mother's prior meeting with Mr. Markle years ago, when both were young; her daydreams and fantasies in later years; her own death; Mr. Markle's old age, and his own abandonment of the home.

(10:00.) In your terms it seems that all of that had to happen before the house was put up for sale, so that Joseph, passing by only a few days ago, could see the sign and decide to look at the house. In much more basic terms all events exist at once, even as atoms and molecules appear at once in all probable positions. The body, behaving in time, uses a time structure and acts in it naturally as its "constant" structure endures in time. So in that framework time was experienced—and using that organizational structure, time seems to unite those events.

Give us a moment... Those events then arise into significance[3] because of the peculiar kind of organization chosen. Other quite-as-valid events do not seem significant—they do not rise into perception, or reality. They exist, however. In one reality, for example, Joseph's mother married Mr. Markle. Joseph inherited the home. In that reality Mr. Markle died before Joseph's mother did, so there was no need for a Joseph, here, to even look for a house; he had one. In that reality Joseph did not marry Ruburt. And in this reality [the one you and Ruburt know] Ruburt instinctively felt apart from that house.

("Can I ask a question?" I disliked interrupting the flow of material, but this was a good time to mention what had been on my mind since Monday night.)

Yes.

("Well, I know you said in the last session [just before 10:33] that from her nonphysical reality my mother isn't trying to coerce Jane and me into buying Mr. Markle's house—yet I

keep wondering what others will think about the idea of in-
fluence being felt in our reality from 'the other side,' you might
say—")

Write your question down, and I will answer it.

("Go ahead. I can write it out later." And Seth pro-
ceeded to deal with the question in his own way.)

I made it clear that the decision rested with Joseph and
Ruburt. But more than that, the whole question of a house of
that kind brought into their own lives questions of values and
prerogatives that were of great importance. They needed to
encounter their own positions on such issues. Joseph was unconsciously aware of the first house [of the two in Sayre], and could
have chosen not to drive down that particular street, for example. Both he and Ruburt have thought relatively little about
money or social status. They have lived an apartment life instead,
with little care for appearances. Yet there is always pressure in
your society toward the acquisition of fashionable homes, and
material possessions are often considered the medal of ability.

Give us a moment . . . Financially, Ruburt and Joseph
were beginning to do well. Only then did conventional ideas
come to the forefront. Those ideas themselves emotionally
attracted certain aspects of Joseph's mother. Quite simply, in her
terms, she wanted her son to do well, and to her that meant
possessing an excellent home. Period. On her part it was an
innocent enough ambition.

When she sensed any strong feelings that Joseph also
wanted such a home, then—in your terms now—she began, from
her different framework after death, to bring that opportunity
into his experience. This is not manipulation. It does show, however, that one portion of Joseph's mother, the portion connected
to her son, still relates to him in a certain fashion. It also shows
that his desires for a house in Sayre *(deeper and stronger)* helped
bring about certain events: He could have such a house if he
wanted one.

The episode also mirrored his beliefs, for to his way of
thinking he would have to relinquish certain freedoms, and this
he was not ready to do. The events basically exist at once,
though at your level you have to perceive them in time. As your
intimate daily reality can be involved with and colored by probabilities, brought into your experience by your own desires
and beliefs, so is your mass culture, world history, and species

orientation colored by probable events that do not fit into your officially recognized idea of physical reality.

Alternate man, probable man, alternate you's, probable you's—these issues apply individually as well as in terms of the species, and they apply to your future as well as to your past. Give us a moment, and give yourself a moment.

(*A one-minute pause.*) The greatest scientific discoveries are always "accidents." They come from intuitional creativity, when suddenly a new kind of significance is seen that was not "earlier" predictable. You accept all data that fit your theories, and ignore clues to the contrary. Yet underneath it all you are significance-making creatures, pattern-formers, immersed in time but basically apart from it, and so new insights come into your awareness and literally change the quality of any given reality at any given time.

Take your break.

(*10:34. Jane, in a deep trance, had spoken for over an hour. I told her I thought "Unknown" Reality was excellent. "But I'm out of it on this one," she said, explaining that she didn't know it well consciously, had little idea of its structure, and couldn't particularly say what was to come in it. In contrast, her involvement with Seth's last book,* Personal Reality, *had been much more intimate during its production.*

(*We discussed the general implications of Seth's material on my mother—that she was not only "alive" after her "death," but that a portion of her was focused upon Jane and me. Jane had allowed Seth to talk about the whole situation in a more personal way than she usually does; the result is that we already have more data on Stella Butts than on the earlier deaths of Jane's own parents [in 1971 and 1972], for instance.[4] We knew that Seth wouldn't continue describing my mother and her present reality indefinitely; such a study could easily grow into a book by itself. In addition, Jane holds deeply felt convictions about giving material on survival personalities; the information in Appendix 10 at (2. has a bearing here. I also think that Seth will be able to say more on the beliefs behind her feelings as this book progresses.*

(*Seth delivered the information in the next three paragraphs quite forcefully. Resume at 10:50.*)

Joseph's mother is not only alive in another level of reality, but still learning. She is quite aware, therefore, of his decision not to buy the [Markle] house.⁵ In her level of reality, she was aware of the fact that Joseph wanted the house strongly; that one portion of him thought of possessing a large home, even though this would require upkeep and attention that <u>another part of him</u> did not want to provide because he felt it would take too much time from his painting and our work.

The portion that momentarily desired the house immediately attracted <u>the same kind of desire</u> always felt on the part of Joseph's mother. This, <u>on another level of activity than physical</u>, reactivated old conflicts between them. For a while their desires united them. Now, however, Stella Butts is better able to understand her son's reactions. Through his decision in this reality, she is finally beginning to glimpse the reasons for his actions in the past, that before were incomprehensible to her.

Try to understand that all of these reactions are really happening at once . . . Joseph's desire at this end attracted his mother's like desire. *(Pause.)* In your terms, however, the reactions continue.

Now give us a moment . . .

(11:00. Book work was over for the evening. Jane paused in trance, then proceeded to deliver a good amount of material on several other matters. The session ended at 11:43 P.M.)

NOTES: Session 694

1. In the Glossary for *Adventures*, Jane defines prejudiced perception as "The propensity for organizing undifferentiated data into specific differentiated sense terms." Also see Chapter 14 in *Adventures*.

2. See Note 3 for Session 682.

3. See the 682nd session after 10:21.

4. For a little material on Jane's family background, see Note 4 for the 679th session, as well as the first delivery of the session itself.

5. A note added 10 months later: There were many house ramifications to come, though, concerning not only Mr. Markle's place in Sayre but some here in Elmira, where Jane and I live. In ordinary terms, we could hardly have expected such a mass of "house connections" to develop. The events took place while Seth-Jane was producing Section 6 for Volume 2 of *"Unknown" Reality*, and are described there in some detail; they also provide nearly ideal links between the two volumes.

Session 695
May 6, 1974
9:29 P.M. Monday

(On Saturday evening, May 4, Jane briefly came
through with some trance information of her own. At least Seth
wasn't overtly present. The last time she'd done this had been
early on March 4; her material then was on parallel man, alternate man, and probable man; Seth mentioned it that same evening in the 687th session, and it furnished the basis for Section 2
of this volume. [The material itself is presented as Appendix 6.]

(It isn't necessary to quote Jane's delivery of Saturday
evening, however. It came about because we'd been discussing
our deceased parents and probabilities, in connection with the
first two sessions [679-80] of "Unknown" Reality. To launch his
book Seth had used a childhood photograph of each of us. The
night before last, then, I told Jane about my idea of asking Seth
to comment upon early photographs of her parents, Marie and
Delmer,[1] to see what would develop in the material.

(We discussed the data given above as we waited for tonight's session to begin. "Seth's book reminds me of an old-fashioned diary," I remarked, "but with a new twist—that of probabilities." I continued that I was somewhat concerned because the notes for Unknown" Reality *were running considerably longer than they had for either* Seth Speaks *or* Personal Reality. *Yet I felt there were reasons for this, and had chosen to go along. Jane agreed. She said the notes were intended to furnish a mundane account of our lives that would "parallel" Seth's more complicated data on probabilities and other concepts. She thought he would have more to say on the subject of notes later in the book.*

(Right after this exchange ended tonight at 9:03, Jane told me that she was going to dictate additional material "herself." She asked me to write it down:

("What we know of the species can be compared to what we know about ourselves as individuals. In one way both concepts are on the same level, and deal with realities in consecutive time sequences. The individual, like the species, exists in <u>multidimensional</u> *terms; and hovers around focuses of probabilities, weaving in and out of alternate realities constantly.*

("A photograph of a given person represents one experienced probable identity, focused in a recognized time sequence. Its validity is dependent upon the other <u>invisible</u> *snapshots not taken, even as the given notes that make up a symphony are important because of the implied notes* <u>not</u> *actually used.*

("In the same way, a 'picture' of the species represents only one version of the species, 'snapped' in a particular time sequence, valid because of the invisible realities not focused upon, but upon which reality rides."

(In a few moments Jane left her altered state of consciousness. "I don't know where that came from," she said, laughing, "but anything you want to know, just ask . . ." At this time we're content to keep a record of such instances while "Unknown" Reality grows. Echoes of Saturday night's experience do show up in tonight's session, although it doesn't appear that the material will have the long-range effects of Jane's March 4 delivery.

(At 9:15 I read the last session to Jane from my notes, since I hadn't started typing it yet. She was in a most relaxed

state as she listened, yet intended to have a session. "I'm just
waiting to get it clear . . .")
Now, Good evening—
("Good evening, Seth.")
—and dictation:

PRACTICE ELEMENT 2

I would like each reader to try two exercises. First of all, take any incident that happens to you the day you read this page. See the particular chosen event as one that came into your experience from the vast bank of other probable events that could have occurred.

Examine the event as you know it. Then try to trace its emergence from the thread of your own past life as you understand it, and project outward in your mind what other events might emerge from that one to become action in your probable future. This exercise has another part: When you have finished the procedure just given, then change your viewpoint; see the event from the standpoint of someone else who is also involved. No matter how private the experience seems, someone else will have a connection with it. See the episode through his or her eyes, then continue with the procedure just given, only using this altered viewpoint.

No one can do this exercise for you, but the subjective results can be most astonishing. Aspects of the event that did not appear before may be suddenly apparent. The dimensions of the event will be experienced more fully.

Give us a moment . . .

(Now Seth went into material that Jane had touched upon during our conversation last Saturday evening, in addition to giving her dictated information.)

PRACTICE ELEMENT 3

For the second exercise, take a photograph of yourself and place it before you. The picture can be from the past or the present, but try to see it as a snapshot of a self poised in perfect focus, emerging from an underneath dimension in which other probable pictures could have been taken. That self, you see, emerges triumphantly, unique and unassailable in its own experience; yet in the features you see before you—in this stance, posture, expression—there are also glimmerings, tintings or shadings, that are echoes belonging to other probabilities. Try to sense those.

PRACTICE ELEMENT 4

Now: Take another photograph of yourself at a different age than the first one you chose. Ask yourself simply: "Am I looking at the same person?" How familiar or how strange is this second photograph? How does it differ from the first one you picked this evening? What similarities are there that unite both photographs in your mind? What experiences did you have when each photograph was taken? What ways did you think of following in one picture that were not followed in the other one? Those directions were pursued. If they were not pursued by the self you recognize, then they were by a self that is probable in your terms. In your mind follow what directions that self would have taken, as you think of such events. If you find a line of development that you now wish you had pursued, but had not, then think deeply about the ways in which those activities could now fit into the framework of your officially accepted life.[2] Such musings, with desire—backed up by common sense—can bring about intersection points in probabilities that cause a fresh realignment of the deep elements of the psyche. In such ways probable events can be attracted to your current living structure.

(9:40.) We have been speaking about probable men, and do intend to deal more deeply with probable man [or woman], as that is applied to your species. The events of the species begin with the individual, however. All of the powers, abilities, and characteristics inherent in the species are inherent in any individual member of it. Through understanding your own unknown reality, therefore, you can learn much about the unknown reality of the species.

PRACTICE ELEMENT 5

Now: Choose another photograph. I want you to look at this one somewhat differently. This should also be a photograph of yourself. See this as one picture of yourself as a representative of your species in a particular space and time. Look at it as you might look at a photograph of an animal in its environment. If the photograph shows you in a room, for example, then think of the room as a peculiar kind of environment, as natural as the woods. See your person's picture in this way: How does it merge or stand apart from the other elements in the photograph? See those other elements as characteristics of the image, view them as extended features that belong to you. If the photograph is dark, for example, and shows shadows, then in this exercise see those as belonging to the self in the picture.

Imaginatively, examine your image from the viewpoint of another place in the photograph. See how the image can be seen as a part of the overall pattern of the environment—the room or furniture, or yard or whatever.

When you see a picture of an animal in its environment, you often make connections that you do not make when you see a picture of a human being in his or her environment. Yet each location is as unique as the habitat of any animal—as private, as shared, as significant in terms of the individual and the species of which that individual is a part. Simply to stretch your imagination: When you look at your photograph, imagine that you are a representative of a species, caught there in just that particular pose, and that the frame of the photograph represents, now, "a cage of time." You, from the outside looking down at the photograph, are now outside of that cage of time in which your specimen was placed. That specimen, that individual, that you, represents not only yourself but one aspect of your species. If you hold that feeling, then the element of time becomes as real as any of the other objects within the photograph. Though unseen, time is the frame.

Now: Look up. The picture, the photograph, is but one small object in the entire range of your vision. You are not only outside yourself in the photograph, but now it represents only a small portion of your reality. Yet the photograph remains inviolate within its own framework; you cannot alter the position of one object within it. If you destroy the photograph itself, you can in no way destroy the reality that was behind it. You cannot, for instance, kill the tree that may be depicted in the picture.

Give us a moment . . .

(*10:11. In trance, Jane abruptly fell silent for well over a minute. Her eyes remained closed as she gently rocked back and forth. Her delivery had been good since the start of the session.*)

The person within the photograph is beyond your reach. The you that you are can make any changes you want to in your experience: You can change probabilities for your own

purposes, but you cannot change the courses of other probable
selves that have gone their own ways. All probable selves are
connected. They each influence one another. There is a natural
interaction, but no coercion. Each probable self has its own free
will and uniqueness. You can change your own experience in the
probability you know—which itself rides upon infinite other
probabilities. You can bring into your own experience any number of probable events, but you cannot deny the probable experience of another portion of your reality. That is, you cannot
annihilate it.

As you are looking at one photograph in your personal
history, that represents your emergence in this particular reality—
or the reality that was accepted as official at the time it was
taken—so you are looking at a picture of a representative of your
species, caught in a particular moment of probability. That
species has as many offshoots and developments as you have
privately. As there are probable selves in private terms, there are
probable selves in terms of the species. As you have your recognized, official personal past, so in your system of actuality you
have more or less accepted an official mass history (see Note 2).
Under examination, however, that history of the species shows
many gaps and discrepancies, and it leaves many questions to be
answered.

Now take your break.

(10:23. And during break, neither of us realized that
Seth had just ended Section 2.)

Section 3

THE PRIVATE PROBABLE MAN,
THE PRIVATE PROBABLE WOMAN,
THE SPECIES IN PROBABILITIES,
AND BLUEPRINTS FOR REALITIES

Session 695

May 6, 1974
(continued)

(Break was over at 10:45.)
This is the beginning of the next section—
("3.")
—to be called *(pause):* "The Private Probable Man, the Private Probable Woman, the Species in Probabilities, and Blueprints for Realities."

Give us a moment . . . We have been using Ruburt and Joseph's private experience here. For now, however, I would like each reader to consider the members of his or her family, so that in a more direct fashion the reader can find in private experience a realization of some ideas I want to present.

PRACTICE ELEMENT 6
(Pause.) In your terms, think of those ancestors in your family history. Now think of yourself and your contemporary

family. For this, try to imagine time as being something like space. If your ancestors lived in the 19th century, then think of that century as a place that exists as surely as any portion of the earth that you know. See your own century as another place. If you have children, imagine their experience 50 years hence as still another place.

Now: Think of your ancestors, yourself, and your children as members of one tribe, each journeying into different countries instead of times. Culture is as real and natural as trees and rocks, so see the various cultures of these three groups as natural environments of the different places or countries; and imagine, then, each group exploring the unique environment of the land into which they have journeyed. Imagine further of course that these explorations occur at once, even though communication may be faulty, so that each group has difficulty communicating with the others. Imagine, however, that there is a homeland from which our groups originally came. Each expedition sends "letters" back home, commenting upon the behavior, customs, environment, and history of the land in which it finds itself.

These letters are written in an original native language that has little to do with the acquired language that has been picked up in any given country. (Pause, then humorously:) Mama and Papa, back at the homestead, know where their children have gone, in other words; they read with amusement, amazement, and wonder the communications from their offspring. In this homespun analogy, Mama and Papa send letters back—also in the native language—to their children. As time goes by, however, the children lose their memories of their home tongue. Mama and Papa know that times are like places or countries, but their children begin to forget this, too, and so they grow to believe that they are far more separate from each other than they actually are. They have "gone native" in a different way. Mama and Papa understand. The children forgot that they can move through time as easily as through space.

Give us a moment . . . Remember, in this analogy the various children represent your ancestors, yourself, and your own children. They are exploring the land of time. Now in your physical world it is obvious that nature grows more of itself. In the land of time, time also grows more of itself. As you can climb trees, both up and down the branches, so you can climb times in the same way. Back home, Mama and Papa know this. The family tree exists at once—but that tree is only one tree that appears in the land of time. It has branches that you do not climb and do not recognize, and so they are not real to you. There are probable family trees, then. The same applies to the species.

(A pause lasting almost two minutes, starting at 11:12.) Give us a moment . . . There are alternate realities, and these exist only because of the nature of probabilities. Now give us a moment . . .

The potentials of the true self are so multidimensional that they cannot be expressed in one space or time. Any person who loves another recognizes the infinite potential within that other person. That potential needs infinite opportunity; the true self's reality needs an ever-new, changing situation, for each experience enriches it and, therefore, enhances its own possibilities. En masse, in your terms, the same is true of the race of man. Mama and Papa, in our analogy, represent the infinite potential within one basic unit (CU) of consciousness.

Then think of your ancestors, your immediate family, and your children, and sense in them the vast potential that is there. Now: Imagine your species as you think of it, and the literally endless capacities for expression and creation simply in the areas of which you are aware. No single time or space dimension could contain that creativity. No single historic past could explain what you are now as an individual or as a member of a species. Period.

Now give us a moment . . . End of dictation.

(11:23. Once again, Seth wound up the evening with some material on another subject. Lately Jane and I have taken to requesting that he finish each session this way, until we're caught up on some projects we've been letting go. End at 11:33 P.M.)

NOTES: Session 695

1. Once again, see Note 4 for the 679th session.

2. The "officially accepted life" mentioned here reminded me that in the last (694th) session Seth used the phrase "your officially recognized idea of physical reality" in discussing the role probable events played in our world history. In the 686th session he referred to "official data" when he considered ancient man's selection of certain mental and biological

pulses as physical reality; later in the same session, he used the self-explanatory "official history." In the 684th session he discussed our "official activity" when he compared our reaction to hunches and premonitions with our acceptance of normal psychological reality.

Then, in the 681st session, see what Seth has to say about individual biological history and the basic unpredictability of consciousness.

Session 696
May 8, 1974
9:58 P.M. Wednesday

(Today is Jane's birthday. She is 45 years old. I didn't ask her to have a session tonight, but she volunteered. While we waited for Seth to come through, she talked about the deaths of her parents.[1] Her father, Delmer, died on November 16, 1971, when he was 68; her mother, Marie, died on May 10, 1972, at the same age.

(When Jane was young Marie had in all seriousness often warned her: "When I die, I'll come back and haunt you." During those years Marie was in her late 20's and early 30's, and already incapacitated by arthritis; and, to quote Seth from a session held in 1964, she had ". . . often spoken vehemently of Ruburt's birth being a source of disease, and pain, that is of her arthritis . . . If Ruburt's mother had it to do over, she would not have the child—and the child hidden within the adult still feels that the mother actually has the power, even now,

189

to force the child back into the womb and refuse to deliver it ..."

(Jane said tonight that she still feels a strong emotional charge in connection with the idea of the "dead" returning in those stereotyped, banal terms. Yet, although Seth has said very little to date about ghosts, hauntings, and possession [we link them together], it doesn't seem that Jane's early family experiences have led her to set up any blocks against such topics. "Seth just hasn't gotten around to them yet," she said. "When he does, they'll make a great series of chapters—or maybe a whole book some day.")

Good evening.

("Good evening, Seth.")

Now: Dictation ... Each probability system has its own set of "blueprints," clearly defining its freedoms and boundaries, and setting forth the most favorable structures capable of fulfillment.

These are not "inner images of perfection," and to some extent the blueprints[2] themselves change, for the action within any given system of probabilities automatically alters the entire picture, enlarging it. The blueprints are actually more like inner working plans that can be changed with circumstances, but to some extent they are idea-lizations, with a hyphen.

As an individual you carry within you such a blueprint, then; it contains all the information you require to bring about the most favorable version of yourself in the probable system that you know. These blueprints exist biologically and at every level—psychically, spiritually, mentally. The information is knit into the genes and chromosomes, but it exists <u>apart</u>, and the physical structures merely represent the carriers of information.[3] In the same fashion the species *en masse* holds within its vast inner mind such working plans or blueprints. They exist apart from the physical world and in an inner one, and from this you draw those theories, ideas, civilizations, and technologies which you then physically translate.

Platonic thought saw this inner world as perfect.[4] As you think of it, however, perfection always suggests something done and finished, or beyond surpassing, and this of course denies the inherent characteristics of creativity, which do indeed always seek to <u>surpass</u> themselves. The Platonic, idealized inner world would ultimately result in a dead one, for in it the models for all exteriorizations were seen as already completed—finished and perfect.

Many have seen that inner world as the source for the physical one, but imagined that man's purpose was merely to construct physically these perfect images to the best of his abilities. *(Very forcefully:)* In that picture man himself did not help create that inner world, or have any hand in its beauty. He could at best try to duplicate it physically—never able, however, to match its perfection in those terms. In such a version of inner-outer reality the back-and-forth mobility, the give-and-take between inner and outer, is ignored. Man, being a part of that inner world by reason of the nature of his own psyche, automatically has a hand in the creation of those blueprints which at another level he uses as guides.

(Long pause, eyes closed.) To some extent great artists not only capture a physical picture of Inner Idea, capitalized, but they also have a hand in creating that idea or inner model to begin with.

In your terms, the inner world does represent Idea Potential as yet unrealized—but those ideas and those potentials do not exist outside of consciousness. They are ideals set in the heart of man,[5] yet in other terms he is the one who also put them there, out of the deeper knowledge of his being that straddles physical time. Existence is wise and compassionate, so in certain terms consciousness, knowing itself as man, sent future extensions of itself out into the time scheme that man would know, and lovingly planted signposts for itself to follow "later."

Give us a moment . . . Man is himself made as much of God-stuff as earth-stuff, so in those terms now the god in himself yearned toward the man in the god, and earth experience. Not understanding yourselves,[6] you have tried to put the idea of God outside of yourselves and your living framework. Through various exercises in this book, I hope to acquaint each of you with the inherent oneness of the inside and outside realities, to give you a glimpse of your own infinite nature even within the bounds of your creaturehood—to help you see the god-stuff in the man-stuff. In other terms, this can help you see the potentials of your species and break down the barriers of limiting thoughts. I would like to change your ideas of human nature. To some extent this will entail humanizing your idea of divinity. But oddly enough, if that is done you will end up seeing the divinity in man.

Ideals that before seemed beyond the reach of individuals or of the species will change their character, and become working models that can be used effectively and joyfully.

Now take your break.

(10:35. Jane's delivery had been average; and, she said now, the session would be a short one. It was. When Seth came through again in a few minutes he said, humorously: "Tell Ruburt I said 'Happy birthday' "—then gave a page of material for Jane on another subject. End at 10:48 P.M.

(Within that deleted information were a few lines I'd like to present here for the record. When Jane finished with certain challenges, Seth remarked, ". . . there will be a 'birth' of seemingly new concepts, simply because his [Jane's] old mental barriers kept him from making certain important connections, and an increasing system of communication between waking and dreaming states. "

(Perhaps the latter happening is already underway: Jane's recall of, participation in, and benefits from such an exchange between her waking and dreaming selves has increased considerably in recent weeks. So have her records, since she keeps detailed accounts of all of her dream activities and correlating "conscious" events. All of this activity appears to be more than transient.)

NOTES: Session 696

1. For material on Jane's family background, see the 679th session, including notes 4 and 8, as well as Appendix 1 for the same session.

2. Seth talked very briefly about such blueprints in Chapter 20 of *Personal Reality*—see the 672nd session after the end of break at 10:28. He concluded his material by stating: "A system of checks and balances exists, however, so that in certain dreams you are made aware of these blueprints. They may appear throughout your lifetime as recurring dreams of a certain nature—dreams of illumination; and even if you do not remember them you will awaken with your purposes strengthened and suddenly clear.

"When you are working with your beliefs, find out what you really think about the dream condition, for if you trust it, it can become an even more important ally because of your conscious cooperation."

3. Seth's material here reminded me of what Jane had told me last week about her own objectified perception of information; see her quoted notes prefacing the 694th session for May 1.

4. Plato, the Greek philosopher, poet, and logician, lived from about 427 to about 347 B.C. Throughout his mature life he treated what he considered to be man's God-given ideas in a series of Dialogues, or free conversations.

5. See Note 3 for Session 679, concerning Seth's male name for Jane (Ruburt), and his comments that "Sex, regardless of all your fleshy tales, is a psychic phenomenon . . ."

Every so often Jane hears from a female reader who wants to know why Seth often uses the male gender in his books, especially in passages like those in tonight's 696th session. A little reflection will show that in spite of the "sexist" implications it would be quite difficult to present such material in other ways, so common is the use of "man," "he," "his," and "him." In the English language we often don't have the right *word*, one meaning male and female equally, with which to represent the species. Many times "humanity" doesn't fit. Nor do we like to substitute "it," since it's neuter and devoid of feeling as far as we're concerned. We also don't want to become involved with rewriting Seth's material: We're sure that when he produces passages cast in the male gender, his intentions are anything but prejudiced in favor of that sex.

While Jane and I talked about the situation, she spontaneously produced the following written material:

"Seth is using the English language (my native one) to discuss issues that often involve concepts most difficult to describe in the language itself—or, indeed, in any language.

"Obviously, Seth's purpose is to explain what he can within the framework of that language, rather than to change the language *itself*—as would be necessary, for example, to escape its often prejudiced nature. This prejudice appears most obviously in its sexual aspects: '*Man*kind' for the species in general, and 'he' in referring to the individual member. Linguistically this leaves the female out in the cold—and in more ways than one—for the masculine intent is clear.

"Using that language, however, Seth's intent is also clear: Individual identity comes *before* sexual affiliation. That affiliation is a mixture of 'female' and 'male' elements that are complementary, not opposing. Neither is superior. Male and female also represent psychic and biological faces and a sexual stance. Through all of Seth's books runs one common thread: Our sexual prejudice is the result of certain aspects of consciousness that we as a species long ago began stressing over others."

6. Among others, in Section 1 see the 684th session after 11:11, and the 686th session from 9:55 to 11:26.

Session 697

May 13, 1974
9:18 P.M. Monday

Good evening.

("Good evening, Seth.")

Now: Dictation . . . These idealizations *(as discussed in the last session)* are certain kinds of psychic patterns, then, occurring at different levels. In certain terms they become the cell's private "idea" of its own growth and development, a picture alive <u>within</u> the cell in terms of physical information, a part of its structure. Such idealizations provide their own impetus; that is, they will grow toward their own greatest fulfillment.

The idealizations <u>themselves</u> are made of "conscious" stuff. These are not inert data,[1] then. The nature of probabilities determines the framework in which these fulfillments can take place, and "frames" living developments. The structure of probabilities provides on the one hand a system of barriers, in which practical growth is not chosen or significant; and on the other hand it insures a safe, creative, rich environment—a reality—in which the idealization can choose from an almost infinite variety of possible actions those best suited to its own fulfillment.

In any system the idealization has already accepted certain kinds of events as significant, and has rejected other (quite-as-probable events) as nonsignificant. This simply provides a workable focus in which achievement and experience can happen.

(9:27.) In simple terms, you will not try to achieve something that you believe impossible within your concepts of reality. The conscious mind, with its normally considered intellect, is meant to assess the practicality of action within your world. You will literally see only what you want to see.[2] If the race believed that space travel was impossible, you would not have it. That is one thing; but if an individual believes that it is literally impossible for him to travel from one end of the continent to another, or to change his job, or perform any act, then the act becomes practically impossible. The idealization of motion, however, in that person's mind, or of change, may be denied expression at any given time—but it will nevertheless seek expression through experience. This applies in terms of the species as well as individuals. Because you are now a conscious species, in your terms, there are racial idealizations that you can accept or deny. Often at your particular stage of development as a race, these appear first in your world as fiction, art, or so-called pure theory.

Thoughts have their own kind of structure, as cells do, and they seek their own fulfillment. They move toward like thoughts, and you have as a species an inner mass body of thought. Privately your thoughts are expressions of your idealizations; and while expressing those inner patterns they also modify and creatively change them. Each cell in your body is to some extent altered with each thought that you think. Each reaction of the cells alters your environment. The brain then responds to the alteration. There is a constant give-and-take. As the cells respond at certain levels to ever-changing streams of probabilities, so do your thoughts. Your body responds as you think it should, however, and so your conscious beliefs about reality have much to do with those probable experiences that you accept as a part of your intimate living.

The private blueprint, yours at birth, is in certain terms

far greater than any one physical materialization of it that could occur in your space and time. This provides you with areas of choice, gives you manipulability, and allows for the myriad of probable activities "possible." You are the judge and the final word in that regard, so that as your ideas change, as you move toward one probable self and decide upon that as your official[3] self, you will always have a rich bank of probable actions to choose from. If only one were provided you would have no choice. The same applies to the species. Now give us a moment . . .

(9:45. A pause lasting well over a minute.) Your current decisions to accept one specific line of consciousness as real, and to ignore others, makes such concepts difficult to understand. You train yourselves—biologically, even—to inhibit certain stimuli, yet often the body itself responds to the very stimuli that you consciously ignore. By opening up your minds to new kinds of significances, however, you can begin to glimpse other orders of events[4] with which you are quite intimately concerned.

Often, for instance, you handle probabilities very well, while remaining consciously blind to them because of your concepts. Even then, however, on other levels your unconscious reaction will follow your own conscious intents. You may make a move in physical life, for example, seemingly for one reason. You may also be unconsciously reacting to quite pertinent data regarding the probable actions of others. Because you do not really fully accept the fact that you can so react, you may block this unofficial information on the one hand, even while on the other you take it into consideration. You are far more aware than you realize of the probable future in areas with which you are concerned. This is true on all levels. If your purposes do not involve illness, for instance, and yet if you believe in contagion, you will automatically avoid circumstances that can lead to epidemics. In terms of probabilities that particular kind will not enter your experience.

Give us a moment . . . All of this applies en masse in terms of diseases, for example, that run rampant through a species.

Take your break.

(10:00. Jane said that noise in the house had interfered with her trance state toward the end of her delivery, then added that she wasn't at her best tonight anyhow. As far as I could tell,

*though, neither the noise nor her feelings had had any influence
on the material. Resume quietly at 10:14.)*
     I will have more to say concerning illnesses, epidemics,
and mass disorders in this book.
     Consciousness, by its nature, continually expands. The
nature of consciousness as you understand it as a species will, in
one way or another, lead you beyond your limited ideas of
reality, for your experience will set challenges that cannot be
solved within your current framework. Those problems set by
<u>one</u> level of consciousness will automatically cause breakthroughs
into other areas of conscious activity, where solutions can be
found.
     Many of your global dilemmas seem so desperate only
because in those areas you have gone as far as you can go—
without going further. The problems act as stimuli in that regard.
This doesn't mean that you <u>have</u> to experience disasters. They
are not preordained. It does mean that you have chosen certain
experiences, but that these will automatically lead to further
creative development if you allow them to. The idealization is
one of brotherhood, in terms of your species. Biologically, in
your terms, such "brotherhood" operates instinctively in the
cooperation of the body's cells, as they function together to
form the private corporal structure. At your viewpoint you lose
appreciation for the great <u>individuality</u> of each cell. You take it
for granted that because the cells work so well together, they
have no private uniqueness.
     In other terms, however—social terms—you have yet to
achieve the same kind of spiritual brotherhood possessed by your
cells; and so you do not understand that the experience of your
world is intimately connected with your own private experience.
If you burn your finger it hurts immediately. Your body instantly begins a cooperative venture, in which adjustments are
made so that the wound begins to heal. If a portion of the <u>race</u> is
hurt it may take a while before "you" feel the pain, but the
entire unconscious mechanism of the species will try to heal the
wound. Consciously you can facilitate that development, and
admit your brotherhood with all other living beings. The healing
will take place far quicker if you do. A biological brotherhood
exists, an inner empathy on cellular levels, connecting all individuals of the species with one another. This is the result of a biological idealization. It exists in all species, and <u>connects</u> all species.

The race suffers when any of its members die of starvation or disease, even as a whole plant suffers if a group of its leaves are "unhappy." In the same way all members of the species are benefited by the happiness, health, and fulfillment of any of those individuals who compose it. Man can be aware of the vast medium of probabilities in which he exists, and therefore consciously choose those best suited to those idealizations that point toward his greatest fulfillment. One part of the species cannot grow or develop at the expense of the other portions for very long.

(10:36.) Give us a moment . . . A photograph is to some extent a materialization of an idealization carried to a certain degree. At another level, your body and your experience is a far richer fulfillment, a living, presently experienced materialization. The picture of your world is still another.

PRACTICE ELEMENT 7

If you can, find a photograph of yourself as a member of a class—a graduation picture, perhaps, or a photograph of club members. Examine what you see there. Then contemplate what is not seen. Imagine the emotional reality of each person present, in the time that the photograph was taken. Then try to feel the emotional interactions that existed between the various individuals. Take your time. When you are finished, try to get a glimpse of those intimate relationships that each person had with other persons not present in the picture, but contemporary. Let your mind, after that, follow through by imagining contacts involving family interactions reaching back through time prior to the taking of the photograph. Then think of all of the probable actions that were either accepted or discarded, so that in time terms these people assembled (for the photograph).

Biologically, there were illnesses avoided, deaths that could have occurred but did not. In space there were endless varieties of probabilities and decisions. People could have moved and did not, or others did move, and so came into that particular space area. There were an infinite number of ideas behind all of those decisions. You form your own experience. In greater terms, therefore, those people decided to be at that particular time and place, so that the photograph is the result of multitudinous decisions, and represents a focus of experience, rising from myriad probabilities. The picture of the world represents in a greater dimensional fashion the same kind of focus. Your most intimate decision affects the species. You are the creator of yourself in space and time. You also have your hand in the larger creativity of mankind's experience.

Now give us a moment, and that is the end of dictation. Take your break.

("Okay."

(10:50. Jane said her trance state had been "much better" for the second delivery; certainly her manner was more forceful. Returning at 11:03, Seth finished his evening's work by speaking on other subjects until 11:28 P.M.)

NOTES: Session 697

1. Jane referred to the concept of living information from another angle in her quoted material at the beginning of the 694th session, in Section 2. Also see Seth's material on units of consciousness at 10:06 in the 682nd session, in Section 1.

In *Personal Reality,* too, Seth tells us: "Information does not exist by itself. Connected with it is the consciousness of all those who understand it, perceive it, or originate it. So there are not records in terms of objective, forever-available banks of information into which you tune. Instead the consciousness that held, or holds, or will hold the information attracts it like a magnet ... The information itself wants to move toward consciousness. It is not dead or inert. It is not something you grab for, it is also something that wants to be grabbed, and so it gravitates to those who seek it. Your consciousness attracts the consciousness that is already connected with the material." See the notes following the 618th session, in Chapter 3 of *Personal Reality.*

2. See Chapter 2 (among many that are applicable here) of *Personal Reality.*

3. Note 2 for Session 695 lists some of the ways in which Seth uses "official" and "officially" in connection with our ideas of physical reality.

4. In *Adventures,* see Chapter 15: The Inner Order of Events and "Unofficial" Perceptions.

Session 698
May 20, 1974
9:28 P.M. Monday

(The regularly scheduled session for last Wednesday night wasn't held because of Jane's very relaxed state. She's been enjoying this letting-down often during the past couple of weeks. On Friday, however, while in an altered state of consciousness, she tuned into some material on Seth, dreams, and other species of consciousness; she calls it The Wonderworks, *and excerpts from it are presented as Appendix 11.*

(Jane had been in another lackadaisical mood most of the day, yet she'd told me after supper that she wanted to have a session tonight. At 9:15, as we sat waiting, she had her first intimation from Seth that a session would actually take place. "And it'll be on the book . . . I'm not used to being so relaxed beforehand, though . . ." What developed was a very short session, and contrary to her expectations, Seth devoted half of it to Jane herself. I had two questions prepared, both growing out of

material in "Unknown" Reality, *but had to lay them aside until next time.)*

Now, good evening.

("Good evening, Seth.")

Dictation: These blueprints for reality are relatively invisible because you have allowed yourselves to forget their existence.

To pursue certain goals, you pretended that they did not exist. Now, however, your global situation as a race requires the new acquisition of some "ancient arts." These can help you become aware again of those inner idealizations that form your private reality and your mass world. They can permit you to become acquainted with other inward orders of events, and the rich bed of probabilities from which your physical existence emerges.

These arts are useless if they are not practiced—useless in that they lie ever latent, that they are not brought out into the exterior framework of your world. To use these arts requires first of all the knowledge that beneath the world you know is another; that alongside the focus of consciousness with which you are familiar there are other focuses quite as legitimate.

You dream, each of you, but there are few great dream artists. Many of the true purposes of dreams[1] have been forgotten, even though those purposes are still being fulfilled. The conscious art of creating, understanding, and using dreams has been largely lost; and the intimate relationship between daily life, world events, and dreams almost completely ignored. The "future" of the species is being worked out in the private and mass dreams of its members, but this also is never considered. The members of some ancient civilizations, including the Egyptians, knew how to be the conscious directors of dream activity, how to delve into various levels of dream reality to the founts of creativity, and they were able to use that source material in their physical world.[2]

(9:41.) Cellular life is affected by your dreams. Healings can take place in the dream state, where events at another order of existence alter the cells themselves. Ruburt has been exploring the reality of dream levels,[3] and in so doing he is beginning to glimpse their significance. To some extent each reader can initiate such private journeys. They will, these dream expeditions, throw great light on the nature of personal daily

experience, and they will also provide personal knowledge of the ways in which probabilities operate.

Give us a moment . . . I said earlier in this book that the world you know arises from basic unpredictability, from which significances then emerge.[4] No system of reality is closed. The particular string of probable actions that you call your official experience does not just dangle, then, out in space and time—it interweaves with other such strands that you do not recognize. In the waking state the conscious mind must focus rather exclusively upon that one particular point of concentration that you call reality, simply so that it can direct your activities properly in temporal life. It is quite equipped, however, also to direct you to some extent in other levels of reality <u>when</u> it is not needed for specific survival duties.

Because you have in the past convinced yourselves that the conscious mind <u>must</u> of necessity be <u>cut off</u> from inner reality, you think that it must be alienated from the dream state. Following such beliefs, you find yourselves thinking of dreaming as chaotic, unreasonable, and as completely divorced from normal conscious direction, purpose, or function. It often seems that sleep is almost a small death, and psychologists have compared dreaming with controlled insanity.[5] You have so divorced your waking and dreaming experience that it seems you have separate "lives," and that there is little connection between your waking and dreaming hours. The rich tapestry of probable actions from which you <u>choose</u> your official life becomes just as invisible. This is quite needless.

Take your break.

(9:56. See the notes at the beginning of the session. As stated, Seth returned after break with a discussion of the reasons for Jane's excellent state of relaxation. Most of his material is deleted here, but I can write that her situation was tied in to her work with the challenges presented by her physical symptoms [as described in Note 8 for the 679th session, in Section 1]. As she comes to understand her own belief systems more and more, Jane very gradually continues her physical improvement. In the personal part of this session, then, Seth explained how her very beneficial state of ease "now began in a dream state last night, was further accelerated this morning, and further so in the relaxation just before the session. . . . The [recent] dreams also provide additional assurance;

*and while dreaming, body states are altered—something physi-
cians do not recognize."*

(Seth's last statement had to do with his contention
that "hormones are also automatically released into the system,
encouraging either periods of activity or tranquilizing periods,
according to the specific portions of the overall process [of
healing]. The dreams provide a steady give-and-take between
conscious and so-called unconscious activity. This is also a time
of deep unconscious creativity. . . ."
(End at 10:43 P.M.)

Notes: Session 698

1. See Note 1 for the 687th session, in Section 1. In the next
paragraph I'd like to review from a slightly different angle some of the information presented there.

Seth began talking about dreams and related subjects from the
time these sessions began over 11 years ago. His material led Jane to do
some excellent work with dreams on her own: See, for example, chapters
4 and 5 in *The Coming of Seth,* and Chapter 14 in *The Seth Material.*
Actually, Seth and Jane dream data run through all of the books those two
have produced so far, either singly or together.

The 92nd session for September 28, 1964, was a basic one for
information on dreams, and Jane quotes various portions of it in chapters
5 and 14, as listed above; I ask the reader to review that material especially (and in both books). In connection with that session, here is some
follow-up dream information that Seth gave in the 97th session:

"The dream world is indeed a natural by-product of the relationship between the inner self and the physical being. Not a reflection,
therefore, but a by-product involving not only a chemical reaction but the
transformation of energy from one state to another.

"In some respects all planes or fields of existence are indeed
by-products of others. For example, without the peculiar spark set off
through the interrelationship existing between the inner self and the physical being, the dream world would not exist. But conversely, the dream
world is a necessity for the continued existence of the physical individual.

"This point is extremely important. As you know, animals
dream. What you do not know is that all consciousnesses dream. We have
said that to some degree even atoms and molecules have consciousness, and
each one of those minute consciousnesses forms its own dreams, even as on
the other hand each one forms its own physical image. Now, as in the
physical field individual atoms combine for their own benefit into more

complicated structure gestalts, so do they also combine to form such gestalts, though of a somewhat different nature, in the dream world.

"I have said that the dream world has its own sort of form and permanence. It is physically oriented, though not to the degree inherent in your ordinary universe. In the same manner that the physical image of an individual is built up, so is the dream image built up.

"The dream world is not a formless, haphazard, semiconstruction. It does not exist in bulk, but it does exist in form. This is not a contradiction nor a distortion. The true complexity and importance of the dream world as an independent field of existence has not yet been impressed upon you. Yet while your world and the dream world are basically independent, they still exert pressures and influences, one upon the other.

"It is essential that you realize that the dream world is a by-product of your own existence. And because it is connected to you through chemical reactions, this leaves open the entryway of interactions, in animals as well as men. Since dreams are a by-product of any consciousness involved within matter, this leads us to the correct conclusion—that trees have their dreams, that all physical matter, being formed about individualized units of consciousness of varying degrees, also participates in the involuntary construction of the dream universe."

2. We've come across some material in our reading lately that at least hints at what Seth tells us here.

3. See the notes on Jane's growing dream activity at the end of the 696th session. Her very active dream life, with its attendent daily record keeping and interpretations, is continuing. She's amassing a good amount of information. (I remind the reader to check Appendix 11.)

4. Seth discussed the basic unpredictability from which significances arise in sessions 681-82, in Section 1. After break at 11:47 in the 681st session, he incorporated this line in his material: "From the 'chaotic' bed of your dreams springs your ordered daily organized action."

5. Seth's statement reminded me of an article I read in a newspaper a few years ago. Actually I've never forgotten it because of the negative impression it made upon me; I remember bringing it to Jane's attention at the time. The piece was about a European psychologist, and included his considered opinion that "dreams are the junk of the mind." Jane and I still think it amazing that a man in such a position could make a statement displaying so little insight . . .

Session 699
May 22, 1974
9:20 P.M. Wednesday

(*The moods of relaxation that Jane has been experiencing often since early this month seemed to have passed, at least for now. The evening was very warm as we waited for tonight's session to start. I reminded Jane of the two questions I'd put off from Monday's abbreviated session, but Seth made only a brief reference to them at the end of tonight's material.*)

Good evening.

(*"Good evening, Seth."*)

Dictation: In your terms a photograph freezes motion, frames the moment—or all of the moment that you can physically perceive.

In usual circumstances you may remember the emotions that you felt at the time a picture of yourself was taken, and to some extent those emotions may show themselves in gestures or facial expression. But the greater subjective reality of that moment does not appear physically in such a photograph. It completely escapes insofar as its physical appearance within that structure is concerned. In the same way the past or the future is closed out. The particular focus necessary to produce such a picture then necessitates the exclusion of other data. That certainly is obvious. Because you must manipulate within specific time periods, you do the same kind of thing in daily life, and on a conscious level ignore or exclude much information that is otherwise available.

In a way, one remembered dream can be compared to a psychological photograph, one picture that is not physically materialized, not frozen motion, not framed by either space or time; therefore many of those ingredients appear that are necessarily left out of any given moment of waking conscious activity.

A remembered dream is a product of several things, but often it is your conscious interpretation of events that initially may have been quite different from your memory of them. To that extent the dream that you remember is a snapshot of a larger event, taken by your conscious mind. There are many kinds or varieties of dreams, some more and some less faithful to your memories of them—but as you remember a dream you automatically snatch certain portions of subjective events away from others, and try to "frame" these in space and time in ways that will make sense to your usual orientation. Even then, however, dream events are so multidimensional that this attempt is often a failure. It might be easier here, perhaps, if you compare a scene from a dream with a scene in a photograph. A photograph will show certain events natural to the time in which it was taken. It will not show, for example, a picture of a Turk at the time of the Crusades. A dream scene might portray just such a motif, however.

It will help if now and then you imaginatively think of vivid dream imagery[1] as if it appeared in a photograph instead. As during your lifetime you collect a series of photographs of yourself, taken in various times and places, so in the dreaming state you "collect" subjective photographs of a different kind. They do not appear in sequence, however. Nevertheless, at a conscious level they can provide you with valuable information about your future and your past.

In those normal, generally accepted terms, the images in photographs do not change, move, or alter their relationships.

The living subjective photography of dreams, however, provides a framework in which these "images" have their own mobility. They represent creativity in far different terms than you usually understand. You know what physical issue is *(intently)*, because you see the children of your loins, but you do not experience the children of your dreams in the same physical way, nor understand that your dream life is continuous. It has organization on its own levels that you do not comprehend, and from its rich source you draw much of the energy with which you form your daily experience. Your conscious mind is the director of that experience.

In your terms, however, you dream whether you are living or dead. When you are alive, corporally speaking, what you think of as dreaming becomes subordinate to what you refer to as your conscious waking life. You always examine your dreams then from an "alien" standpoint, one prejudiced in favor of the ordinary waking state. However, the dreaming condition is consequently experienced in distorted form. Often it does not seem clear. By contrast to waking consciousness it can appear hazy, not precise, or off-focus. This does not always apply, because in some dreams the state of alertness is undeniable.

(9:50.) For many reasons, some mentioned here and some not as yet discussed, you have closed your dreams out of your lives to a large extent. While you must of course hold accurate focus in time and place, there is still no basic reason why you must so divorce yourselves from dream experience.

Give us a moment . . . Some inventors, writers, scientists, artists, who are used to dealing with creative material directly, are quite aware of the fact that many of their productive ideas came from the dream condition. They see the results of dream activity in practical physical life. Many others, though untrained, can clearly trace certain decisions made in waking life to dreams. Few understand, however, that private reality is like a finished product, rising out of the immense productivity that occurs in the dreaming condition. Ruburt calls this *The Wonderworks,*[2] and with good reason. In waking life there are fluctuations in your consciousness, periods when you are more or less alert, in your terms, when your attention wanders from issues at hand; or when, instead, you are certainly brilliantly focused in the moment. So there are gradations of consciousness in the waking state. Usually you pay little attention to them.

The official[3] line of consciousness that you accepted blithely ignores any deviations, and when such events occur usually continues merrily on as if nothing had happened. In the dreaming state, such fluctuations also happen. It should be obvious that there you can leap from time to time.

Much more is involved, however, for there are "separate" strands,[4] if you prefer, of consciousness that are naturally pursued in the dream state, and these can be followed with some training and diligence. They involve probable "series" of events. For example, if one particular dream event is chosen for physical materialization, then in your reality other events will appear in due time, and in serial fashion.

You may take your break.

(10:05 to 10:25.)

Dictation: You have yourselves painted a pretty enough picture of what you think of as your own reality, as individuals and as a species. All of your institutions, beliefs, and activities seem to justify your picture, because everything within the overall "frame" will of course seem to agree.

The picture is a relatively simple one, all in all—one in which each consciousness is assumed to be directed toward a particular focus, is ensconced in one body, with its existence bounded by birth at one end and by death at the other. *(Pause.)* Unfortunately, that picture is as limited as any one of your photographs. You are used to examining your dream state from the viewpoint of your "waking" condition, but some time in the dream state try to examine your normal waking reality. Simply give yourself the instructions to do so. You may be quite surprised with the results. Speaking as simply as I can, and using concepts that you can understand, let me put it this way: From the other side—within what is loosely called the dream state—there is an existence quite as valid as your own, and from that viewpoint you can be considered as the dreamer. "You" are the part of you concentrating in this reality. You form it through information and through energy that on the one hand has its source outside this system, and that on the other constantly flows into this system—and so in that respect the systems are united.

Give us a moment... The same applies to all consciousness of any type or variety. In a manner of speaking, then, your cells dream. There are minute variations of electrical discharge, not now perceivable, that could pinpoint this kind of fluctuation on the part of cells, and also on the part of atoms and molecules.

In your terms, obviously, atoms do not dream of cats chasing dogs, yet *(intently)* there are indeed "lapses" from physical focus that are analogous to your dreaming state. Give us a moment... In those conditions the atoms pursue their own probable activities, and indeed make astounding calculations, bringing into your actuality the necessary probable actions to insure official life forms. But neither are they limited otherwise, for their other probable directions are also actualized. Period. On different levels in the dream state, then, you are also subjectively aware of other probable realities. Your conscious intent is unconsciously brought into the dreaming condition, and that intent helps you sort the data. *(See Note 4.)*

So, from other streams of actuality you choose those events that you want physically materialized; and you do this according to your beliefs about the nature of reality. A photograph is taken, and you have before you then a picture of an event that in your terms has already happened. In dreams you take many subjective "photographs," and decide which ones among them you want to materialize in time. To a certain extent, therefore, the dreams are blueprints for your later snapshots.

Now take a brief break—and *(humorously)* tell Ruburt he will be amazed with the organization of this book.

(10:50. Jane's state of dissociation had been excellent, her delivery rather fast around the indicated pauses. She said that Seth's last remark came about because at the supper table this evening she'd told me, as she has before, that she still hasn't read this book straight through, and has little idea of its organization. [See the appropriate note at 10:34 in the 694th session.] Then, as we ate, Jane had asked me once again if "Unknown" Reality had any organization—or purpose: "Where's Seth going with it?" I suggested she forget such worries and let the work come out in its own way, explaining that portions of these notes were concerned with recording the circumstances surrounding just that procedure.

(After the end of break at 11:17, Seth came through with a fairly long block of material on another matter. He closed out the session at 11:43 P.M. with this line about the questions I had waiting for him: "I bid you a fond good evening—and I know

when your material will fit." Since I take this to mean that some time may pass before the questions enter into the scheme of this book, I'll briefly note their subjects below.

(1. Seth's reference, after 9:27 in the 697th session, to our race as "a conscious species." I wanted to get his comments as to how, in our terms at least, we could be in a state other than a "conscious" one. I had trouble visualizing such a situation.[5]

(2. A photograph of Jane and her parents, Marie and Delmer. It was taken in the summer of 1932, when Jane was 3 years old, and as far as we know it's the only one of the Roberts family in existence. I anticipated hearing what Seth would say about some of the probable paths since taken by the photograph's three subjects. I've had the question in mind ever since Seth discussed separate, childhood snapshots of Jane and me in the same terms during the first session for "Unknown" Reality. [See the 679th session, with the notes relevant to Jane and her family background. In that session, Seth told us that the 12-year-old Jane in the photo under discussion was to become probable to the one I eventually met and married.] Beside whatever Seth could tell us about her parents, I was curious to know whether the Jane who was shown at the age of 3 might be—or was destined to become—another probable Jane . . .[6])

NOTES: Session 699

1. Seth's evocative material on dream images reminded me of an equally evocative poem about the dreaming self that Jane wrote in 1965, a year and a half or so after the sessions began. I've always wanted to see the poem published; I think it very rich in both subject matter and visual content.

My Dreaming Self

My dreaming self
Looked in the window
And saw me on the bed.
Moonlight filled
My sleeping skull.
I lay nude and still.

My dreaming self
Came in
And walked about.

I felt as if doorknobs turned,
Opening rooms up
In my head.

My dreaming self
Had eyes like keys
That glinted in the dark.
There was no closet
Within my bones
That they could not unlock.

My dreaming self
Walked through
The framework of my soul.
He switched lights on as he passed.
Outside the night
Was black and cold.

My dreaming self
Lay on the bed.
I stood aside with awe.
"Why, both of us are one,"
I said. He said,
"I thought you knew."

2. See Appendix 11 for Session 698.

3. See Note 2 for the 695th session.

4. In Appendix 4 for Session 685, Jane wrote of her attempts while in the dream state to sort out multidimensional, probable data of her own, and of how they collected for processing in sidepools of experience "before flowing into the 'official pool of consciousness.' " Then, she added a bit later, through bypassing direct neurological activity, and using the "side pockets or pools where data are still unprocessed . . . you can pick up several other strands of consciousness 'at once,' though retention may be difficult."

And, of course, while writing this note I found that Seth's material in tonight's 699th session, as well as Jane's in the whole of Appendix 4, are very reminiscent of what I call double dreaming. See the 692nd session, with its Note 2.

5. A note added better than five months later: Seth *did* answer the question—in the 718th session, Section 5, Volume 2.

6. And added after Volume 2 of *"Unknown" Reality* was completed in April, 1975: Interesting as it is, I never pursued this question, and Seth volunteered no information on it.

Session 700

May 29, 1974

9:28 P.M. Wednesday

(No session was held Monday night.)
Good evening.
("Good evening, Seth.")
Dictation: You must first of all understand that your own greater reality exists whether you are in flesh or out of it, and that your subjective experience has a far greater <u>scope</u> than the physical brain itself allows.

This—apart from corporal living—continues of course while you are a creature in space and time. It presents a parallel noncorporal existence, so to speak, that your brain does not register. In the sleep state you are in a connective area, where bleed-throughs occur.

New paragraph: The blueprints for reality will not be found in the exterior universe. Some other civilizations experimented with a different kind of science than the one with which you are familiar. They met with varying degrees of success in their attempts to understand the nature of reality, and it is true that their overall goals were different than yours. Such people were focusing their consciousnesses in a completely different direction. Your own behavior, customs, sciences, arts, and disciplines are in a way uniquely yours, yet they also provide glimpses into the ways in which various groupings of abilities can be used to probe into the "unknown" reality.

Art is as much a science, in the truest sense of the word, as biology is. Science as you think of it separates itself from the subject at hand. Art identifies with the subject. In your terms, then, other civilizations considered art as a fine science, and used it in such a way that it painted a very clear-cut picture of the nature of reality—a picture in which human emotion and motivation played a grand role.

Your scientists spend many long years in training. If the same amount of time were spent to learn a different kind of science, you could indeed discover far more about the known and unknown realities. There are some individuals embarked upon a study of dreams, working in the "dream laboratories"; but here. again there is prejudiced perception, with scientists on the outside studying the dreams of others, or emphasizing the physical changes that occur in the dream state. The trouble is that many in the sciences do not comprehend that there is an inner reality. (*Intently:*) It is not only as valid as the exterior one, but it is the origin for it. It is that world that offers you answers, solutions, and would reveal many of the blueprints that exist behind the world of your experience.

(*9:53.*) The true art of dreaming is a science long forgotten by your world.[1] Such an art, pursued, trains the mind in a new kind of consciousness—one that is equally at home in either existence, well-grounded and secure in each. Almost anyone can become a satisfied and productive amateur in this art-science; but its true fulfillment takes years of training, a strong sense of purpose, and a dedication—as does any true vocation.

To some extent, a natural talent is a prerequisite for such a true dream-art scientist. A sense of daring, exploration, independence, and spontaneity is required. Such a work is a joy. There are some such people who are quite unrecognized by your societies, because the particular gifts involved are given zero priority. But the talent still exists.

Give us a moment, and rest your hand ... A practitioner of this ancient art learns first of all how to become conscious in <u>normal</u> terms, while in the sleep state. Then he[2] becomes sensitive to the different subjective alterations that occur when dreams begin, happen, and end. He familiarizes himself with the symbolism of his own dreams, and sees how these do or do not correlate with the exterior symbols that appear in the waking life that he shares with others. I will have more to say about these shared symbols later, for they can become agreed-upon signposts.

There are inner meeting places, then, interior "places" that serve as points of inner commerce and communication. Period. In a completely different context, they are quite as used as any city or marketplace in the physical world. This will be elaborated upon later in the book.[3] Our dream-art scientist learns to recognize such points of correlation.

In a manner of speaking, they are indeed learning centers.[4] Many people have dreams in which they are attending classes, for example, in another kind of reality. Whether or not such dreams are "distorted," many of them represent a valid inner experience. All of this, however, is but a beginning for our dream-art scientist, for he or she then begins to recognize the fact of involvement with many different levels and <u>kinds</u> of reality and activity. He must learn to <u>isolate</u> these, separate one from the other, and then try to understand the laws that govern them. As he does so, he learns that some of these realities nearly coincide with the physical one, that on <u>certain</u> levels events become physical in the future, for example, while others do not. He is then beginning to glimpse the blueprints for the world that you know.

(Heartily:) Take your break.

(10:10. "He just stopped so you could rest your fingers," Jane said after coming out of an excellent trance. The rate of her delivery had been average. "It's sure funny: I can feel a whole lot more right there now, waiting to be given—but before the session, nothing. This book is different. I have to get into it in a certain deliberate way that I didn't have to for the others [Seth Speaks and Personal Reality]." Jane snapped her fingers several times. "In ESP class Seth comes through trigger fast, like he did all those times last night. But not here; yet once I get started I want to keep going ..."

(Resume in the same manner at 10:26.)

Now: You manufacture articles. It has taken you centuries to reach your point of technological achievement. It seems to you then that objects come from the outside, generally speaking—for after all, do you not make them in your factories and laboratories?

In a way it seems that "artificial" or synthetic fabrics are not natural. You produce them from the outside. Yet your world is composed of quite natural products, objects that emerge, almost <u>miraculously</u> when you think of it, from the inside of the earth.

You work with material that is already there, provided. You mix, change, and rearrange what is already given. The entire physical universe emerges from an inside, however, and none of your manufacture would provide you with even one object, were it not for those that appeared as source materials long before. Wood, plants, all the species of the earth, the seasons and the planet itself, come from this unidentifiable inside. Physical events have the same source.

(10:35.) Give us a moment... The true scientist understands that he must probe the interior and not the exterior universe; he will comprehend that he cannot isolate himself from a reality of which he is necessarily a part, and that to do so presents at best a distorted picture. In quite true terms, your dreams and the trees outside of your windows have a common denominator: they both spring from the <u>withinness</u> of consciousness.[5]

(10:39.) Simply as an analogy, look at it this way: Your present universe is a mass-shared dream, quite valid—a dream that presents reality in a certain light; a dream that is above all <u>meaningful,</u> creative, based not upon <u>chaos</u> *(with a knowing look),* but upon spontaneous order. To understand it, however, you must go to another level of consciousness—one where, perhaps, the dream momentarily does not seem so real. There, from another viewpoint, you can see it even more clearly, holding it like a photograph in your hands; at the same time you can see from that broader perspective that you do indeed also stand outside of the dream context, but in a "within" that cannot show in the snapshot because of its limitations.

Now: That is the end of dictation. Give us a moment, and we will continue.

This is personal material. First of all, however, this book will open up many very important areas, and provide guidelines for many others to follow.

(Through Seth, Jane now proceeded to deliver three pages of information for herself. The session ended at 11:02 P.M.

(Much of tonight's private material is the kind that eventually appears in Jane's "own" works, such as Adventures, *or is translated in her poetry. Within it are a few hints about certain more general aspects of her abilities, and those can be presented here. "Ruburt," Seth commented, "is just beginning his own dream endeavors, which could not seriously start until he learned to have faith in his own being." [Appendix 11 contains excerpts from* The Wonderworks, *the paper Jane wrote almost two weeks ago on Seth, dreams, and the creation of our reality. In my notes for* The Wonderworks *I described her own recent dream series— which still continues, by the way.] And: "In our case," Seth said a bit later, "Ruburt almost 'becomes' the material he receives from me. If certain other beneficial alterations occur, and further understanding on Ruburt's part, we may be able to meet at* other *levels of consciousness—in the dream state, when he is not co-operating in the production of our book material." For Jane has never met Seth, face to face, you might say, in a dream. The closest she's come to this situation is in giving a session for him in the dream state, as she does in waking life.*

(Now for a couple of references concerning portions of the book material in tonight's session. Like the dream information given above, these instances demonstrate how "Unknown" Reality and the events of Jane's daily living are interwound.

(1. At the end of the paragraph of material begun at 10:35, where Seth touched upon the "withinness of consciousness": I thought his data there echoed Jane's own, as she recorded it in The Wonderworks.

(2. Then almost immediately after 10:39, when Seth referred to "chaos": His rather sly emphasis on the word didn't escape me. Currently Jane and I are reading a book written by a biologist. It has many good things in it, but we're disturbed when we come to passages in which the author describes "life" as opposed to "nonlife"; or in which he postulates an ultimate chaos—the running-down of our universe into a final random distribution of matter—as inevitable. Such ideas are surely the

*projections of a limited human view, we think, and are quite
misleading. Also, as we grew up independently of each other,
Jane and I gradually dispensed with conventional scientific ideas
that life had occurred by chance; the emotional natures of our
creative endeavors led us to question the theory. Now we don't
think it's true even in ordinary scientific terms.*

*(Nor is the biologist's chaos the same thing as Seth's
"unpredictability." As Seth tells us in the 681st session in Section 1: "Science likes to think that it deals with predictable
action. It perceives such a small amount of data, however . . .
that the great inner unpredictability of any molecule, atom, or
wave, is not apparent. . . ." In connection with this, we suggest
the reader study especially Seth's material from 10:00 to 10:36
in the 681st session.)*

NOTES: Session 700

    1. See the 698th session to 9:41.
    2. Since from this point Seth uses the masculine pronouns "he"
and "him" while discussing representatives of the race, I refer the reader to
Note 5 for Session 696, in Section 3.
    3. A note added later: Unfortunately, Seth didn't keep his
promise to elaborate upon dream/symbol meeting places.
    4. Chapters 9 and 10 in *Seth Speaks* contain much information
on dreams. For material on the classes held at after-death training centers,
see in particular the 537th session in Chapter 9. While out of body during
the sleep state, some people from our reality, Jane among them, assist those
who have just died in adjusting to their various new environments. And
from Seth in the 536th session: ". . . I had spent many lifetimes acting as
[such] a guide under the tutorship of another in my daily sleep states."
    5. And trees have their dreams, too. See Note 1 for Session
698.

Session 701

June 3, 1974

9:17 P.M. Monday

(I finished typing last Wednesday night's session after supper this evening; in fact, Jane just had time to read it before we sat for this one at 8:50.

(Softly:) Good evening.

("Good evening, Seth.")

Now: Give us a moment . . . We are speaking quietly to keep Ruburt in a particular state—but *(humorously, leaning forward),* we will not whisper.

(Long pause.) The outsideness of the physical world is connected, then, with a multidimensional "insideness." That exterior world is thrust outward, however, and projected into reality in line with your conscious desires, beliefs, and intent. It is important that you remember this position of the conscious mind <u>as you think</u> of it. Each physical experience is unique, and while the energy for it and the creation of it come from within,

218

the pristine, private, and yet shared quality of that experience could not exist in the same way (more emphatically) were it not so exteriorized.

The exteriorization has great purpose and meaning, then, and brings forth a different kind of expression. Though I may emphasize the importance of inner reality in this book, therefore, I am in no way denying the great validity and purpose of earthly experience. Any exercises in this book should help you enrich that experience, and understand its framework and nature. None of the exercises should be used to try to "escape" the connotations of your own earthly reality.

New paragraph: Nevertheless, the blueprints lie within. Give us a moment... We will have more to say very shortly about our dream-art scientist (see the last session); yet there are also other important ways that could be used to study the nature of reality. One in particular does not involve the dream state per se. It does include the manipulation of consciousness, however. To some extent it includes identification with, rather than separation from, that which is being studied.

Give us a moment... While connected with your own civilization, the man Einstein[1] came closest perhaps in this regard, for he was able to quite naturally identify himself with various "functions" of the universe. He was able to listen to the inner voice of matter. He was intuitively and emotionally led to his discoveries. He leaned against time, and felt it give and wobble.

The true [mental] physicist[2] will be a bold explorer— not picking at the universe with small tools, but allowing his consciousness to flow into the many open doors that can be found with no instrument, but with the mind.

Your own consciousness as you think of it, as you are familiar with it, can indeed help lead you into some much greater understanding of the simultaneous nature of time[3] if you allow it to. You often use tools, instruments, and paraphernalia instead— but they do not feel time, in those terms. You do. Studying your own conscious experience with time will teach you far more. Period.

(Pause at 9:40. Jane's voice had very gradually increased to a near-normal volume.)

PRACTICE ELEMENT 8
Using your conscious mind as a threshold, however, you can discover still more. Figuratively speaking, stand where

you are. Think of that moment of conscious awareness as a path. Imagine many other such paths, all converging; again, imaginatively take one of them in your mind and follow it. Accept what you experience uncritically. To some small extent you are "altering" your consciousness. *(Half humorously:)* Of course, you are not "altering" it at all. You are simply using it in a different fashion, and focusing it—however briefly—in another direction. This is the simplest of exercises.

Suppose that you stood in one spot all of your physical life, and that you had to do this because you had been told that you must. In such a case you would only see what was directly before you. Your peripheral vision might give you hints of what was to each side, or you might hear sounds that came from behind. Objects—birds, for example—might flash by you, and you might wonder at their motion, significance, and origin. If you suddenly turned an inch to the right or the left you would not be altering your body, but simply changing its position, increasing your overall picture, turning very cautiously from your initial position. So the little exercise above is like that.

Give us a moment . . . You are presently little aware of the dimensions of consciousness—your own or those seemingly "beneath" your own. The true physicist is one who would dare turn around inside his own consciousness.

Give us a moment . . . There are inner structures within matter. These are swirls of energy. They have more purposes than one. The structures are formed by organizations of consciousness, or CU's. You have the most intimate knowledge of the nature of a cell, for example, or of an atom. They compose your flesh. There is, in certain terms, a continuum of consciousness there of which your present physical life is a part. You are in certain kinds of communication and communion with your own cells, and at certain levels of consciousness you know this. A true physicist would learn to reach that level of consciousness at will. There were pictures drawn of cellular structures long before any technological methods of seeing them were available, in your terms.

Give us a moment . . . There are shapes and formations that appear when your eyes are closed that are perfect replicas of atoms, molecules, and cells, but you do not recognize them as such. There are also paintings—so-called abstracts—unconsciously produced, many by amateurs, that are excellent representations of such inner organizations.[4]

Ruburt has at times been able to throw his consciousness into small physical instruments *(computer components, for instance)*, and to perceive their inner activity at the level of, say, electrons. Given time, in your terms, a knowledge of the structure of so-called particles could be quite as clearly understood by using such techniques. Now, however, your terms would not match. Yet your terms are precisely what imprison you, and lead you to the "wrong" kinds of questions.

(With amusement:) The wrong kinds of questions are the right ones for you, however, in your civilization and with your beliefs, because you want to stay within that structure to that extent. Only now are you beginning to question your methods, and even your questions.[5] The true physicist would be able to ask his questions from his usual state of consciousness, and then turn that consciousness in other directions where he himself would be led into adventures-with-reality, in which the questions would themselves be changed. And then the answers would be felt.

(10:08. Very forcefully all through here:) But most physicists do not trust felt answers. Feeling is thought to be far less valid than a diagram. It seems you could not operate your world on feelings—but you are not doing very well trying to operate with diagrams, either!

In many cases your scientists seem to have the strange idea that you can understand a reality by destroying it; that you can perceive the life mechanism of an animal by killing it; or that you can examine a phenomenon best by separating yourself from it. So, often, you attempt to examine the nature of the brain in man by destroying the brains of animals, by separating portions of the animal brain from its components, isolating them, and tampering with the overall integrity of both the animal in question and of your own spiritual processes. By this I mean that each such attempt puts you more out of context, so to speak, with yourself and your environment, and other species. Period. While you may "learn" certain so-called facts, you are driven still further away from any great knowledge, because the so-called facts stand in your way. You do not as yet understand the uniqueness of consciousness.

(Very emphatically:) It is absurd to believe that you can learn something about consciousness by destroying it. It is absurd to believe that you can learn one iota about the inner

reality of life when your search leads you to destroy it. Destruction, you see, in your terms (underlined twice), presupposes a
misunderstanding of life to begin with.

Are your hands tired?

*("No," I said, although I was feeling the pace a bit. But
Jane was doing well.)*

There are ways of identifying with animals, with atoms
and molecules. There are ways of learning from the animals.
There are methods that can be used to discover how different
species migrate, for example, and then to duplicate such feats
technologically if you want to. These methods do not include
dissection, for what you learn that way you will not be able to
use *(deeper and much louder)*.

In a way you are simply overexuberant, like children
playing a new game. You will discover that at best you are using
children's blocks. Some of you have already come to that conclusion. As this book continues, I will indeed outline some beginning proposals as to ways in which you can use your consciousness to understand the nature of reality, and to make some
of those inner blueprints clear.

Take a brief break.

· *(10:28 to 10:45.)*

Now: Even in your terms of history and serial time, as
a race you have tried various methods of dealing with the physical world.[6] In this latest venture you are discovering that exterior
manipulation is not enough, that technology alone is not "the
answer." Please understand me: There is nothing wrong with a
loving technology.

If Einstein had been a better mathematician,[7] he
would not have made the breakthroughs that he did. He would
have been too cowed. Yet even then his mathematics did hold
him back, and put a kink in his intuitions. Often you take it for
granted that intuitive knowledge is not practical, will not work,
or will not give you diagrams. Those same diagrams of which
science is so proud, however, can also be barriers, giving you a
dead instead of a living knowledge. Therefore, they can be quite
impractical.

I admit that I am being sneaky here; but if you did not
feel the need to kill animals to gain knowledge, then you would
not have wars, either. You would understand the balances of
nature far better.

If you did not feel any need to destroy reality (in your terms) in order to understand it, then you would not need to dissect animals, hoping to discover the reasons for human diseases. You would have attained a living knowledge long ago, in which diseases as such did not occur. You would have understood long ago the connections between mind and body, feelings, health, and illness.

I am not saying that you would have necessarily had a perfect world, but that you would have been dealing more directly with the blueprints for reality.

(Abruptly:) End of dictation.

(10:56. With hardly a pause, Seth-Jane switched over to some material for me; the session ended at 11:16 P.M. Jane's trances had been excellent throughout the evening.)

NOTES: Session 701

1. Today Jane had been looking at Einstein's own book on his theories of relativity. (*Relativity, The Special and the General Theory,* Tr. by Robert W. Lawson, © 1961 by the Estate of Albert Einstein, Crown Publishers, Inc., New York, N. Y.) She soon laid it aside, telling me that she couldn't understand much of it except by making a strong effort of will. The mathematics it contained were beyond her entirely. I had ordered the book last month after she expressed interest in seeing it. Einstein died in 1955 at the age of 76.

2. Two weeks after this session was held I added "[mental] " to Seth's term, "the true physicist," because he does refer to "mental physicists" in the next three sessions.

3. A note added five months later: For some of Seth's early remarks about time, see the excerpts from the 14th session (for January 8, 1964) in Chapter 4 of *The Seth Material.* I quoted a few lines from the same session midway through the Introductory Notes for Volume 1 of *"Unknown" Reality* (as well as after the 724th session in Volume 2), and considered some thoughts about our attempts to grasp Seth's concept of simultaneous time. The notes introducing this first volume also contain other applicable material having to do with Jane's trance production times for the Seth books.

4. As an artist myself, I've occasionally wondered if some abstract paintings could have such origins. It's quite possible that I've talked about this with Jane, although I don't remember doing so at any particular time.

5. In physics, questioning is certainly the mode of the day, however, even if in its own terms. Two months ago a prominent East Coast newspaper carried a long article about the "turmoil" and "confusion" in which modern physics finds itself because of recent discoveries on atomic and subatomic levels. Many of these new facts contradict respected old facts, and are leading to previously unheard of, or rejected, questions having to do with internal structures for such near-dimensionless processes as the electron, which moves about the atomic nucleus, and for the various "heavier" particles that make up the nucleus itself.

Now it's suspected that, in many cases at least, some of the fundamental laws of nature aren't directly available to us—that often our world presents to us only an approximate representation of its basic qualities. Science needs new theories to unify as many of the four forces of nature (gravity, electromagnetism, and the atomic "strong" and "weak" forces) as possible, instead of separating them as in the past. We are now told that simplicity is the thing.

(And, very simply, the idea that the "event horizons" of black holes may radiate detectable light could be a step in the unification of some of those forces—gravity and electromagnetism—as they are treated in relativity theory and quantum theory, respectively. See Note 4 for Session 681, and Note 4 for Session 688.)

6. In Section 1, see the 683rd session to 10:11.

7. Evidently Albert Einstein wasn't a great mathematician. He often commented upon his poor memory. He did much of his work through intuition and images. Not long after the outline for his Special Theory of Relativity was published in 1905, it was said that Einstein owed its accomplishment at least partly to the fact that he knew little about the mathematics of space and time.

In the 45th session for April 20, 1964, I find Seth saying: "Einstein traveled within and trusted his own intuitions, and used his inner senses. He would have discovered much more had he been able to trust his intuitions even more, and able to leave more of the so-called scientific proof of his theories to lesser men, to give himself more inner freedom."

The inner senses, as described by Seth, are listed in Chapter 19 of *The Seth Material.*

Session 702
June 10, 1974
9:19 P.M. Monday

(*Last Tuesday afternoon, in our living room, Jane and I participated in a filmed television interview that is to be aired by a New York City station. The program's host and his cameraman stayed to film Jane's ESP class that night. Seth came through during class, as he often does, and was at his jovial—and serious—best. Jane also sang in her trance language, Sumari.*

(*This will be the first time Seth has appeared on television since we did some promotional work for The Seth Material after its publication in 1970. At that time Jane spoke for Seth on two occasions from cities in the East. Reactions were excellent; she still receives an occasional call or letter about one of those shows in particular. I might add that since Seth launched "Unknown" Reality in February of this year, Jane and I have fulfilled another television commitment, and that she was the subject of a lengthy radio interview. But the pressures of work,*

225

plus our own conservative attitudes about personal publicity,
have led us to pass by other such opportunities.

(The regularly scheduled session for the next night,
Wednesday, was not held so that Jane could rest.)

Good evening.

("Good evening, Seth.")

Now to begin with, dictation. Give us a moment . . .

Ultimately your use of instruments, and your preoccu-
pation with them as tools to study the greater nature of reality,
will teach you one important lesson: The instruments are useful
only in measuring the level of reality in which they themselves
exist.[1] Period.

They help you interpret the universe in horizontal
terms, so to speak. In studying the deeper realities within and
"behind" that universe, the instruments are not only useless but
misleading. I am not suggesting that their use is futile, however—
merely pointing out the limitations inherently involved.

So-called objective science gives you a picture, a
model, that has served well enough in its own fashion, enabling
you to travel to the moon, for example, and to advance in a
technology that for a time you set your hearts upon. In the
framework of objective science as it now exists, however, even
the technology will come up against a stone wall. Even as a
means, objective science is only helpful for a while, because it
will constantly run up against deeper inner realities that are
necessarily shunted aside and ignored simply because of its
method and attitude.[2] No objective science or splendid technology alone will keep even one man or woman alive, for example, if that individual has decided to leave the flesh, or finds
no joy in daily life.

(Pause.) A loving technology, again, would always add
to the qualitative and spiritual deepening of experience. The
inner order of existence and true science go together. The true
scientist is not afraid of identifying with the reality he chooses to
study. He knows that only then can he dare to begin to understand its nature. There are many unofficial scientists, true ones in
that regard, unknown in this age. Many are quite ordinary people
in exterior terms, with other professions. Yet it is no accident
that greater discoveries are often made by "amateurs"—those
who are relatively free from official dogmas, released from the
pressure to get ahead in a given field—those whose creativity

flows freely and naturally in those areas of their natural interest.

(9:42.) Give us a moment... Without an identification with the land, the planet and the seasons, all of your technology will not help you understand the earth, or even use it effectively, much less fully. Without an identification with the race as a whole, no technology can save the race. (Pause, during an intent delivery.) Unless man also identifies himself with the other kinds of life with which he shares the world, no technology will ever help him understand his experience. I am speaking in very practical terms. Gadgets will, ultimately, teach you nothing about the dimensions of your own consciousness. When you use them (biofeedback, for instance) even to attain alterations of consciousness, you are programming yourselves, stepping apart from yourselves.

Give us a moment... Such gadgets can be useful only if they show you that such alterations are naturally possible. Otherwise, with your ideas of applied science and technology, the gadgets will be the pivoting point, and the ideas of manipulation will be stressed. In other words, unless the ideas behind objective science are altered, then gadget-produced altered states will almost certainly be used to manipulate, rather than free, consciousness.

I am not making a prediction here. I am simply pointing out one probability that exists. There have indeed been civilizations upon your planet[3] that understood as well as you, and without your kind of technology, the workings of the planets, the positioning of stars—people who even foresaw "later" global changes. They used a mental physics. There were men before you who journeyed to the moon, and who brought back data quite as "scientific" and pertinent. There were those who understood the "origin" of your solar system far better than you. Some of these civilizations did not need spaceships.[4] Instead, highly trained men combining the abilities of dream-art scientists and mental physicists cooperated in journeys not only through time but through space. There are ancient maps drawn from a 200-mile-or-more vantage point—these meticulously completed on return from such journeys.

There were sketches of atoms and molecules, also drawn after trained men and women learned the art of identifying with such phenomena. There are significances hidden in the archives of many archaeological stores that are not recognized by you because you have not made the proper connections—and in some cases you have not advanced sufficiently to understand the information.

Give us a moment . . . The particular thrust and direction of your own science have been directly opposed to the development of such inner sciences, however, so that to some extent each step in the one direction has thus far taken you further from the other. Yet all sciences are based on the desire for knowledge, and so there are intersections that occur even in the most diverse of paths; and you are at such an intersection.

Your own science has led you to its logical conclusion. It is not enough, and some suspect that its methods and attitudes have a built-in disadvantage. Physicists are going beyond themselves, so to speak, where even their own instruments cannot follow and where all rules do not apply. Even the prophet Einstein did not lead them far enough. You cannot stand apart from a reality and do any more than present diagrams of it. You will not understand its living heart or its nature.

The behavior of electrons, for example, will elude your technological knowledge—for in deepest terms what you will "perceive" will be a facade, an appearance or illusion. So far, within the rules of the game, you have been able to make your "facts" about electrons work. To follow their multidimensional activity however is another matter—(humorously:) a pun—and you need, if you will forgive me, a speedier means.

(Pause.) The blueprints for reality lie even beneath the electrons' activity. As long as you think in terms of [subatomic] particles, you are basically off the track—or even when you think in terms of waves. The idea of interrelated fields comes closer, of course, yet even here you are simply changing one kind of term for one like it, only slightly different. In all of these cases you are ignoring the reality of consciousness, and its gestalt formations and manifestations. Until you perceive the innate consciousness behind any "visible" or "invisible" manifestations, then, you put a definite barrier to your own knowledge.

Take your break.

(10:20. "I don't know what he said about electrons and things like that," Jane told me as soon as she was out of her hour-long trance state, "but all of this is general, and it's leading up to something more. I carried it as far as I could. Maybe we'll get more on it after break . . .")

(I thought it very interesting that Seth had talked about subatomic waves and particles in the last paragraph of his delivery tonight. Such ideas involve the physicists' ongoing conception of the duality of nature. For instance: Is light made up of waves or particles? A contemporary accommodation, called complementarity, leads experimenters to accept results that show either aspect to be true. As noted in the last session, Jane had attempted to read Einstein's book on his theories of relativity earlier that day. We had briefly discussed Einstein's work and some allied subjects before tonight's session, but I hadn't asked her to give material on physics through Seth.[5] In her own way, Jane is quite interested in the field, however, and has done a little work in it with scientists. We may have more to say about those efforts later in "Unknown" Reality.

(Now, however, we had time to just touch upon the data involving electrons when Jane told me that she was suddenly aware of more information on the same subject. Seth was ready. "I'll do the best I can with this," she said, as she took off her glasses. Resume at 10:22.)

Ruburt's vocabulary is not an official scientific one. Nor <u>for our purposes should it be</u>—for that vocabulary is limiting.

In as simple a language as possible, and to some extent in your terms, the electron's spin determines time "sequences" from your viewpoint. In those terms, then, a reversed spin is a reversed time motion. There is much you cannot observe. There is much that is extremely difficult to explain, simply because your verbal structure alone presupposes certain assumptions. Electrons, however, spin in <u>many directions at once</u>,[6] an effect impossible for you to perceive. You can only theorize about it. There are "electromagnetic momentums thus achieved and maintained," certain stabilities that operate and maintain their own integrity, <u>though these may not be</u> "equal" at all portions of the spin. There are equalities set up "between" the inequalities.

Time, in your terms then, is spinning <u>newly</u> backward as surely as it is spinning newly *(the telephone began to ring)* —ignore it—into the future. And it is spinning outward <u>and</u> inward into all probabilities simultaneously.

(10:34. The ringing persisted for almost two minutes. I found the situation very irritating—especially since I'd forgotten to turn off the telephone's bell before the session. If there was one time when we didn't need an interruption, I thought, it was

*while Jane was dealing with the present kind of material. Yet she
continued to speak for Seth:)*

There are, nevertheless, unequal thrusts in all directions, though "equalities" can be ascertained by concentrating
only upon certain <u>portions</u> of the spin.

Take your break.

*(10:36. "I heard the phone, and tried to hold the
trance through it," Jane said. "But I don't know about this book,
and ordinary people reading it. I'm just letting it all come out . . .
It's great fun, though. I feel like I'm in the heart of things. It's
only a little after ten-thirty, but I feel that I've really traveled a
long way since the session started . . ."*

*(Using conventional reincarnational terms, I half-
jokingly asked Jane if she'd ever been a dream-art scientist, say, or a
mental physicist. She said she didn't know. [We hardly ever talk
about whatever personal involvement either of us might have
had with reincarnation, incidentally, regardless of whether any
such lives would be based upon Seth's ideas of simultaneous time
and probabilities, or upon time as a series of successive
moments.] Jane did know that the rest of the session would be
for her, though. She was right; Seth came through at 10:55, then
said good night at 11:30 P.M.*

*(A note: Jane's very rich and vivid dream series is still
underway, and she continues to keep detailed records. At times
the paperwork involved keeps her busy for a couple of hours a
day. She recorded five dreams last night, for instance. I last mentioned her recent dreams in Appendix 11, for Session 698. That
appendix contains excerpts from* The Wonderworks—*material
which Jane wrote last month while in an altered state of consciousness, and which was at least partly inspired by her dream
series. In some of the deleted portions of these sessions, Seth has
rather extensively discussed Jane's dream work and related activity. He did so again tonight. It's important to note here that
Jane's dream-connected experiences include some new, and very
exciting, psychic developments for her.)*

NOTES: Session 702

1. Once again (as in Note 7 for the last session), I quote Seth
from the 45th session: "Any investigation of the basic inner universe, which

is the only real universe, must be done as much as possible from a point outside your own distortions . . . To get outside your own universe, you must travel inward . . . Your so-called scientific, so-called objective experiments can continue for an eternity, but they will only probe further and further with camouflage [physical] instruments into a camouflage universe . . . The subconscious, it is true, has elements of its own distortions, but these are easier to escape than the tons of distortive camouflage atmosphere that weigh your scientific experiments down."

(See Note 3 for Appendix 11, concerning Seth's use of "camouflage" in the early sessions.)

2. Seth's material about technology and science leading to inner realities reminds me of two related examples that I've become aware of recently through my own reading. The first one involves a more intimate inner reality than the second, yet both pose interesting questions. Each reader can probably give similar illustrations. (However, as I wrote in Appendix 1, "I'm not interested in knocking our technology, but in pointing out coexisting inner factors that I'm sure are just as important.")

My first example concerns the development of biofeedback machines in the 1960's. With one of these devices the individual was to learn to control, when necessary, his or her own blood pressure, or any of certain other involuntary body functions. Doubtlessly such self-monitoring is an example of the "loving technology" that Seth mentioned in his final delivery for the last session; yet we now understand that the early claims for biofeedback were considerably exaggerated. Within a more reasonable context the technique will take its place in our medical systems, but in each case what we learn will surely point up the need to understand our individual inner realities; i.e., what caused the high blood pressure, or whatever, in the first place?

My second example grows out of a recent book on astronomy. The author explains the various theories for the origin of our observable universe of planets, galaxies, quasars, and so forth, presenting the evidence for and against each theory. Yet when the question arises as to what prevailed before the advent of our universe (or of whether it has existed "forever"), we are told that science doesn't deal with ultimate origins and endings; we are referred to the realms of theology and/or philosophy for whatever answers are available.

Strange but inevitable, I think, how the conscious mind, developing such disciplines as biofeedback and astronomy (to use the examples considered here), finds itself led back to its own inner sources.

3. Four little notes, the last two of which are added later from Volume 2 of "Unknown" Reality:

See Chapter 15 of Seth Speaks for Seth's material on the art and technology of the ancient civilization of Lumania (as well as his references to those that came before and after it). Even now, he tells us, the Lumanians' attributes are incorporated in our own heritage.

Seth discusses some "species of consciousness," starting at 11:08 in Session 692, Volume 1.

From the 715th session in Section 4 of Volume 2: "There are civilizations of the psyche, and only by learning about these will you discover the truth about the 'lost' civilizations of your planet—for each such physical culture coincided with and emerged from a corresponding portion of the psyche that you even now possess."

From the 742nd session in Section 6: "Atlantis is a land that you want to inhabit, appearing in your literature, your dreams, and your fantasies, serving as an impetus for development . . . It carries also, however, the imprint of your fears, for the tales say that Atlantis was destroyed. You place it in your past while it exists in your future. Not the destruction alone, but the entire pattern seen through the framework of your beliefs. Beside this, however, many civilizations have come and gone in somewhat the same manner, and the "myth" [of Atlantis] is based somewhat then on physical fact in your terms."

4. In the 40th session for April 1, 1964, Seth had something to say about the challenges space travel will present to our own civilization: ". . . you are severely hampered as far as space travel is concerned, by the time elements involved . . . In your terms it will simply take you too long to get where you want to go. Scientists will begin to look for easier methods. They are even now being forced to consider the possibilities of telepathy as a means of communication, and they will be forced further and further along these lines.

"It is very possible that you might end up in what you intend as a space venture only to discover that you have 'traveled' to another plane [probability]. But at first you will not know the difference."

And from the 45th session, 20 days later: ". . . your present theory of the expanding universe is in error. Space travel will be dumped when your scientists discover that space as you know it is a distortion, and that journeying from one so-called galaxy to another is done through divesting the physical body of camouflage [matter]. The vehicle of so-called space travel is mental and psychic mobility, in terms of psychic transformation of energy . . ."

5. In the last session see the material, with notes 1 and 7, on Einstein, as well as Note 5; in the 684th session the material on the multidimensional activities and fluctuations of Seth's CU's (or units of consciousness), electrons, and other such phenomena; and in the 681st session the material, with Note 7 especially, on science, probable atoms, and the basic unpredictability behind all systems of reality. In the same session Seth also comments on Jane's vocabulary, as he does after break tonight.

6. Seth, in the 681st session: "Atoms can move in more directions than one at once." In Note 7 for that session I wrote that as an artist my intuitional reaction to that statement was to associate the multidirectional ability of the atom with Seth's notions of simultaneous time and

probabilities. Since electrons are the particles or processes moving about the nucleus of the atom, I now make the same association for them. Thus, according to Seth, we have a most complicated and profound dance of units or essences—behavior not really amenable to translation in words.

In the 688th session, in Section 2, see the material on time and the backward and forward, inward and outward motion of the CU's, or units of consciousness.

Physicists began talking about the spin of electrons in 1925; shortly afterward they began to consider the spin of the components of the nucleus itself. This spin isn't the orbital motion of the electron around a nucleus, however, but (very briefly) is actually more a measure of the electron's magnetic field.

Time reversal or particle symmetry, the equivalence of space and time, is a tenet of relativistic physics and quantum theory. In the material I have on file on electron spin itself, though, I haven't found any discussion of Seth's ideas of: (a) a reversed electron spin and a consequent time reversal, or (b) electrons spinning in many directions at once (even if we could grasp such a situation). Such concepts in association with electron spin may be dealt with in the literature of physics, but are unfamiliar to me or outside my limited understanding. I'm sure also that in ordinary terms Jane knows nothing of them.

Instead, I'd say that Seth's material after break grew out of her own intuitive, mystical understanding that space and time are interwound.

Session 703
June 12, 1974
10:01 P.M. Wednesday

(In a whisper:) Good evening.

("Good evening, Seth.")

We will begin, at least, with dictation. Give us a moment . . .

The multidimensional aspects of the electron cannot be perceived within your three-dimensional system, using instruments that are already predisposed or prefocused to measure only certain kinds of effects.

While this may sound quite sacrilegious scientifically, it is possible to understand the electron's nature and greater reality by using certain <u>focuses of consciousness:</u> by probing the electron, for example, with a "laser" [beam] of consciousness finely focused and attuned—and more will be said about this later in the book. So far in any of your investigations, you have been probing exterior conditions, searching for their interior nature.

To make this clear: When you dissect an animal, for instance, you are still dealing only with the "inside" of exterior reality, or with another level of outsideness. *(Pause.)* In a manner of speaking, when you probe the heavens with your instruments you are doing the same thing. There is a difference between this and the "withinness" out of which all matter springs. It is there that the blueprints for reality are found. There are various ways of studying reality. Let us take a very simple example.

Suppose a scientist found a first orange, and used every instrument available to examine it, but refused to feel it, taste it, smell it, or otherwise to become personally involved with it for fear of losing scientific objectivity.

In sense terms he would learn little about an orange, though he might be able to isolate its elements, predict where others might be found, theorize about its environment—but the greater "withinness" of the orange is not found any place inside of its skin either. The seeds are the physical carriers of future oranges, but the blueprints for that reality are what formed the seeds. In such dilemmas you are always brought back to the question of which came first, and begin another merry chase. Because you think in terms of consecutive time, it seems that there must have been a first egg, or seed.[1] The blueprints for reality exist, however, in dimensions without such a time sequence.

Your closest point to the withinness of which I speak is your own consciousness, though you use it as a tool to examine the exterior universe. But it is basically free of that reality, not confined to the life-and-death saga, and at other levels deals with the blueprints for its own physical existence.

In the entire gestalt from cellular to "self" consciousness, there is a vast field of knowledge—much of it now "unconsciously" available—used to maintain the body's integrity in space and time. With the conscious mind as director, there is no reason why much of this knowledge cannot become normally and naturally available. There is, therefore, a quite valid, vital, real and vastly creative inner reality, and an inward sequence of events from which your present universe and life emerges. Any true scientist will ultimately have to learn to enter that realm of reality. So-called objective approaches will only work at all when you are dealing with so-called objective effects—and your physicists are learning that even in that framework many "facts" are facts only within certain frequencies,[2] or under certain conditions.

You are left with "workable facts" that help you manipulate in your own backyard, but such facts become prejudice when you try to venture beyond your own cosmic neighborhood and find that your preconceived, native ideas do not apply outside of their context.

Because of your attitudes, ideas do not seem as real to you as objects, or as practical. Thoughts are not given the same validity as rocks or trees or beer cans *(two of which sat on the coffee table between us at the moment)* or automobiles. In your terms an automobile gets you somewhere. You do not understand the great mobility of thought, nor grasp its practical nature. You make your world, and in an important manner your thoughts are indeed the immediate personal blueprints for it. When you manipulate objects you feel efficient. The manipulation of thoughts is far more practical. Here is a brief example.

(10:36.) Your medical technology may help you "conquer" one disease after another—some in fact caused by that same technology—and you will feel very efficient as you do heart transplants, as you fight one virus after another. But all of this will do nothing except to allow people to die, perhaps, of other diseases still "unconquered." People will die when they are ready to, following inner dictates and dynamics. A person ready to die will, despite any medication. *(Emphatically:)* A person who wants to live will seize upon the tiniest hope, and respond. The dynamics of health have nothing to do with inoculations. They reside in the consciousness of each being. In your terms they are regulated by emotions, desires, and thoughts. A true doctor cannot be scientifically objective. He cannot divorce himself from the reality of his patient. Instead, usually, the doctor's words and very methods literally separate the patient from himself or herself. The malady is seen almost as a thing apart from the patient's person—but thrust upon it—over which the patient has little control.[3]

The condition is analyzed, the blood is sampled. It becomes "a blood sample" to the doctor. The patient may silently shout out, "That is not just a blood sample—it is my blood you are taking." But he [or she] is discouraged from identifying with the blood of his physical being, so that even his own blood seems alien.

The blueprints for reality: In greater terms they reside within you. In private terms they are part of your being.

To some extent I am suggesting in this book a different approach. So far the blueprints for reality have been largely unknown. Your methods make them invisible, so here I am suggesting ways in which the unknown reality can become a known one. I have mentioned the dream-art scientist and the [true] mental physicist *(in sessions 700-1)*. I would like to add here the "complete physician."

Give us a moment . . . The complete physician would be a person who learned to understand the dynamics of being, the soul-body relationship—one who was healthy in his or her own body. Unhappy people cannot teach you to be happy. Sick ones cannot teach you to be well. Psychiatrists have a high suicide rate. Why do you think they can help you live happily, or add to your vitality? Physicians are not the healthiest of men by far.[4] Why do you think they can cure you?

(With emphasis:) Now in your framework of beliefs the psychiatrists and the doctors are helpful. They know more than you do about the techniques upon which you all agree. While the society accepts these techniques, then you are to some extent dependent upon them, and you had better think twice before you let them go. But in greater, more vital issues, the sick doctor does not know as much about health as an "uneducated, untrained," but healthy person—and I am speaking in quite practical terms. The person who is healthy understands the dynamics of health. In your framework it seems that his or her understanding can be of little practical value to you if you are, for instance, unhealthy. But a true medical profession would be, literally, a health profession. It would seek out people who were healthy and learn from them how to promote health, and not how to diagram disease.

This is on the most surface level, however. A true healing, or health profession, would deal intimately with the powers of the psyche in healing the body, and with the interrelationship among the desires, beliefs, and activities of the conscious mind and its effects upon the cellular behavior.

The "unknown" reality. Unknown or not, it is what you are working with.

You may take your break.

(11:09. Jane had been in a deep trance for over an hour, yet she was out of it before I finished writing Seth's last sentence. While delivering the material she'd had an overall

glimpse of the plan of "Unknown" Reality, but lost it as soon as break came. We had been talking about the book's organization before the session.

(Once again now, Jane wondered why the "more elaborate or complicated qualities" of her trances [she couldn't really explain what she meant here] were necessary in order for her to deliver this book, as opposed to the "easier" ones she'd experienced for Personal Reality. *I suggested she forget such comparisons and think that "Unknown" Reality simply required a different approach, for whatever subjective reasons, and that perhaps her constant questioning would be taken care of as her work on it progressed.*[5]

(During her delivery Jane had also "picked up" that Seth would soon finish this third section, and that the first three sections would make up Part 1 of the book. So far, Seth hasn't designated or titled a Part 1.[6] *Jane had received more, but she was vague on it: ". . . something to do with how each of us could be our own dream-art scientist, mental physicist, and complete physician. And there's more to come on the three classifications of man that Seth gave in that earlier session . . . And stuff on the lands of the mind, I think, which leads to our ancient civilizations and how they're embedded in our minds now . . ."*

(That "earlier session" is the 687th, in Section 1, and in it Seth mentioned parallel man, probable man, and alternate man. But actually his material therein [and part of the heading for Section 2] grew out of the discourse Jane had come through with on her own the night before the 687th session was held. See Appendix 6.

(Seth returned now at 11:40, delivered some material on my painting, among other subjects, and ended the session at 12:15 A.M.)

NOTES: Session 703

1. While discussing probabilities and his units of consciousness in the 682nd session, in Section 1, Seth told us: "The idea of one universe alone is basically nonsensical. Your reality must be seen in its relationship to others. Otherwise you are always caught in questions like 'How did the universe begin?' or 'When will it end?' All systems are constantly being created."

Also see the material about astronomy and origins in Note 2 for Session 702.

2. Physicists assign a frequency, or vibration in periodic motion, to all objects in our universe—galaxies, stars, planets, subatomic wave/particles, and so forth. Form is thought to be an expression of frequency. Some scientists say now that the familiar "vibrations" mediums talk about represent or approximate this quality. Seth first mentioned frequencies soon after these sessions began.

To me there are connections between such periodic activity and Seth's information in the 684th session, in Section 1: "Your bodies blink off and on like lights . . . For that matter, so does the physical universe." For additional references on the way atoms and molecules—consciousness itself, in other words—can phase in and out of our probable reality, see Note 3 for the 684th session.

And yet, very rarely do I hear Jane speak of vibrations (the "vibes," in popular jargon) or frequencies.

3. See the 661st session in Chapter 17 of *Personal Reality*. In his material after 11:23 especially, Seth discusses the doctor-patient relationship, and the feelings of powerlessness that can beset the individual during times of illness.

4. Current statistics show that in the United States the suicide rate for psychiatrists, doctors, and dentists is three to four times higher than it is for the rest of the population. There's much discussion now of the additional stresses and frustrations encountered by those in the medical disciplines, aside from personality traits or conflicts that can lead an individual to take his or her own life; the suicide of a doctor, for instance, may be triggered by his inability to fulfill the role society expects of him.

The bulk of the material in *Personal Reality* concerns the nature of beliefs, and the physical and mental environments that are created, both individually and *en masse,* as a result of those beliefs. It follows, then, that a number of the sessions in that book either deal with health and illness, or with subjects that approach those topics in various ways. Chapters 16 and 17 in particular contain material on what Seth calls natural hypnosis, and on Western medicine, physicians, the suggestions associated with medical insurance and "health" literature, diet, childbirth, hospitals, natural death, good and evil, and so forth.

5. See these two notes, in sections 1 and 2 respectively: at 11:26 for Session 686, and at the start of Session 694.

6. A note added later: It turns out, of course, that there is no Part 1 in *"Unknown" Reality*. Instead, as explained in my Introductory Notes, Jane and I decided to publish the first three sections as Volume 1.

Session 704

June 17, 1974

9:27 P.M. Monday

Now—good evening.

("Good evening, Seth.")

(With many pauses:) Dictation . . . The unknown reality, probable man, dreams, the spin of electrons, the blueprints for reality—all of these are intimately related.

Your daily personal lives are touched, are changed, are created from the interrelationships that exist among those phenomena. So, of course, your mass world is also affected. You do have free will, and in a certain fashion it can be said to be dependent upon the nature of probabilities and the multidimensional behavior of electrons.[1]

Unpredictability does not mean chaos. All order rises out of the creative elements of unpredictability. In fact, the behavior of any object in your universe is "predictable" only because you concentrate upon such a small portion of its reality.[2]

Unpredictability assures uniqueness, and is the opposite of predetermined motion. The great saga of recognized physical activity arises from a vast unrecognized, unpredictable dimension in which probabilities are allowed full freedom.

The full practical implication here should be understood: No course is irrevocably set or beyond change. Within the limited framework of your usual operations, however, so-called predictions[3] may be made. They will be workable to some degree. In deeper terms however no action is set beyond alteration. The unknown reality is the source for the known one. If you want to "discover" how things work, then your journey must eventually lead you into the dimensions that lie within the world you know.

You must therefore explore the psyche, the living consciousness. It will lead you to the withinness. This is not an impractical, but very practical, endeavor in all areas. Scientifically, such studies would vastly enlarge your concepts so that a loving technology could follow the most beautiful contours of the mind, rising on the natural mountains of human abilities and then more easily into fulfillment.

Medicine would gently and expertly encourage healing processes as it more fully understood the psyche's great emotional being and needs. Learning would take advantage of the latent inner knowledge of the subjective self, and help it interpret itself in terms of physical life. The dream state would be seen as an inexhaustible fountain of information. Efforts could then be made to understand and interpret private symbolism, and individuals within a society would be taught to take advantage of their own inner data to enrich their personal lives and help the community.

I am aware that some of this sounds "retrogressive," for I am even suggesting a situation in which politicians or statesmen would learn to "dream wisely"—and become aware of the psyche, the mass psyche, of their people, and tune into the "private oracle."

Now all of this certainly sounds unscientific to many people, yet most of my readers have already picked up a different version of the nature of science, or they would not be reading this book to begin with. The private oracle: What does that mean? And what does it have to do with the unknown reality? More, what does it have to do with the practical world? The private oracle is the voice of the inner multidimensional self—the part of each person not fully contained in his or her personhood, the part of the unknown self-structure out of which personhood, with its physical alliance, springs. Basically that portion of the psyche is outside of space and time, while enabling you to operate in it.[4] It deals intimately with probabilities— *(louder:)* the source of all predictable action.

Because of its position it has great powers of communication, both as a receiver and as a sender. Unfortunately, science as it has developed in your time has resulted in a mistrust of the individual, and saddled him or her with a sense of powerlessness, subjectively, even while it has added a seeming sense of objective power. I say that it has seemingly added a sense of objective power *(intently during a fast delivery)*. For instance, your sophisticated techniques allow you to say that conditions are right for a tornado, and you will have a tornado watch *(as we had in our Elmira area not long ago),* or your instruments will pick up faint earthquake tremors, and following fault lines you will then "predict" that an earthquake will appear in another area. So it seems that you have some power over your environment. The individual person can then prepare for a potential disaster. It seems that you can seed the clouds with chemicals and bring forth rain when it is needed, and therefore obtain a power over the environment that is quite practical. You believe that you need scientific paraphernalia to achieve such ends—yet many animals are aware of such phenomena, and without such instruments. And mankind itself is innately equipped to "foresee" such potential disasters.

The physical organism itself is so equipped. Blood pressure rises in whole populations—stress signals in terms of hormones are activated, but you are not taught to recognize these natural signals. There is a give-and-take between all portions of nature. You are as natural as an animal, and as "tuned in" to the deep rhythms of the earth—those that you consciously perceive and those that are perceived by your body consciousness, but are screened out by the "official mind."

I am simply suggesting that you become more natural. Because science has made an effective barrier to that method of approach, the power seems to reside in the gadgets rather than in man. Man no longer identifies with a storm, for example, and has lost his sense of relationship with it, and therefore his natural power over it. The same applies to storms of the psyche. The dream-art scientist, the true mental physicist, the complete physician—such designations represent the kinds of training that could allow you to understand the unknown, and therefore the known reality, and so become aware of the blueprints that exist behind the physical universe. The proof is in the pudding, of course. Largely, it seems that your techniques work a good deal of the time. Let us look at medicine, for instance.

(10:16.) Your physicians can point to lives saved by sophisticated technology. You can point to diseases stamped out because of inoculations or other preventive measures, such as the intake of certain vitamins, or sanitary procedures. It seems the worst kind of idiocy to suggest that the individual has any kind of effective protection against illness or disease. (Long pause.) Almost anyone can name a family member or friend who died 30 or 40 years ago of a disease that is now completely conquered. It seems that such lives would have been saved with modern procedures. In your society a medical checkup is a must every so often.

Again, many can thankfully praise a given doctor for discovering a disease condition "in time," so that effective countering measures were taken and the disease was eliminated. You cannot know for sure, of course, what would have happened otherwise. You cannot know for sure what happened to those people who wanted to die. If they did not die of the disease, they may have "fallen prey" to an accident, or died in a war, or in a natural disaster.

They may have been "cured" whether or not they had treatment, and gone on to lead productive lives. You do not know. A man or woman who is ready to die, if saved from one disease will promptly get another, or find a way of fulfilling that desire. Your problem there rests with the will to live, and with the mechanics of the psyche. The complete physician would try to understand the inner mechanics of vitality and, as best he could, learn to encourage these.

He would try to ascertain the patterns of the psyche, and follow them. He would encourage the patient to tune into the private oracle in order to ascertain his or her own purposes in physical life, and to reinforce spiritual strength. The complete physician would be an individual, (male or female), who was in superb health, and therefore understood himself the particular dynamics that operate between spiritual vitality and physical well-being. *(Intently:)* That would be his speciality. We are indeed speaking of a somewhat ideal situation here, from your viewpoint. Yet you will not learn the mechanics of health by putting yourself in a hospital. You may be cured of a particular disease, but unless you learn more about the dynamics of your being, you will simply "fall prey" to another. The same applies to all levels of activity. You may discover how to be happy by association with a happy person, but you definitely will not discover that answer by associating with those who are miserable. They will only teach you what unhappiness is like—if you do not know already.

Each individual is a universe in a small package. *(A one-minute pause.)* As the physical planets move in order while being individual, so there can be a social order that is based upon the integrity of the individual. But that order would recognize the inner validity that is within the self; and the inner order, unseen, that forms the integrity of the physical body, likewise would form the integrity of the social body. The self, the individual, being its fulfilled self, would automatically function for the good of itself and for the good of society. The individual's good, therefore, is the society's good, and represents spiritual and physical fulfillment. This presupposes, however, an understanding of the inner self and an exploration into the unknown reality of the individual psyche.

You may take your break.

(10:42 to 11:05.)

Dictation: To some extent, each individual who wants to can become aware of the "unknown" reality—can become his or her own dream-art scientist, mental physicist, or complete physician, and begin to explore those lands of the psyche that are the real frontier.

Such a journey will illuminate not only the private aspects of reality, but the experience of the species as well. Period. End of section.

(11:06. And [added later] end of Volume 1 of "Unknown" Reality. This 704th session continues briefly in Volume 2, where Seth gives the heading for Section 4 [which opens that second volume]; then he adds a few words of personal material for Jane and me before saying good night at 11:21 P.M. The notes for tonight's session are presented below, however, since all of them refer to material already given.

(The three sections that will make up Volume 2 are listed in the Epilogue for this book.)

NOTES: Session 704

    1. See Session 702 after 10:22, with Note 6, as well as Note 2 for Session 703. More references to material on the fluctuations of atoms among realities can be found in Note 3 for Session 684.

    2. See the 681st session after 10:00.

    3. In Note 6 for Session 681 I quoted Seth on his own ability to predict (which he seldom indulges), and on the subject in general. He also commented on predictions in a more amused way in ESP class for January 5, 1971; see the transcript in the Appendix of *Seth Speaks*: "Time, in your terms, is plastic. Most predictions are made in a highly distorted fashion; they can lead the public astray. Not only that, but when the predictors fall flat on their faces it does not help 'The Cause.' Reality does not exist in that fashion. You can tune into certain probabilities and predict 'that they will occur,' but free will always operates. No god in a giant ivory tower says 'This will happen February 15 at 8:05.'; and if no god predicts, then I do not see the point of doing so myself."

    4. A note added later: Jane dealt with her "own" ideas of the inner multidimensional self in Part 2 of her *Adventures in Consciousness: An Introduction to Aspect Psychology.* See chapters 10 and 11, among others. Seth's private oracle is analogous to her basic nonphysical source self, from which numerous Aspect selves simultaneously emerge into various realities. All Aspects of a source self are in communication with each other, even if unconsciously. The Aspect self that appears in our reality is the focus personality, "earthized" in physical form. I made a number of diagrams to illustrate Jane's material in Part 2 of *Adventures,* and several of these show a schematic source self with its attendant Aspects.

    In very simplified terms, then, Jane regards Seth as a personagram, "a multidimensional personification of another Aspect of the entity or source self, as expressed through the medium." Aspects like Seth, she wrote in Chapter 11, "would have to communicate through the psychic fabric of the focus personality. They would have to appear in line with our idea of personhood, though their own reality might exist in quite different terms. I think that I always sensed this about Seth. It wasn't that I mistrusted the Seth personality, but I felt it was a personification of something else— and that 'something else' wasn't a person in our terms ... Yet in an odd way I felt that he was more than that, or represented more; and that his psychological reality straddled worlds ... I sensed a multidimensionality of personality that I couldn't define."

APPENDIX 1
(For Session 679)

(April, 1976. In this appendix I've put together some material on mysticism from Jane, Seth, and myself. I wrote the first tentative notes for it shortly after the 679th session was held, in February, 1974, with the idea of adding to them later if necessary. As events worked out, Seth was halfway through Volume 1 of "Unknown" Reality before I realized that these supplementary notes would work well as the first appendix in the first volume. The notes may have their own kind of order, but unlike most appendix material aren't presented in a chronological sequence. As in the Introductory Notes, I want to stress Jane's role as the creative artist, disseminating her personal view of a larger inner reality, and her intuitive and conscious comprehension of at least some aspects of that reality; for such understanding can easily elude our Western-oriented, materialistic, technological outlook.

(I'm not interested in knocking our technology, however, but in pointing out coexisting inner factors that I'm sure are just as important. After all, our technology is responsible for the very existence of this physical book, thereby making it possible for Seth, Jane, and me to communicate with many others.

(Since Jane began delivering the Seth material, I've become more and more interested in questions about the origins of creative [meaning artistic] endeavors. When we start looking for such beginnings in ordinary terms, we usually end up reaching back into the subject's childhood. But, paradoxically, the origins aren't to be found there, either, or grasped in regular terms, for according to Seth they'd lie outside the reach of physical life. Without going into Seth's ideas that time is simultaneous, or that any endeavor is creative, the kinds of origins I'm discussing here wouldn't have any beginning or end. More likely than not, they'd be chosen by the personality before birth, or outside the physical state.

(As soon as Seth mentioned Jane's "deeply mystical nature" in the 679th session, I thought of some personal material he'd given us six months earlier. I've slightly rearranged excerpts from that session for presentation here:)

Even in his poetry, before our work, Ruburt's energy led him way beyond "himself" at certain times. He tried to hold himself down because, he felt, the energy was so strong that allowed freedom in almost any direction, it would bring him into conflict with the mores and ways of other people.

Ruburt is literally a great receiver of energy. He attracts it, and it must therefore go <u>through</u> him, translated into outward experience. He is himself. He cannot turn himself or his abilities off . . . His activities would be strong in whatever level of activity he <u>focused</u> his energy, exaggerated in terms of <u>others</u> by comparison. He <u>is</u> a great mystic. Naturally, that is, a great mystic. That is reflected through his poetry as well as our specific work. So that expression would come through poetry also with its "psychedelic" experience, regardless of specific sessions. . . .

(At about the time that personal session was held, we'd been reading a book on the lives of some of the well-known mystics of the past. Most of them had functioned within religious frameworks, and Jane and I saw how their various environments had given color and shape to their transcendent experiences. [I would add that in turn those experiences obviously enriched those environments.] But in spite of Seth's material, Jane told me: "I'm not a mystic. I don't think of myself as one at all—not like those church people." She smiled. "I don't have a vision every time I want to do something important.

("In fact," she continued, "I'm embarrased that Seth called me a mystic—a great one, I mean—like that. No matter whether it's natural or not . . ." Rather reluctantly, she agreed to let me present that personal material here; but only, I think, because she understood my desire to give what I consider to be pertinent background material for the Seth books. Yet, at the same time, she could say to me: "I hope to go further into consciousness than anyone else ever has."[1]

(I reminded Jane that since she belonged to no religion now [having left the Roman Catholic Church when she was 19 years old], her mystical nature would choose other avenues of expression than religious ones; as in these sessions, for instance. Perhaps, I suggested, it would turn out that one of her main endeavors would be to enlarge the boundaries of "ordinary" mystical experience itself, to show it operating outside of accepted religious frameworks. I added that within those religious boundaries, mystics across the centuries and throughout the world have given voice to the same ideas in almost the same words, and that as an "independent" mystic Jane was in a

*position to approach the situation from a freer, more individual
standpoint: She would be able to add fresh insights to what is
certainly one of the species' all-pervasive, unifying states. For the
mystical way surely speaks about our origins.*[2]

 *(Yet, somewhat ironically, Jane's inherent abilities first
began to show themselves, even if on unrealized or "unconscious" levels, within the very disciplined structure of Cathol-
icism. And she had reinforced that framework by demanding her
transfer from a public to a Catholic grade school.*

 *(I asked her about her childhood feelings, in line with
Seth's description of her mystical nature in the 679th session.
Jane told me that during those years she'd had no idea that she
might be anything so esoteric as a "mystic." She was simply
herself, and her sense of self, with her individual abilities and
appreciation of the world she created and reacted to, grew in a
very natural manner as she matured. Through her involvement
with the Catholic church, she became aware of the quality called
"mysticism" in connection with the saints of that church—but
still she had no idea of attributing such a quality to herself. Her
desire, her drive, was to write.*

 *(My own point in all of this is that Jane was different
from her contemporaries in more ways than she realized. It was
obvious to her in her youth that none of her friends wrote
poetry, or talked about the subject matter of much of her own
poetry.*[3] *Jane intuitively felt her own nature, without trying to
define it. Concurrently as a child, she would take long walks at
night and pray, especially when she'd "been bad."*

 *(Throughout her formative years, however, Jane's
grandfather—her "Little Daddy," as she called him—played an
important part. To some extent he replaced the father she'd lost
at the age of two when her parents were divorced. Joseph
Adolphe Burdo was of Canadian and Indian stock, and grew up
speaking French. His ancestors had originally spelled the family
name "Bordeaux." In certain ways Jane identified strongly with
him, as Seth explains in the excerpts to follow from the 14th
session for January 8, 1964.*

 *(When Seth gave us this information, the sessions had
barely started. Yet we could relate to it at once; in this instance
especially Seth's insights "fit" Jane's conscious knowledge and
extended it in most interesting ways.*

 (To initiate the material [in the 14th session] I asked

*Seth: "Jane has been very curious to learn something about her
grandfather. Can you help her with this?" Seth replied:)*

Part of a very strong entity. However, extremely inar-
ticulate in last life, due to an inability to synthesize gains in past
lives.

*("Why was Jane so attached to him when she was a
child?")*

Besides normal reasons, he was psychically inclined, at
a time when Jane was young and herself close to a past life. She
sensed his deep and personal inner awareness. It confused and
haunted him, since his inarticulateness applied also to thoughts
within himself. He felt strongly but could not explain. In his
solitary nature he came close to being a mystic, but he was
unable to relate his personality as Joseph Burdo with the social
world at large, or even to other members of the family. There
was a block, regrettably. He felt strongly his connection with the
universe as a whole and with nature as he understood it. But to
him, nature did not include his fellow human beings. The soli-
tariness that besieged him—because it did besiege him—is dangerous to any personality unless it comes after identification with
the human race.

That is, in his feeling of unity with All That Is, he
excluded other human beings, and on your plane it is necessary
for the personality to relate to its fellows. Only after such relationships are established is isolation of that nature beneficial.
Jane sensed her grandfather's feeling of identification with the
rest of nature, however, and since as a young child she had not
yet developed a strong ego personality, she felt no sense of
rejection as did, for example, the other members of the family.
When he spoke of the wind, she felt like the wind, as any child
will unself-consciously identify with the elements.

Her grandfather responded to his own attraction for
her, and was able to expand in her direction because she was not
an adult. He was essentially childlike in one manner, and yet he
had little use for most people. Had he lived to see Jane mature,
the feeling between them might well have dissipated. He could
not relate to another adult, and when in his eyes Jane joined the
league of adulthood he would not have been able to retain his
strong leaning toward her.

He never forgave his own children for growing up . . .
Yet he related his own body, at least until the very end, very well

with nature. He considered that he aged as a tree will age, but perversely he felt that others aged to spite him . . . From an early age, however, Jane drank in his feeling of completeness with nature, and it had much to do with her later development . . .

(*Joseph Burdo died in 1948 at the age of 68. Jane was 19 years old. Just two years later, she wrote the following poem.*

I Shall Die in the Springtime

I shall die in the Spring
Time, grandfather.
Earth, feeding her desire,
Will welcome the still warm flesh.

There will be cool winds
That will be my thoughts, grandfather.
They will rush through my skull
Like shadows or gray birds.

Wait and listen for me, grandfather.
As once we walked through forests,
Lend your hand.
The wind of eternity blows through my hair,
And I feel it touch my palms with ice.

I shall be part of earth and spring again, grandfather.
I shall be wind again. I shall be tree and flower.
I shall be free of the wheel again.
Grandfather, why does this cause me pain?

Published in Patterns, A
Verse Quarterly, *October 1954.*

(*Even so, through her school years Jane didn't particularly talk about her thoughts, or the abilities she sensed within herself—not with her mother, the priests she came to know well [and who didn't approve in any case if she carried her religious devotion, her mysticism, "too far"], or even with her grandfather. Jane wrote about her inner world instead. She had boyfriends, but no dreams of marriage, children, or keeping house. Essentially, then, she "felt alone" in her constant desire to write.*

(After she left the church, she distrusted organized religion in general, and had no idea that her writing would lead to any kind of "mystic experience." In fact, when Seth began to speak about immortality, Jane was disturbed and said that she wanted the sessions to stay away from any religious connotations.

(She hasn't undergone a classical religious conversion of the kind William James describes in his The Varieties of Religious Experience,[4] *yet more than once she's known her own forms of ecstasy, or deep alteration of consciousness, or illumination—whatever one chooses to call such states. From two perspectives she rather briefly describes one such episode, which actually lasted several hours, in her* Dialogues, *and in* Adventures in Consciousness.[5]

(Jane often enjoys being up and alone in the early hours of the day. She rises before dawn and makes herself "a simple quick breakfast"—just so she can read, make some notes, and watch the sky lightening outside the kitchen window. She listens to the first songs of the birds. The telephone is quiet. And, as she just wrote for me, on April 3, 1976, "I always feel an odd, right, somehow sturdy satisfaction, as if someone should be up to watch the day come; and it's me."

(The night before I'd been working on these notes, and we talked about mysticism, among other things. Because of our discussion, Jane rose early that morning and produced several pages of material. When I got up I found within her output the paragraphs presented below. They make an excellent ending for this appendix. Although she begins by once again expressing doubts, or at least qualifications, about her mystical status, I think her comprehension that she's part of the day, of the earth, and of time, is surely a description of her independent pursuit of the mystical way. Jane wrote:)

"Rob asked me about mysticism, though, and it's very hard to think of the word in connection with me because I confuse the various definitions or implications placed upon the word. To me it's a sort of . . . yes, sturdy connection of one person to the universe . . . a one-to-one relationship; a yearning to participate in the meaning of existence; a drive to appreciate nature and salute it while adding to it; but the knowledge that nature is also a touchstone to a deeper unknowable essence from which we and the world spring.

"But as I think the word is interpreted, I'm not a mystic. In usual terms the state implies a far greater compassion and goodness than I possess; an inner graciousness that I sense but rarely achieve; and a patience with people that I lack. A piousness that I dislike, too. These are the Christian versions; but a certain fanaticism often goes with them that I would find most distasteful. Some forms of Zen extoll the virtues of good rambunctious humor, which I favor, but then ideas of renunciation clutter up both Eastern and Western mystic philosophies, as far as I know . . .

"The idea of the priestess used to fascinate me, before my own involvement in our sessions. But I thought of a priestess-poetess, mixing this with the idea of the mistress when I met Rob. Wherever we live is significant to me; a privileged place; our domestic platform in the universe.

". . . I have more sympathy and love for myself now. By making myself better I can really do something to . . . change a small part of the world. Maybe that's all I'm responsible for—odd thought—what else did I, do I, feel responsibile for? But if people loved the part of the earth that makes up their bodies, then they'd treat themselves more gently. And the earth would know. Like I feel the day knows, when I watch the dawn come.

"I was going back to bed when my last lines suddenly reminded me that I still feel the way I did when I was a young girl; that some part of the dawn does come for *me*; personally; and that to some extent time didn't exist before I was born. My birth brought a certain element into the world that wasn't there before. And with me, I brought time. This happens when anyone is born, but most people don't feel it—or don't seem to . . . Together all of us on earth form time and contribute to its design and to history. This happens whenever one of us is born or dies. I guess I've always felt that way.

"I thought that life was a gracious gift, and that we were 'given' the natural world along with it. I've always been grateful for that. I felt that each person had a purpose, but I didn't think you had to search for it, because I naturally wanted to write; and that was my purpose. I never questioned it."

NOTES: Appendix 1

1. Jane made her remark while we were talking about the "daemons," or guardian spirits, of Socrates. The Athenian philosopher (470?-399 B.C.) believed that happiness was the goal, that one should be "well-daemonized," that the guidance for life came from God.

2. The mystical way is one of the natural feedback systems that operate between the body and the psyche, as Seth reminds us in Chapter 10 of *Personal Reality*. See the 640th session for February 14, 1973: "Natural 'mystical' experience, unclothed in dogma, is the original relgious therapy that is so often distorted in ecclesiastical organizations, but it represents man's innate recognition of his oneness with the source of his own being, and of his experience."

Two years later, while working on Chapter 22 of *Psychic Politics*, Jane herself wrote: "No one has really tried to map the *natural* contours of the psyche. Few even wonder if it can be done . . . The visions that don't agree with the various religious and mystical dogmas, that aren't couched in terms of Christ, Jehovah, or Buddha, might well represent holes in the official picture through which a glimmer of inner reality seeps. . . . But again, the insisted-upon literal interpretation [of a psychic or mystical event] hounds us."

3. When she was 16, for instance, Jane wrote: "The gods have not lost their way, nor have I!" And: "I can't find time. I've looked everywhere . . ." But her friends in school asked her to write love poems for their "crushes" of the moment.

4. Longmans, Green and Co., London, 1908.

5. Jane deals with her profound alteration of consciousness in Part 2 of *Dialogues*: "The Paper and Trips Through an Inner Garden," and in Chapter 9 of *Adventures*.

APPENDIX 2
(For Session 680)

(In mentioning my "sportsman self," Seth referred to information he'd given about three of my probable selves in a private session on January 30, 1974—just a few days before starting "Unknown" Reality. *The session contains many personal insights that I now recognize as being quite true. But even without Seth's help, interesting results can flow from an awareness of the probable-self concept: The reader can begin to intuitively consider his or her own probable selves, or those of others who may be closely related psychically or physically. I'm not writing here about rationalizing the existence of one or more probable selves to account for personal shortcomings in this reality, however, but of simply using the idea to enlarge our basic notions of the human potential. See Note 1 for Session 679.*

(Here's Seth to me in that January session:) You, for example, could have excelled at certain sports, where Ruburt had no such inclinations. You chose to concentrate on artistic endeavors as you grew and learned through various areas and periods—that is, you tried and enjoyed sports, and writing; and after a while you decided upon the painting self as the particular focus upon which you would build a life.

The sportsman that you might have been would have gathered, from that same available background, other attitudes and ideas that would have fit in with his concept of <u>himself</u>, and with his core focus. The childhood camping background served as a rich source material, to be used in any way <u>you</u> chose. The sportsman, the writer or the artist—any of them would utilize that background differently, but well, and in such a way that it peculiarly suited each of them.

Give us a moment . . . Your father's inventiveness would also be used in the same manner, as source material, by whichever self you chose to become. There are many choices. I am using here three only to show you how those primary aspects of your personality operate now in your present condition . . .

The painting also, innately now, involves going outdoors, though you seldom paint from nature out in the landscape. Nevertheless, you would be determined to be free enough to do so. The sportsman that you might have been still lives within you enough so that, for example, you automatically stay trim and limber.

Your father's creativity, as mentioned [in earlier, unpublished sessions] had its side of secrecy, privacy and aloneness . . . you identified creatively with his private nature. The writing self became latent as the sportsman did, yet the writing self and the artist were closely bound. You felt conflicts at times. It never occurred to you that the two aspects could release one another—one illuminating the other—and both be fulfilled. Instead you saw them as basically conflicting. Time spent writing meant time _not_ spent painting. You believed the painting self had to be protected . . . as you felt that your father had to protect _his_ creative self in the household. . . .

The time is right for you to enlarge your focus. You must realize it is futile to say, "Why does understanding take so much time?" or, "Why have we been so opaque?" or, in your case, "Why has it taken me so long to be a good painter?"

There are comprehensions, illuminations, that cannot be verbalized, that arise as a result of . . . solving problems or challenges that seem to have nothing to do with the original challenges. These, however, are quite unpredictable fulfillments that come about as you solve what appears to be one main problem. They are achievements that arise out of a given situation, while often in your terms the given challenge may not seem to be solved.

There are unpredictable levels of understanding that are the creative results of certain courses of action that you take. These can exist whether or not the course itself seems advantageous, and can even overshadow the benefits [that] a _successful_ course might have given, in those terms . . . Though it would seem, then, that you have made errors, the errors in themselves are creative, and have brought about unforseen probabilities that now enrich—and also change—your original course.

Ruburt's writing abilities have blossomed because of his psychic experiences. Your painting abilities have also . . . The psychic breakthrough did not just occur. Your deepest natures called it out of the probable sequence into your joint reality—for a reason, because each of you knew that it could best help you to develop all of your respective abilities to their fullest, and also help others.

APPENDIX 3
(For Session 681)

(Jane finds her "massive feelings," as she calls them, not only instructive psychically, but exhilarating indeed when they encompass revelatory or transcendent states of consciousness. One day in April, 1973, she had a fine series of encounters with massiveness, many of them embodying those extra qualities; see her own account of the whole adventure in the notes for the 653rd session in Chapter 13 of Personal Reality.

(In my notes preceding the 39th session for March 30, 1964, I described the first massive state Jane experienced after beginning the Seth sessions. That material contains passages that are of special interest here, and I've combined them in these excerpts:)

"At 8:45 I walked into the living room to waken Jane for the evening's session. She continued to lie quietly on the couch, eyes closed, but in a few minutes told me she'd just been visited by a most strange sensation. From her description of it I thought she might have been exploring an ability related to the inner senses. So far, Seth has explained six of these. (Several years later, Jane was to list nine such inner senses in Chapter 19 of *The Seth Material.*) Jane said that upon coming slowly awake from her nap she'd had the very peculiar feeling of 'growing larger.' The laughing phrase she used was that she'd felt as 'big as an elephant.' Her boundaries of awareness seemed to have expanded. Holding her hands up on either side of her head, she indicated a width of almost three feet; her head had literally felt that wide to her.

"Jane added that when we close our eyes we're aware of a certain 'area of blackness,' one we're used to. While she'd been in this unusual state, that area was much enlarged—she used the words 'infinitely large' to describe it. Jane said it was as though her eyes had actually moved further apart to create this expanded field of awareness, of infinite black. She hadn't sensed anything happening within this area, but thought that she might have, given more knowledge and experience. She hadn't been frightened by the sensation, and went along with it. She didn't have it now that her eyes were open, yet the physical feeling of enlargement had been so strong there could be no doubt of it . . .

"As we talked, Jane suddenly announced that her

experience had triggered her memory: She'd had similar sensations of enlargement twice before. Both took place before she
started the sessions late in 1963; one about six months ago, in
October, 1963, say, and the other one over a year before that—
perhaps in March, 1962. She couldn't be sure of either date. She
felt each one upon awakening from a nap, but with her eyes still
closed. Neither event had made as much of an impression on her
as tonight's experience, for she hadn't sensed the odd, infinite
black within the expanded area of the skull. Since she'd been
alone on each occasion, she simply forgot to tell me about either
one of them."

(In that 39th session, Seth confirmed that Jane had
been experimenting with one of the inner senses. Surprisingly,
she'd tuned into one he hadn't told us much about yet: Expansion or Contraction of the Tissue Capsule.)

I am rather surprised that Ruburt hit upon this one at
this time, as it is usually a rather difficult ability to attain. . . .
Ruburt experienced this on a physical level, trying to translate
inner data into sensation that could be recognized by the outer
senses. This seventh inner sense represents an extension of the
self, a widening of its conscious comprehension . . . or a pulling
together into . . . a minute capsule that enables the self to enter
other fields.

(And from the 40th session:) The tissue capsule is
actually an energy field boundary . . . At the same time it pro-
tects the whole self from certain radiations which do not here
concern you. No living consciousness exists on any plane without
this tissue capsule enclosing it . . . To some inhabitants of other
planes [realities] that have access to your plane, all that can be
seen of you is this capsule, since such inhabitants have had no
experience in your particular type of camouflage [physical] construction. Therefore your camouflage patterns are invisible to
them, but the tissue capsules are not.[1]

These capsules can be seen by you under certain circumstances and have been called astral bodies . . . a term which
does not meet with my pleasure . . .

(So Jane experienced a modest series of unusual
psychic events before the sessions themselves began; some details
on these have been given in earlier notes. Her first massive sensations in March [estimated], 1962, were followed by these phenomena in 1963: our York Beach experiences in August; her

reception of Idea Construction *in September; her massive feelings in October [estimated]; the outline she produced for* ESP Power *[or* The Coming of Seth*] as a result of the* Idea Construction *adventure; and the beginning of these sessions in November, through our trying certain experiments listed in that outline [as Jane explains in Chapter 1 of* The Seth Material*]. It didn't occur to us to label any of those events as "psychic" until the event of* Idea Construction. *Listing them as I've done here is also apt to artificially set them aside from the flow of insights within the poetry Jane has written since childhood; actually, of course, all are related.*

(And finally, I can note that in recent years I've had some experiences of my own with the seventh inner sense. These have been very pleasant, but not nearly as deep as Jane's. While immersed in them I've always been exceptionally sensitive to sound.)

NOTES: Appendix 3

1. Seth had more to say about perceptions between realities in the 42nd session for April 8, 1964: ". . . forms vary on different planes, are visible or invisible according to your own situation. A form that may be perceived by you as solid may be seen merely as an electrical unit on another plane, or as color on a third. You, for example . . . are perceived by others on other planes at this moment, but to them you are not seen in the form with which you are familiar.

"The universe as you think of it contains innumerable planes, all taking up, in your terms, the same amount of space. The forms within these planes are in constant motion, as are the planes themselves. There is a continual exchange of energy and vitality, in other words, of actual atoms and molecules between one plane and another . . . the interaction and movement of even one plane through another results in effects that will be perceived in various ways . . . as necessary distortive boundaries, in some cases resembling a flow as if a plane were surrounded by water, or in other cases a charge as of electricity. But on each plane the effects . . . of this interchange of energy will take on the camouflage [physical appearance] of the particular plane.

"Using the senses developed on a particular plane to perceive its characteristic camouflage patterns, it is almost impossible to see beyond these boundary effects. The inner senses are inherently equipped to do this, but for many reasons they do not. The appearance of an expanding universe is also caused, therefore, by this distortive boundary effect . . .

"In some cases the distortion could be likened to the reflection of a solid tree in water. The outer senses, observing the reflection, might try to judge the depth of the water by the height of the tree, supposing it to be as deep as the tree is high . . ."

APPENDIX 4
(For Session 685)

(As she often has following recent sessions, after the 685th session Jane discovered herself delivering Seth material in the sleep state. This time her involvement was so vivid and insistent that the next morning I asked her to write her own account of it for a verbatim presentation in this appendix. That request alone had some very interesting and creative results. Jane:)

"February 26, 1974. Since the first session on Seth's book (the 679th) was held—and before we knew it *was* a book— I've been getting material on it in my sleep after each session. I've also done this on a few nights when sessions weren't held. Last night was different in some way, though now I remember hardly anything. I just know I 'woke myself up,' saying rather angrily, 'My consciousness just can't handle . . . this stuff . . . this way,' or something like that. I'm sure about the first part of that sentence but not about the last part. The material was on probabilities. I think I saw some of it written down—was I writing it? Anyway, I was getting too much of it at once. I didn't know . . . where to put it . . . or how to express it with my kind of consciousness.

"Now I *do* recall something: I was getting a whole bunch of material and it *was* multidimensional. I was confused. I thought part of it went with stuff already given . . . but in a . . . probable way. I didn't see how it could be inserted into a normal manuscript because it had this extra dimension. It was here that I got angry and woke myself up. As I opened my eyes, I realized that the material hadn't been given yet in *'Unknown' Reality*— though in the sleep state I was sure it had been.

"The whole thing had been going on for some time before I finally woke up with my objections. Several times earlier I'd awakened also, sat up, and smoked a cigarette. Each time as I lay down again, the material started coming. So the last time I said: 'Now, look, Seth, if you want to take me to some of these probabilities, great; with you leading the way; but my consciousness is having a hell of a time handling whatever it is we're doing.' Then I fell asleep and the material stopped."

(Within 15 minutes of finishing her statement, Jane spontaneously began writing a second, longer one. She produced it in an altered state of consciousness—albeit a sort of grudging

260

one, as her subsequent notes show. But first the material: She regards its method of reception, as well as its content, as representing breakthroughs of a kind for her; and because both that reception and content are related to "Unknown" Reality *we're presenting considerable portions of the statement here:*)

"February 26, 1974. I'm getting something like this . . . that data comes through to us multidimensionally, then is sifted through neural connections, where it's transformed into time-segmentation or strung-out experience. Next it flows into our probable (physical) reality (which itself changes all the 'time.') We inherently possess separate pockets or pools of experience (biologically valid among the cells' characteristics), sidepools where information collects for processing before flowing into the 'official pool of consciousness.'

"There are ways to bypass this process and dip directly into these sidepools.

"Usual memory is as much a sifting process as it is anything else, in which experience's intensity varies—sometimes 'alive' neurologically and sometimes not—just to focus our consciousness in one probable action or series. (As I type I add: We forget anything not pertinent to our selected series of probable actions. The psyche knows its own parts. Seth says so in his books, but we ask the psyche the wrong questions.)

"In these side pockets, memory, so-called, is not so structured. Its ever-present living elements are apparent; and its growth. Its material is ever-fresh. Here the past still happens. Usually we experience it through neurological connections; that's when it seems vivid or alive, but actually it's that way all the time. Past motion and acts still go on, not recurring—it's hard to explain—but those past actions are still exploring other probabilities, while our nervous structure focuses us in the one (physical) probable reality we've chosen. To us those other actions seem terminated . . . but that's only because usually we can't follow them.

"Writing, as a linear form, itself imposes limitations here.

"These 'past' probabilities are not fleshed out in our terms, but they're brilliantly focused in their own life. In the Saratoga experience[1] I felt ghostly because *there* I was a future probability . . . At certain levels of consciousness, through bypassing direct neurological activity and impact, you can then glimpse other portions of your own probable experience—both in the future and the past.

"Using these side pockets or pools where data are still unprocessed, in our terms, you can pick up several other strands of your own consciousness 'at once,' though retention may be difficult. Explaining the experience to the normal consciousness automatically helps expand it (the normal consciousness), so that each time the process becomes easier. Until, with practice, experience and data from several areas can be held simultaneously. The difficulty then is a translation in linear terms, hence Ruburt's trouble in the Saratoga episode."

(Now here, Jane told me later, she began moving into a different, hard-to-define, "strange" state of altered awareness. At the same time she began casting her material in the third person. Ruburt "him" "he"—entered in; yet [as she was to note in a subsequent statement] she wasn't picking up on Seth:)

"Now, physically, neurological action is a code for other actions that usually can't be experienced at once because of the selectivity mentioned earlier.[2]

"The ghostly, off-center Saratoga adventure bypassed and blurred usual neurological processes, allowing him to slip through. The blurring is—was—also necessary to aid in distinguishing another reality from the normally accepted one, particularly in the beginning of such activity. He was tuning into probable neurological materializations . . . that are ghost images inherent in the normal nervous structure . . . latent connections biologically part of the cells' realities. He was moving into other selectivities. Actual complete impact is unlikely under most conditions, though various degrees of interception and intermixing can occur.

"Ruburt's difficulty, anger, and impatience last night[3] resulted from initial problems of translating multidimensional experience into linear terms and thought patterns. Fresh material *was* being born anew in the past, and he didn't know how to fit it into his time scheme."

(Here in the last paragraph, then, is a pertinent clue, and one that Jane arrived at without asking Seth: She's experienced such translation challenges often since beginning "Unknown" Reality—hence her talk before many of these sessions [from the 679th on] about attaining that "certain clear focus," or "the one clearest place in consciousness," before she began speaking for Seth.

(I kept Jane busy! That afternoon, after we'd discussed her second statement of the day, I asked her to write a description of the circumstances surrounding her reception of it. So for the third time that day she led off a page with the date:)

"February 26, 1974. At Rob's request this morning I wrote a statement about my experience in the sleep state last night. Today, Tuesday, is my ESP class day, which means that I have a little less time for my writing, so after giving Rob the small description I intended to type a chapter of *Adventures in Consciousness*.[4] I'd lost some writing time lately because of business matters, and because I was trying to catch up on the mail, so I was particularly concerned about getting back to *Adventures*.

"Instead, I felt myself entering another level of consciousness. I grumbled for a minute, wondering if I wanted to go along or end it and type. Then I thought that something important might be up; and I 'knew' that this—whatever it was—was connected with my experiences of last night. So I went along, and wrote my second statement of the day.

"While doing it, I felt mildly exhilarated. My consciousness gets a smooth feeling at such times, an easiness. Yet I was also aware of the same kind of reluctance I'd felt in the sleep state last night; as if I was trying to do something . . . difficult, or translate information that was more distant than usual from our ordinary concepts. I almost felt stubborn, like a reluctant child, wanting to do the thing but not wanting to make the effort at the same time. The easiness won over, though.

"Toward the end of the material (in the second statement) I briefly thought the Seth level might be involved, but the wording didn't come through as automatically and smoothly as it does with Seth, and I didn't feel his . . . personality. The information referred to me as Ruburt, though, which automatically meant that it was from a 'higher' or other level than the Ruburt one. Yet I dislike the connotations called up by my use of the word 'higher' here.

"Actually I think today's experience was a different kind of approach to what happened to me when I was sleeping last night . . . After reading over all of this material, I see that on both occasions I was experimenting with the process it describes—trying to dip directly into a 'sidepool' of data and bypass *usual* neural connections."

(There's much to be learned here, Jane said in conclusion,

*providing she can find the time for study. An interesting ques-
tion: According to the feelings she expressed toward the end
of her third statement, Seth himself evidently isn't represented
by [or called out of] such a sidepool of consciousness—yet what
sort of connection* might, or does, *he have with one? We haven't
asked yet.)*

NOTES: Appendix 4

    1. Jane's description of her "Saratoga experience," as she calls
it, is given in the notes preceding the 685th session. See the first paragraph.

    2. Once again, refer to the 682nd session at 10:36.

    3. See the second paragraph of the notes before the 685th
session.

    4. See Note 5 for Session 680.

APPENDIX 5
(For Session 686)

(This appendix is an extension of the opening notes for the 686th session.

(9:10 P.M. Jane began her own dictation before to-night's session by saying that as she'd typed her statements yesterday [for Appendix 4] she would "get glimpses" of some of the concepts Seth was going to talk about in "Unknown" Reality—yet they would immediately vanish from her consciousness, so that all she had left was the knowledge that she'd experienced the insight.

(She started coming through with her material as soon as we sat for the session, so it took me a few moments to get my pen and notebook ready. But from here on I was able to take notes on most of what she said, so the following is pretty close to a verbatim report:)

"Now I'm getting ideas from so many places at once, so fast, that I can't express them all. I need you to coach me, to ask, 'What's happening now?' to keep me focused on one channel. . . . Because our mental habits automatically block out such material, we only recognize one series of neurological happenings—it takes time for the message to leap the nerve endings [the synapses] . We just recognize *one speed*: Other messages leap too fast or too slow for us to focus upon them. By altering our consciousness in the way I'm learning to do now, though, we can line up our focuses with these other 'ghostly' messages, that are quite as real as the neurological validity we usually accept."

(By now Jane was dictating steadily, almost as she does when speaking for Seth.) "Now everything I just said came in a flash while I was waiting for you to write down what you just wrote; but what I got originally was like a ball of string, so that as I explained it the string unraveled into the words . . .

"I had all kinds of sudden flashes about this when I was doing the dishes *(less than half an hour ago)*—about Seth's book, and that in a strange way it was difficult for me to get this book material. It was new, maybe; it would involve concepts that by themselves went against the grain of usual conscious thought, which wants to go consecutively. It's as though my consciousness is trying to use a new kind of organization—for me, for it—and so there's a kind of unfamiliarity. No scientific language would be

265

used—not that I know any—but that would structure what I'm trying to do; and unwittingly, perhaps, it might lead me into a scientific dogma without recognizing it. Besides, that would put an unnecessary burden on the reader, who might feel he or she needed a particular vocabulary. The use of a normal vocabulary would put the ideas within the reach of the ordinary person as much as possible. Although most people might need to work at it to understand the material, there'd be no automatic difficulties with words."

(9:24.) "Now while giving all of that, I'm in some kind of altered state of consciousness that I can't quite identify. What's so strange about it, I guess, is that I don't seem able to verbally put my fingers on it." (*Jane laughed, scrambling her syntax.*) "I can't pick it up, and for that reason it can get quite exasperating when I talk about it. I feel, though, that all of this is part of tonight's session."

(*She laughed again.*) "I also have an awful feeling that I'm going to get some kind of instructions from Seth about what I'm to do physically in order to get this material, and so compensate for this new way of receiving things . . . but don't put that in the notes . . .

"I almost feel that if you asked me at any time of the day, 'Jane, what are you getting now?' that I could tune into any of these areas of information, and tell you . . . As the messages leap the nerve ends they form certain pulses; we recognize these as messages and ignore all the others. I feel as though I'm learning to jump in between the recognized pulses and pick up usually inaccessible ones. Trying to make all this verbal is very difficult."

(*Once new developments in Jane's psychic abilities begin to show themselves, one can start backtracking to find possible origins. I'd say that her own awareness of multiple channels has grown out of her initial sensing of the channels available from Seth, as described in the 616th session in Chapter 2 of* Personal Reality; *and that her material on neurological speeds is related to the observations of Jane that were noted by Sue Watkins in* Seth Speaks; *see the 594th session in the Appendix of that book. I also think that a thorough search of earlier sessions would turn up many other clues, foreshadowing both eventualities.*

(*I'd like to add here that the flood of material issuing from Jane lately, both in and out of trance, has been extraordinary—and I note that as one who is used to her strong bursts of creative activity. There seems to be no end to it. She's also been very active in her ESP class this month, with extensive singing in Sumari—which is her own musical trance language[1]— and with long sessions via Seth in each class; the transcripts of some of the latter have run to five or six single-spaced type-written pages. It takes physical time and great physical energy to deliver all of that material . . .)*

NOTES: Appendix 5

1. Much Sumari material can be found in Chapter 7 of Jane's *Adventures,* and in the Appendix of her novel, *The Education of Oversoul Seven.*

APPENDIX 6
(For Session 687)

(Yesterday, in the magazine section of a leading metropolitan newspaper, Jane and I read a long article on the evolution of ancient man—"ancient" here meaning "true man" at least 2.5 million to 3 million years old. Aside from the question of whether "evolution" in ordinary linear terms has been scientifically proven [concerning which point Jane and I have many reservations], we were drawn to the article because we thought its "factual" information might eventually supplement some of Seth's material for "Unknown" Reality. Both of us ended up more incensed than informed, however; it seemed to us that even on its own terms the piece contained many unjustified conclusions that were based on very flimsy evidence—and assumptions—at best.

(While watching television last night we periodically discussed the trite thinking embodied in the article. Then, as we made ready to retire, Jane announced that she was "getting" information on the subject of ancient man—but not necessarily from Seth. She asked me if I wanted her to continue doing so. We were both tired, but I wondered if this could turn out to be an episode like the one she'd experienced before the last session, when she dictated material on the various neurological actions, or speeds, that she sensed. [See Appendix 5.] Tonight's opportunity, concerning a subject of such interest to us, implied something too good to pass by without investigation. I found a pen and some paper in Jane's desk. We sat down at 12:10 A.M.

(There would be material in this book, Jane told me, about:

1. *Parallel Man*
2. *Alternate Man*
3. *Probable Man*[1]

(She added that her situation this evening was like the one mentioned by her in the material presented in Appendix 5. She was open to my suggestions: If I prompted her, she could go right into a session and get the information. She continued:)

"For a long time these varieties of ancient men shared our earth and history, in varying terms. Right now, though, in our time, all of the different kinds of consciousness that we might expand into are here with us . . . some of them appearing as pathological to us . . .

268

"We consider anything that doesn't seem like usual consciousness to be pathological in one way or another. Many individuals show variations that actually represent future developments of consciousness; we're experimenting with these probabilities . . . There are actually *species* of consciousness, but we don't recognize them as such. Yet they shape our neurological history."

(*12:19.*) "Some of the experiments with man-animals didn't work out along our historic lines, but the ghost memories of those probabilities still linger in our biological structure, and in our terms can be activated according to circumstances.

"The growth of ego consciousness by itself set up both challenges and limitations. This automatically meant that emerging man, in that framework, must let go of a certain kind of animal comprehension that was extremely valuable *overall*, but could inhibit ego growth . . . For many centuries there was no clear-cut differentiation between various species of man and animal . . . There were also, of course, parallel developments in the emergence of physical man. Again, for many centuries, there were innumerable *species* of man-in-the-making, in your terms; various postures, and even types of manipulation, as well as alterations in brain size and activity. In some, different kinds of senses predominated. At the same time a great give-and-take was occurring at all levels—including vegetation, for example—so that together the creatures and the earth worked out the kind of stability best suited for the particular kind of developments that were to emerge.

"The known races are a dim reminder of that larger difference and activity."

(*12:27 A.M. Jane paused. She said she could continue, but we decided to end her dictation here, if somewhat regretfully. I hadn't suggested that Seth come through, so we could see what she'd produce otherwise. "Well," she commented, "I gave the material while I was in an altered state of consciousness, but I don't know where it came from. It seems Seth-like, but also really strange. It's like the stuff I got the other day. Maybe I'm opening up now so that I can get part of the information this way, as well as through Seth. An odd experience . . ."*

(*By "the other day," Jane actually referred to the half-hour just before the 686th session last Wednesday night, when she produced the dictation given in Appendix 5 [but also see Appendix 4, for the 685th session].*

(Portions of the article in yesterday's newspaper, I should add, dealt with the recent discoveries of skeletal fragments in East Africa that indicate the coexistence of several varieties of ancient man and preman; the latter being creatures who looked rather human but whose brains, it is believed, remained apelike. This part of the article is approximately in line with the material Jane came through with some hours later. Her material, however, wasn't influenced by the news story, for just about a year ago Seth-Jane delivered a session for Personal Reality on the mixing of animal and man: the 648th for March 14, 1973, in Chapter 12. I'd say that this evening Jane elaborated upon that session—especially upon the impressions she gave then during the 11:30 break, on "animal doctors . . . a bridge between animals and human beings." But then, for some years Seth has been reiterating that even in our terms there is no well-defined evolutionary path leading from our ancient state to our present one.)

NOTES: Appendix 6

1. One might say that Seth himself provided for Jane's material here when, back in the 681st session, he talked about parallel events, alternate realities, and probable selves and worlds.

(The following material is, in part, an outgrowth of certain effects described in Personal Reality; *see my notes for the 616th session, bridging chapters 2 and 3. That session was held on September 20, 1972, and the notes I'm referring to concern a new development in Jane's abilities: her initial realization that on at least some occasions she would have more than one channel of information available from Seth. I quoted her as saying she believed that "Seth could do three books at once, a chapter at a time on each, and with no confusion among them."*

(Jane had some other insights into Seth's multiple channels as she continued dictating Personal Reality *after that session,[1] yet we continued to think of the new development as one of mostly theoretical interest. Close to 18 months passed. Then on the morning of March 10—the Sunday before last—we learned that we may have to rethink the idea of Seth-Jane producing more than one major work at a time; for on that day Jane received the outline for another book, along with the knowledge that she'd need Seth's help in producing it. The book's title is* The Way Toward Health. *Jane wrote at the time, then told me, that she almost felt "the book could be* Personal Reality *Number Two." She added that her experience in "getting it" was related not only to her ability to sense that sometimes more than one stream of material was available from Seth, but to the way that she herself had tuned into the information on neurological speeds late last month. That episode had taken place just before she delivered the 686th session for this volume of "Unknown" Reality, and is described in Appendix 5.*

(As quickly as she could once she became aware of what was happening that Sunday morning, Jane typed a 3-page summary or outline of the contents for The Way Toward Health, *including chapter headings, then wrote a very condensed statement about how the whole thing came to her. We're presenting the statement below, and a few examples from the outline, in order to show some of her other activities while producing "Unknown" Reality. Thus, everything she's received so far on the health book is on file, ready to be used should she choose to follow this new idea any further.*

(As of now, however, I'd say that she doesn't have

much inclination to do so. Nor do I. Perhaps, even knowing Jane's unique creative abilities as well as we do, we're each somewhat daunted by the thought that consciously we might not be able to concentrate enough on two such projects at once. I do believe it possible for Jane to deliver "Unknown" Reality *and* The Way Toward Health *concurrently through Seth, and to carry on her "regular" writing, for I think we have yet to learn the limits of her abilities [although as she continues to develop them she increases our knowledge of human potential]. Right now she's working on the final draft of Chapter 5 of her own theoretical work on psychic matters,* Adventures in Consciousness.

(In this appendix the emphasis is more on the circumstances surrounding Jane's reception of the outline for the new possible book, than on its contents. In reverse order, therefore, I'll present first the statement she wrote describing that process of reception once it was completed, then return to the outline itself.)

"Sunday, March 10, 1974. 3:50 P.M.

"I have all the material for a new book, suddenly, after breakfast. Read something in the paper about concentration on illness causing pain, and that reminded me of some ideas I had last night. Then while doing dishes this morning I had the feeling a whole book on health is there or here. Went to my study, got chapter headings and outline, more or less, but I don't know yet how to get the rest of it; I feel almost that it's a Seth book, that I need him to bring it in. But Seth's doing a book! I know this new book has application to me most practically, too, giving methods of breaking out of my own patterns.[2] Could feel the bulk and immediacy of the book, but also frustrated that what I've got down is so little and sketchy—WHEN IT'S ALREADY HERE. Yet of course it must be *there* and I have to get it *here.* I feel caught between relaxation—want to lie down—and ambition, that if I just sit here the book will somehow clearly burst out in one way or another. Rob wondered if it's part of *"Unknown" Reality,* but I don't think so."

(Now, after just a little organizing on my part, here are a few samples from the 35 chapter headings in Jane's outline for The Way Toward Health. *Chapter contents are sometimes indicated.)*

Sunday, March 10, 1974. 10:00 A.M.

Illness and Neurological Prejudice
> Thoughts and beliefs as stimulating and directing probable cell reactions.

The Body as a Planet
>Its archaeology of ideas and beliefs. Its private idea of history as alive in cellular memory, upon which the body's current present is based. Prejudiced official histories.

The Naming of Diseases as Structuring Experience Into Permanent States and Socially Recognized Organizations

Medicine and Therapy as Used to Perpetuate Illness

The Community Recognition of Illness. The Hospital as a Social Institution

Illness as a Way of Focus—an Organizer of Experience
>Conversion, love, etc., as alternate organizers.

The Need for an Organized Structure for Experience
>If one vanishes, an illness may take its place while a new one forms.

Excitement Illnesses as Providing Necessary Stress

The Present Development of Ego Consciousness, and Why We're at This State
>The connections with health and illness.

Crisis Points, the Mechanics of Self-Healing, and the Psyche. False Sympathy
>Often the patient doesn't want to get well, and the doctor knows it.

The Creative Aspects of Illness
>The steps involved as symptoms replace the problem.

Illnesses of Childhood and Old Age
>The connections between schizophrenia in the young, and senility. The child tries to project inner reality outward, and finds outside structures too small.

The Way Out of Illness?
>A title or chapter heading? No, that's negative. I'd rather be more positive: *The Way*

Toward Health. A feeling this could be *Personal Reality* Number Two.

(After Jane finished her outline and statement she slept for several hours. Upon awakening, she told me that she remembered receiving hints about the new possible book in two dreams during the previous week. She'd written the dreams down, as usual, while wondering about their significance without being able to explain them: "But this material doesn't go into Adventures," *she noted after one of the dreams, since she'd thought of that possibility first.*

(Jane had produced her statement so quickly that after reading it I was left with several questions. I took notes on our conversation about it that Sunday night. Yes, she had been in an altered state of consciousness during her reception of The Way Toward Health *"on a real high"—both while the outline for it was coming through and while she wrote her description of the process. No, she hadn't heard Seth, or sensed his presence while this was going on; she'd just realized that his help would be necessary if she decided to do the book. Nor was it connected with "Unknown" Reality. "I wrote down what I could snatch from the whole book," she said, "but I knew that what I got was nothing compared to what was there. If I could have immediately spoken the whole thing, it would have been done at once—that's what was so frustrating! While I was in the altered state, I sensed not only the physical bulk of the book, but the actual contents within it. Those contents were immediately available. I can't tell you how frustrated—how blocked—this made me feel at the time.*

(We'll see what, if anything, develops concerning The Way Toward Health.*)*

NOTES: Appendix 7

1. In *Personal Reality*, see sessions 648, 657, and 673 in chapters 12, 15, and 21 respectively.

2. A review of Note 8 for the 679th session will show why Jane feels that *The Way Toward Health* could be of value to her, too.

APPENDIX 8
(For Session 690)

(Seth began talking about the dilemma posed between the conventional theory of evolution and his ideas about the simultaneous nature of time and existence, soon after these sessions started late in 1963. He dealt with this duality very evocatively in the 45th session for April 20, 1964:)

The value climate of psychological reality can be likened to an ocean in which all consciousness has its being. There are multitudinous levels that can be plunged into, with various life forms, diverse and alien, but nevertheless interconnected and dependent one upon the other. I like the ocean analogy because you get the idea of continuous flow and motion without apparent division.

As temperatures in various depths of ocean change, and as even the color of the water and of the flora and fauna change, so too in our value climate there are quality changes, and senses equipped to project and perceive the changes. There are distortions because of the limitations of the outer senses, but the inner senses[1] do not distort. The inner senses inhabit directly the atmosphere of our value climate; they see through the ever-varying camouflage (physical) patterns, and the flux and flow of apparent change. To some small degree in our sessions <u>you</u> plunge into this ocean of value climate, and to the extent that you are able to divest yourselves of the clothes of camouflage, you can be truly aware of this climate.

What is required is more than a shedding of clothes, however. To plunge into this ocean you also leave the physical body at the shore. It will be there when you get back. Your camouflage patterns can be likened to those cast by sun and shadow upon the the ever-moving waves. As long as you keep the pattern in mind, you create it, and it is there. If you turn your head away for a moment and then look quickly back you can see only the wave. Your camouflage and your world are created by conscious focusing and unconscious concentration. Only by turning your head aside momentarily can you see what is beneath the seemingly solid pattern. By plunging into our ocean of value climate you can dive beneath your camouflage system and look up to see it, relatively foundationless, floating above you, moved, formed, and directed by the shifting illusions caused by the wind of will, and the force of subconscious concentration and demand.

Yet even these camouflage patterns must follow the basic rules of the inner universe, and reflect them, even if in a distortive manner. So does value expansion become reincarnation and evolution and growth. So are all the other basic laws of the inner universe followed on every plane, and reflected from the most minute to the most gigantic spectrum.

Concentrating upon your own camouflage universe, you are able to distinguish only the distortive pattern, and from this pattern you deduce your ideas of cause and effect, past, present and future, and ideas of an expanding universe that bloats . . .

NOTES: Appendix 8

1. See Chapter 19 of *The Seth Material.*

APPENDIX 9
(For Session 690)

(The contents for this appendix, including a short description of Jane's use of Sumari, came through within a month after the 690th session was held.

(In ESP class for April 16, a student asked Seth to comment on "the differences between the male and female [human beings] as we understand them." Seth's answer was a long one. It clearly illuminated his material in this session, as can be seen in the excerpt I've put together for this presentation. [This sometimes happens in class: Seth will elaborate upon book information, or discuss it from a different viewpoint; this in turn makes Jane and me want to see such material used in the book.])

All time is simultaneous *(Seth told the members of class)*, and so you are male and female at once.

In all religions, those that you did not officially adopt in your society, what you would think of as the female religions predominated. Those people did not progress in industrial terms because they were too well aware of their part in nature. They could not dissect it.

Your ideas of sexuality follow both your religions and your sciences, then, for you have created each. But you always know what you are doing, and there are cycles in the earth, and in your being and your soul. And so you are in the process of reuniting yourself, and discovering what the word "humanity" means. You are finding out the meaning of individuality, which is a far more important word than you realize, and when you understand that meaning, then your own individuality will express itself in its natural form. Regardless of what words are put upon your experience in terms of sexual roles, you will be a full human being. When the conscious and the unconscious minds are understood, you will have no more problems with sexuality.

Now I am simply giving you a brief idea of what is involved, and I expect each of you to follow through in your own way, to see the connections and think about them. And now, before you, what do you see? A woman or a man? You see a range of human being and personality that defies conventional ideas of sexuality or of consciousness—that defies all of the ideas that have been handed down to you, and that challenges you each to look for the reality of your own being.

Your sexuality is a point of focus, and that is all. For those of you who need it said, I say it: A woman is as intellectual as a man. A man is as intuitive as a woman. You chose your sexual focus for a reason. The reason has more to do with the flexibility of consciousness than you presently understand. It has to do with the real nature of aggression and passivity,[1] which you have allowed yourselves to forget . . . Birth is an aggressive experience. Passivity is based upon the joyful recognition of natural aggression. To be carried along, each of you must be very sure of yourself. To allow yourself what is now, in your terms, a luxury of passivity, you must have confidence in the nature of your own reality and strength. Otherwise passivity frightens you to the core.

Think of your ideas about your own sexuality in connection with those about your being and consciousness. Regroup your ideas so that you automatically think of sexuality in relationship to your religions and sciences. You have associated the word "female" with the unconscious, while you have been working toward what you now think of as an egotistically based consciousness. There is more in what I am saying than you presently realize. You cannot, each of you, consider the real meaning of your own sexuality unless you understand your own religious history. Follow through, in your own minds, with your memories. Try to be honest with yourselves as to those early experiences in which you forced yourselves to behave differently than you were, because adults told you that you must . . . You had better understand the beautiful, unique quality of your own individuality lest you project upon the other sex—whichever sex you are—those abilities and qualities that you are afraid are your own, or project upon them those abilities and qualities that you wish you possessed and fear you do not.

Each of you must discover what sexuality is, in all of its aspects, and connect it with the nature of your consciousness and your being. The answers must come from within. You have before you now certain hints and signs. Use them. And all of you who look upon me as a sign of great logical thinking (*humorously*), and therefore male-oriented, in your terms, then listen:

(*Without a break Jane went from her Seth trance into another very creative mode of consciousness. For perhaps five minutes she sang to the class in Sumari,[2] the trance language she initiated a few years ago. I've always found the quality of her*

Sumari expression to be of a high order. Each song is unique and thrilling, whether it's muted or powerful, melodic or animated; often the particular delivery is made up of a combination of such attributes, as it was this evening. Class members discussed the song briefly. Then Jane came through as Sumari once more, but this time she spoke in conversational tones.[3] Immediately she was finished, Seth returned:)

You hear, and you do not hear, and yet your inner selves listen and they hear. What you were told was not given you in precise English, in intellectual terms, in paragraphs or in sentences. What you were given brought you into an encounter with your own emotions—those of which you were aware, and those that you hide, each from the other. And *(with humorous emphasis)* I am not giving you any more intellectual clues!

Teachers use many methods, and so we use many methods. We are male and female, ancient and forever new. And so are you!

NOTES: Appendix 9

1. Among other sessions in *Personal Reality*, see the 634th in Chapter 8, and the 642nd in Chapter 11.

2. Sumari is a "family of consciousness" that Jane first contacted in ESP class for November 23, 1971. She and I are both Sumari. Jane describes the whole development in chapters 7 and 8 of *Adventures*. Various Sumari examples can also be found in Chapter 20 and the Appendix of her novel, *Oversoul 7*. (And, I can write later, Seth expands his family-of-consciousness material considerably in Session 732, Section 6, Volume 2 of *"Unknown" Reality*.)

3. Jane also writes poetry in Sumari, and can translate it into English. When they've been recorded she can do the same with her Sumari songs and her verbal prose, as I call it. Later, as we discussed her use of Sumari in the material for this appendix, I asked her if she could describe the subjective feelings involved with her ability to go so quickly from Seth to Sumari, as well as to reverse the order.

"There's nothing I can say," she wrote, "except that the transformation is so smooth and natural to me now that later it's hard—almost impossible—to pinpoint my feelings. I *think* that Seth's energy propels me into Sumari when he initiates a song, as he did here. I just feel great energy, changing from one 'slot' to another."

APPENDIX 10
(For Session 692)

(During the two weeks immediately following the 691st session, Jane kept working with the project involving the missing person; see the notes for that session. Among other things, she took part in a series of lengthy telephone exchanges, usually late at night. She scored some remarkable "hits" psychically and made some errors—yet she ended up thinking that her demonstrated abilities often collided with what our society teaches us is possible in human activity. Jane told me that at times she felt a distinct yearning for understanding by the others involved in the affair; yet, because of her participation in it, her confidence in knowing what she can do was strengthened significantly. And Seth, very briefly commenting upon the search while it was still in progress, remarked to an out-of-town group of visitors that Jane was endeavoring to use her psychic abilities on her own; and that the assurance she was gaining through her efforts would be much more valuable to her than any she might derive from Seth himself "doing all the work."

(To conclude the whole episode I'd like to illuminate, from two additional angles, Jane's feelings and concerns about needing the understanding of others:

(1. "Sometimes," she said to me recently, and with no hint of smugness, "when I talk to a group of people—say on a Friday night, when psychic stuff may or may not be involved—I get the weird feeling that I'm operating on nine or ten different levels at once: The meanings and understandings that are being exchanged, at least between me and the other individuals in the room, are all so different. Those people can't possibly know how I interpret some of the things they say. I do think I'm a lot more aware of this than they are, because of the very nature of what I can do—but I can't explain that to every person I speak to. There isn't time. And it would be too exhausting."

(2. This note was added eight days later. Within some personal material we received following the 694th session for May 1, 1974, Seth said in part:)

He *(Ruburt)* was bound and determined to explore the nature of reality.[1] . . . He wanted to protect himself until he had enough knowledge to know what he was doing. He fears for the gullibility of people, and is rightly appalled at their superstitions—

as you are, Joseph *(as Seth calls me)*. Indeed, as Ruburt became aware of the little that is known, he wondered at his own daring. There was no one he could turn to for instruction. I could have helped him further, but I was [part of what he was investigating] ...

    (Seth continued:) He also began to see two poles in society: one highly conventional and closed, in which he would appear as a charlatan; and another, yearning but gullible, willing to believe anything if only it offered hope, in which his activities would be misinterpreted, and to him [would be] fraudulent ... There was a middle ground that he would have to make for himself ... to make a bridge to those intellectuals who doubted, and yet maintain some freedom and spontaneity in order to reach those at the other end. This required manipulations most difficult for any personality, and a constant system of checks and balances.

    (I think that because of the very nature of the abilities she's chosen to develop in this life, Jane will always find such manipulations necessary. And they are *difficult.)*

NOTES: Appendix 10

    1. Some of Jane's confrontations with reality are explored in various parts of my Introductory Notes, and in Appendix 1.

APPENDIX 11
(For Session 698)

(The heading The Wonderworks *first came to Jane as she sat at her desk last Friday morning, May 17. She realized immediately that it was connected to the extraordinary series of dreams she began having early this month. [These total 33 so far, and their number increases almost nightly. I've barely mentioned them in recent notes—just for sessions 696 and 698—but Seth has had a good deal to say about them in current personal material.] Many of the dreams have been quite long and involved. I'd say that some of them are classics of their kind; Jane's own symbolism is beautifully illustrative of the way dreams can offer insights and solutions to very real physical challenges. Her whole nighttime adventure here is a most practical one, and is worthy of an extended study elsewhere.*

(Jane wrote an intuitive dissertation on the wonderworks idea as soon as she received the title; this took up two single-spaced typewritten pages. She was in "a slightly altered state of consciousness" while transcribing the data. The following excerpts from her paper show the unity that underlies her daily activities; for she thinks that her own dream experiences, "Unknown" Reality, and The Wonderworks—*to use a set of recent examples—are so interrelated that practically speaking it would be futile to try to separate them.*

(We also see creative connections between the way Jane produced The Wonderworks *this month, and the book outline for* The Way Toward Health *last March, as described in Appendix 7: She conceived and delivered the latter while in a dissociated state also. And as with* The Way Toward Health, *she doesn't know whether she'll ever carry* The Wonderworks *any further.*

(Selections from The Wonderworks:)

"Creative expression, from its intuitional spark to objectification, mirrors in our private realities the way the universe was [and is] constantly created.

"Wonderworks—inner experiences just beneath usual consciousness—contain different orders of events.[1] Literally the stuff of all creativity (in miniature).

"The ways in which dream material becomes real, the processes involved, are the same ones by which the universe itself becomes objectified to our views and experience. The universe is the result of a certain kind of focus of consciousness; the stuff of it, the matter, rises out of inner wonderworks—of which the private wonderworks of each of us is a part.

"If we really understand how dreams worked and allowed ourselves to explore dream levels, we'd see how the universe is formed. It is the . . . creative product, *en masse*, of our individual and joint dreams . . . Our world is a dream level for some other types of consciousness; it's shared to some extent, then, and can serve as a meeting point.

"Seth straddles many of these points and appears in the dream levels of others at their personal symbol level. I haven't gotten to the deeper level of dream experience yet, where I could meet him directly. At trance levels we intersect, but we don't meet. This intersection of Seth-Jane in trance also happens in dreams, when book sessions occur there. Sometimes there is some separation, though, as when I'm aware of a Seth giving me material . . . Seth is an ancient entity, however. When he comes into my dreams the automatic intersection takes place, so I'm not aware of him separately.

". . . to meet him personally, I've had to go to another level. I tried this once, and got scared.[2] Seth wasn't known at the location I reached there. He could be scattered into several 'spirit guides'; that's how his reality would be interpreted, or come through . . .

"Other species of consciousness gain their experience at different 'levels'; often we encounter such consciousnesses in the dream state, then interpret their actions in the wrong order of events . . according to our own camouflage[3] system . . . Our bodies are the focuses for only the physical part of our consciousnesses . . . My latest dreams are giving me a picture of the nonphysical inner wonderworks . . ."

NOTES: Appendix 11

1. See Chapter 15 of *Adventures in Consciousness.*

2. Jane has yet to publish her account of what happened when she deliberately set out to find Seth. She isn't holding back from doing so for any particular reason, however, and thinks she may eventually describe her psychic journey in one of her own books.

3. In Note 2 for Session 688, I quoted Seth briefly on the

meaning he attached to the word "camouflage" (in 1970). Jane's use of it here in her own material was rather unusual, however, and took us way back to the first time we heard it from Seth, in the 16th session for January 15, 1964.

Basic nonphysical reality, he told us then, was "like some chameleonlike animal, constantly camouflaging its true appearance by taking on the outward manifestations of each neighboring forest territory [or world] ..." And so this primal vitality expressed itself physically in our environment.

"Camouflage" became a familiar word to us in those early sessions, and we thought it an excellent one for Seth's purposes—but rather oddly, except for using it once in a while in recent years, he's largely dropped it from his vocabulary.

A BRIEF EPILOGUE

I began this piece soon after finishing the Introductory Notes for Volume 1 in the summer of 1976.

So by now Volume 2 of *"Unknown" Reality* is well along toward completion. Seth finished his part of the second volume over a year ago, and since then I've carefully gone over my original notes for it; I've rewritten almost all of them (often many times) in an effort to get them just right, in my view. Those who are interested in the more detailed mechanics of Seth-Jane's production of *"Unknown" Reality,* especially where qualities of time are involved, should review my Introductory Notes. But personally, I think the most important part of those notes is Jane's contribution to them, wherein she discusses her subjective relationship with Seth.

Many good things will be found in Volume 2. Perhaps I can intrigue our readers by giving Seth's headings for the three sections it will contain. In length those sections may somewhat exceed the three in Volume 1, and are rather complicated.

Section 4: Explorations. A Study of the Psyche as It Is Related to Private Life and the Experience of the Species. Probable Realities as a Course of Personal Experience. Personal Experience as It Is Related to "Past" and "Future" Civilizations of Man.

Section 5: How to Journey Into the "Unknown" Reality: Tiny Steps and Giant Steps. Glimpses and Direct Encounters.

Section 6: Reincarnation and Counterparts: The "Past" Seen Through the Mosaics of Consciousness.

The headings can only hint at the mass of material behind each one, of course. But as Jane enthusiastically put it when we were discussing where to divide the six sections of *"Unknown" Reality,* "Volume 1 provides the general background and information upon which the exercises and methods in Volume 2 depend." Then she reminded me of Seth's final lines for this first volume (given after break ended at 11:05 in the 704th session), and I suggest that the reader review that material now.

In Section 4, then, Seth has more to say about CU and EE units, cellular consciousness, ancient man, evolution, space travel, and other seemingly disparate subjects as he continues to develop his thesis that "biologically the species is equipped to deal with different sequences of time while still manipulating within one particular time scheme." The reader is invited to experience his or her own "unknown reality" through the study of dreams and practice elements, and to try for psychic travel into other realities. Jane does her own traveling: The "psychic library" she's learning to visit while in a certain state of altered consciousness is described, and the ways in which the library is related to the birth of her book, *Psychic Politics* (which is to be published in the fall of 1976).

One of Jane's earlier travels through an altered state of consciousness, in September, 1972, resulted in the first session on her unique "slow" and "fast" sounds, then led into information on faster-than-light particles, black holes, white holes, and "dead" holes. The entire episode is presented in an appendix in Section 4. In another appendix I explore the relationship between Jane and Seth, using many quotes from previously unpublished sessions.

Among other information in Section 5, Seth gives considerable material designed to help the reader achieve psychic travel; related here is his session on dreams and dream photography. He also lists more practice elements, and discusses language, personhood, physics, and some of my own reincarnational experiences. Jane initiates information on "world views," with examples: Seth defines that concept as "the view of reality" held in the immortal mind of each of us, the "living picture" that exists outside of time or space, and that can be perceived by others. Seth also offers major material on his theories involving "counterparts." He explains in some detail how we live more than one life at a time, how "the greater self 'divides' itself, materializing in flesh as several individuals, with entirely different backgrounds—yet each embarked upon the same kind of creative challenge." (And yes, I can write here that sometimes counterparts meet.)

In Section 6, Seth develops much of the material in 5. Inevitably new information comes through, as he intends it to. For instance, he lets his ideas about reincarnation and counterparts lead into another main concept—that of the "families of consciousness," as he calls them. The Sumari family that Jane and I choose to be allied with is one of these. Seth names each family, describes it, and shows how its characteristics interlock with those of other families. Thus the combined actions of the families of consciousness make our world as we know it.

Section 6 also contains the story of how Jane and I searched for the "hill house" we bought and moved into before the last section of *"Unknown" Reality* was finished. That material makes an excellent ending for Volume 2. For Jane and me, our house-hunting adventures were an intensely interesting journey through a complicated skein of probabilities. Seth's information and my own notes detail the interdependent, yet spontaneous, psychic and physical relationships within which each of us elects to move; they reveal how a conscious understanding of such factors, some of which may reach back into one's childhood, can help greatly in practical daily living. As Seth comments in the 742nd session for April 16, 1975, in Section 6: "It is obvious that when you move from one place to another you make an alteration in space—but you alter time as well, and you set into motion a certain psychological impetus that reaches out to affect everyone you know . . . Such messages are often encountered in the dream state. Empty houses are psychic vacancies that yearn to be filled. When you move, you move into other portions of your selfhood."

Robert F. Butts
September, 1976

Index

INDEX